PHYSICS
MADE SIMPLE

PHYSICS MADE SIMPLE®

NEW, REVISED EDITION

BY

IRA M. FREEMAN, Ph.D.

Professor of Physics, Rutgers University; Author of *Theoretical Physics, Modern Introductory Physics, Invitation to Experiment, The New World of Physics,* and numerous interpretive books on science for young people.

MADE SIMPLE BOOKS®

DOUBLEDAY & COMPANY, INC.

GARDEN CITY, NEW YORK

Library of Congress Catalog Card Number 65–13090

Printed in the United States of America

A DIFFERENT BOOK ON PHYSICS

This book is intended to be a simple, first introduction to the subject of physics. As such, it can serve you in several ways: It can provide information and understanding leading to advancement in your work, whether this be a job in industry, in one of the arts or in military work. Further, because it has been written in such a way as to make it especially appropriate for self study, it is well suited for use as a refresher course, or for reference work.

The book stresses the essentials of the subject. It concentrates on the main ideas and developments and explains them in simple, straightforward language. The mathematics used is purposely kept simple in order that the physical principles may dominate the discussion. Nothing beyond arithmetic and simple algebra (linear equations in one unknown) is used, and all computations are shown in detail and are fully explained.

Three valuable features contribute to the self-teaching aspect of the book. One of these is the inclusion of detailed instructions for doing fifty-seven basic experiments, using nothing more complicated than objects commonly found about the home. Whenever possible, these experiments should be performed as you come to them in the text. They will add immeasurably to your grasp of the subject and help develop a real feeling for its practical side.

The second self-teaching device is the large number of Practice Exercises, involving questions and simple calculations based on the material of the text and requiring, in many instances, some original thinking with the text material as a point of departure. Be sure to work out these exercises conscientiously. The answers to most of them, together with detailed solutions, are given at the back of the book. For some, only hints to the final solution are presented. In every case, do the best you can "on your own" before looking up the answers and solutions.

Finally, the Summary at the end of each chapter is programmed in the form of a self-testing device.

—IRA M. FREEMAN

CONTENTS

SECTION ONE—MATTER

CHAPTER I 14

Matter and Energy 14

Three Forms of Matter 14
Solid 14
Liquid 14
Gas 14
General Characteristics of Matter 15
Mass and Weight 15
What is Energy? 16
Electrical, Chemical, Mechanical Energy 16

CHAPTER II 18

How We Measure Things 18

Measurement of Length 18
The Metric System: The Meter 18
Measurement of Area and Volume 19
The Units of Measurement 19
Measuring Mass and Weight 20
The Kilogram 20
Time 20
The Second 20
Derived Units; Density 20
Fundamental Units 20
Area and Volume 20

CHAPTER III 23

Liquids 23

Liquid Pressure 23
What is Force? What is Pressure? 23
Pressure Depends on Depth 23
Computing the Pressure 25
Applications of Fluid Pressure 25
Buoyancy and Flotation 26
Archimedes' Law of Buoyancy 27
Applications of Flotation 27

CHAPTER IV 30

The Air and Other Gases 30

Air Pressure 30
The Barometer 30
Toricelli's Experiments 30
The Atmosphere 31
Boyle's Law 32
Buoyancy in Gases 33
Uses of Air Pressure 33
Air Resistance 33
The Airplane; Bernoulli's Law 34
Other Applications 35

SECTION TWO—FORCE, MOTION AND ENERGY

CHAPTER V 38

Forces 38

Representation of Forces; Vectors 38
Resultant of a Set of Forces 38
Equilibrium of Forces 39
Center of Gravity 40
Torque and Rotation 41
Gravitation 42

CHAPTER VI 45

Motion 45

Speed and Velocity 45
Acceleration 46
Motion with Constant Acceleration 46
Falling Motion; Projectiles 46
Force and Motion 47
Newton's Laws 47
Law of Inertia 47
Centripetal Force; Satellites 48
The Second Law 48
The Third Law; Action and Reaction 49
Rotational Inertia 50

CHAPTER VII 52

Work, Energy and Machines 52

Work 52
The Energy Principle 53
Potential Energy 53
Kinetic Energy 53
Power 54
Machines 55
Perpetual Motion Machine 55

CHAPTER VIII 58

Molecules 58

Atoms and Molecules 58
The Kinetic Theory 58
Gas Pressure 59
Molecular Forces in Solids 61
Other Properties of Solids 61
Surface Tension 62
Capillarity 62

SECTION THREE—HEAT

CHAPTER IX 66

The Nature of Heat 66

Temperature and Its Measurement 66
Expansion of Solids and Liquids 67
Expansion of Gases; Absolute Temperature 68
Conduction of Heat 69
Convection 70
Radiation 71

CHAPTER X 74

Heat Energy 74

Quantity of Heat 74
Heat Units 75
Fusion of a Solid 75
Vaporization of a Liquid 76
Moisture in the Air 77
Conservation of Energy 77
Heat Engines 78
Refrigeration 78

SECTION FOUR—SOUND

CHAPTER XI 82

The Nature of Sound 82

Sound Waves 82
Temperature Effects 83
Reflection of Waves 83
Continuous Waves 84
Frequency and Wavelength 85

CHAPTER XII 88

Acoustics 88

Pitch and Frequency 88
Intensity and Loudness 89
Indoor Sound 89
Stationary Waves 90
Vibration of Strings 91
Waves in a Pipe 91
Resonance; Forced Vibrations 92
Quality of Sounds 93

SECTION FIVE—LIGHT

CHAPTER XIII 98

Light and Lighting 98

Light Travels in Straight Lines 98
Speed of Light 99
Light Sources 99
Filament Lamp 99
Carbon Arc 99
Tube-Type Lighting 100
Fluorescent Lamps 100
Illumination 100
Theories of Light 102

CHAPTER XIV 105

Reflection and Refraction of Light 105

Reflection of Light 105
Law of Reflection 105
Plane Mirror 106
Curved Mirrors 107

Refraction of Light 108
Law of Refraction 108
Wave Theory of Refraction 109
Total Reflection; Mirages 110
Lenses 110
Image Formation 111
Diverging Lenses 112
Some Optical Instruments 112
Camera and Eye 112
Microscopes and Telescopes 113

CHAPTER XV 116

Wave Optics and Color 116

The Spectrum 116
Color Mixing 117
Mixing Pigments 118
The Spectroscope 119
Electromagnetic Waves 119
Diffraction 120
Interference 121
Polarization 122

SECTION SIX—MAGNETISM AND ELECTRICITY

CHAPTER XVI 126

Magnets and Electric Charges 126

Magnetism 126
Magnet Poles 126
Magnetic Fields 127
The Earth's Magnetism 128
Static Electricity 129
Electric Charges 129
Atoms and Electricity 130
Conductors and Insulators 130
Electrostatic Induction 131
Electric Fields 132
Potential and Capacitance 132

CHAPTER XVII 136

Electric Currents 136

Current Strength 136
Action of a Cell; Ions 136
Batteries 137
Electrolysis 138
A Simple Circuit 138
Ohm's Law 139
PD in a Circuit 140
Resistors in Series 140
Resistors in Parallel 141
Electric Power and Energy 142

CHAPTER XVIII 144

Heating and Magnetic Effects of Electric Currents 144

Heat Developed in a Conductor 144
Applications of the Heating Effect 145
Oersted's Discovery 145
Field Due to a Current 145
Coils 146
Uses of Electromagnets 147
Force on a Current 147
Moving-Coil Meters 148
Motors 149

CHAPTER XIX 151

Induced Currents 151

Faraday's Experiments 151
Electromagnetic Induction 151
Lenz's Law 152
Generators 153
Generating DC 154
Back Voltage 154
The Transformer 155
The Telephone 156
Other Sound Reproducers 156
Eddy Currents 157

SECTION SEVEN—ELECTRONICS AND NUCLEAR PHYSICS

CHAPTER XX 160

Electronics 160

Cathode Rays 160
Production of X Rays 161

Electron Tubes 161
Radio 162
Amplitude Modulation 162
Frequency Modulation 162
The Transistor 163
Television 164
Radar 164
The Electron Microscope 165
The Photoelectric Effect 165
The Quantum Theory 166

CHAPTER XXI 169

Nuclear Physics 169

Positive Rays; Mass Spectra 169
Isotopes 170
Natural Radioactivity 171
Size of the Nucleus; Bohr's Theory 172
Artificial Nuclear Changes 173
Mass-Energy Equivalence 173
Einstein's Theory of Relativity 173
Radio-Isotopes 174
Cosmic Rays 174
Elementary Particles 174
Nuclear Fission 175
Nuclear Reactors; Fission Bombs 175
Uses of Reactors 176
Nuclear Fusion 177

Answers and Solutions 180

Important Formulas and Relations 186

Index 189

TABLES

1. Metric Units of Length 19

2. Metric Units of Mass 20

3. Densities of Several Materials 21

4. Conversion Factors for Speed Units 45

5. Molecular Magnitudes for Air 60

6. Coefficients of Linear Expansion for Solids 67

7. Temperatures of Various Objects 69

8. Heat Conduction Coefficients 70

9. Specific Heats of Common Materials 74

10. Speed of Compressional Waves in Various Materials 82

11. Sound Intensity Levels 89

12. Illumination Requirements for Various Purposes 101

13. Index of Refraction of Various Substances 109

14. Comparison of Magnetic, Electrostatic and Gravitational Forces 133

EXPERIMENTS

1, 2, 3. General Characteristics of Matter 15

4. Measurement 19

5. Density 21

6, 6a. Liquid Pressure 23, 24

7. Archimedes' Law for Floating Bodies 27

8. Density and Flotation 27

9. Miniature Submarine 28

10. Air Pressure 30

11. Air Resistance 34

12. Airplane Wing Principle 34

13. Making a Coin Jump 35

14. Making a Cylinder Roll Uphill 41

15. Falling Motion 47

16. Action and Reaction 50

17. Horsepower of a Human Being 54

18. Hardness of Materials 61

19, 20. Surface Tension 62

21. Judging Temperature 66

22. Conduction of Heat 70

23. Convection of Heat 71

24. Radiation 71

25. Boiling at Reduced Pressure 76

26. Refrigeration 78

27. Speed of Sound 82

28. Sound Reflection Principle 83

29. Vibrations and Sound 86

30. Reflection of Waves from Flat and Curved Surfaces 86

31. Pitch of Sound 88

32. Stationary Wave Patterns 91

33. Homemade Guitar 91

34. Organ Pipe Principle 92

35. Forced Vibration 93

36. Pinhole Camera 98

37. Simple Photometer 101

38. Plane Mirrors 107

39. The Curved Mirror 107

40. Refraction of Light 109

41. Converging Lens 112

42. Light Through a Prism 117

43. Mixing Pigments 118

44. Diffraction of Waves 120

45. Diffraction Gratings 121

46. Interference of Light 122

47. Mapping Magnetic Fields 128

48. Generating Electrostatic Charges 132

49. Simple Voltaic Cell 137

50. Resistors 141

51. Heat of a Filament Lamp 144

52. Current-Indicating Instrument 148

53. Induced Currents 153

54. Transformer 156

55. Radio Tube 163

56. Light from a Luminous Watch Dial 172

57. Chain Reaction 175

SECTION ONE

MATTER

Chapter I

MATTER AND ENERGY

When we look around us and examine the objects found in our homes, in the streets, in stores and factories, and in Nature everywhere, we realize that the things with which we are surrounded are made of a great variety of materials. Chemists have found that all complex substances—wood, steel, glass, plastics, even the waters of the ocean and the air we breathe—are mixtures of chemical **compounds.** Nearly a million compounds have been identified, and these, in turn, are merely different combinations of only about a hundred chemical **elements** known to science.

THREE FORMS OF MATTER

Some of the substances we meet are **solids,** such as iron or stone. Others are **liquids,** such as oil or water. Still others are **gases,** such as air or steam. These three conditions—solid, liquid and gas—are called the three **physical states** of matter. A solid object can be thought of as one that tries to keep a definite shape and a definite bulk, or volume. A liquid also has a definite volume, because it is almost impossible to pack it into any smaller space. But a liquid will take on the shape of *any* container into which it is poured (see Fig. 1). A gas, on the other hand, has neither a definite shape nor a definite volume: If some air is let into a chamber that was previously pumped out, this quantity of air will fill the whole space uniformly. Unlike water in a jar, a gas does not have a distinct surface.

Some common substances are mixtures of matter in several states. Fine sand or silt mixed with water will not settle out. It forms a **colloidal suspension**—a stable mixture of a solid and a liquid. Ink is another example. Milk is an **emulsion**—globules of one liquid (fat) suspended in another (water). **Foam** is a gas suspended in a liquid.

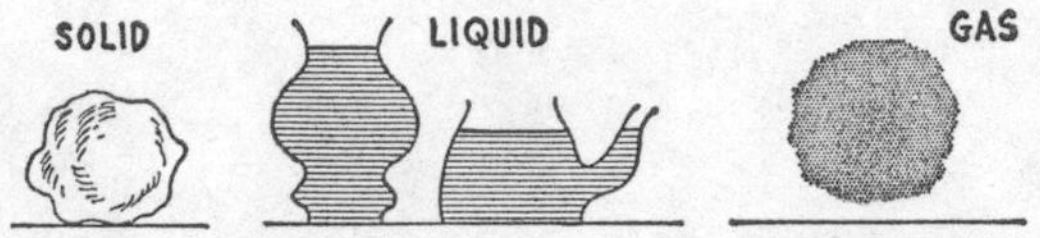

Fig. 1. (Left) Definite volume, definite shape (Center) Definite volume, no definite shape (Right) No definite volume, no definite shape

Often, we know a single kind of matter in all three principal states. Water is a common example. Ordinarily, water is a liquid, but at low temperatures it goes into its solid state (called ice), and at higher temperatures it becomes steam, which is the name for the gaseous state of water. We usually think of air as a gas, but at about 300 degrees below zero it turns into a bluish liquid. Iron, commonly seen in the solid state, becomes a liquid in a foundry and is a gas in the sun and in the stars, where the temperature is many thousands of degrees. These are all **physical changes,** and the material keeps its identifying characteristics all the while. But when wood burns or cement hardens or cream turns sour there is in each case a more permanent change and new substances are formed. These are examples of **chemical change.** Later on in this book (Chap. VIII) you will get to know the modern scientific interpretation for these differences in behavior in terms of the tiny **atoms** and **molecules** of which all matter is built up.

GENERAL CHARACTERISTICS OF MATTER

In studying physics, we are not especially interested in the *special* properties of the many kinds of matter; this is the business of the chemist. What we do want to find out about are the *general* characteristics common to all kinds of matter. One of these is *permanence*. Experience shows that we can neither manufacture nor destroy matter.* All we can do is to change it from one form to another by chemical processes like those mentioned.

Another general fact about matter is the obvious one that it *takes up space*. No two things can occupy the same space at the same time. A boat pushes aside the water as it passes and a chisel forces apart the fibers of a block of wood. Even air acts to keep other intruding material out, as you can see by performing a simple experiment:

EXPERIMENT 1: Float a small cork on water in a basin and push the open end of a tumbler down over it. The water surface inside the glass is found to be pushed down, as shown by the change in position of the cork. The same principle applies to the air pumped into the suit of a deep-sea diver or into a caisson used in underwater construction projects.

Sometimes we meet situations where two pieces of matter *do* seem to occupy the same space:

EXPERIMENT 2: Fill a glass brim full of water. Add salt, from a shaker, a little at a time. With care, a considerable amount of salt can be put in without making the water overflow.

The explanation here is that water—in fact, any substance—is not *continuous* matter; there are spaces between the water molecules, into which other molecules such as those of the salt can enter. More about this in Chap. VIII.

Another general property of material bodies that we shall have more to do with later on is called **inertia.** In some respects, this is the most fundamental of all the attributes of matter. It can best be described as the tendency for any object to stay at rest if it is at rest now, or—if in motion—to continue moving as it is now. When a car in which you are sitting starts up suddenly, you find yourself falling back into your seat. Nothing actually pushed you backward—your body merely tried to stay at rest, as it was originally. If, after getting under way the brakes are quickly applied, you pitch forward; your body obviously tries to persist in its previous motion.

EXPERIMENT 3: Place a heavy rock or a bucket of sand on a board resting on two pieces of pipe, which act as rollers. Tie one end of a piece of heavy cord to the weight and wrap the other end a few times around a short stick, to act as a grip (Fig. 2). A gentle pull on the string will make the board and its load glide along easily, and once in motion it will tend to keep going; but a *sudden* sharp jerk will break the string while hardly moving the weight at all.

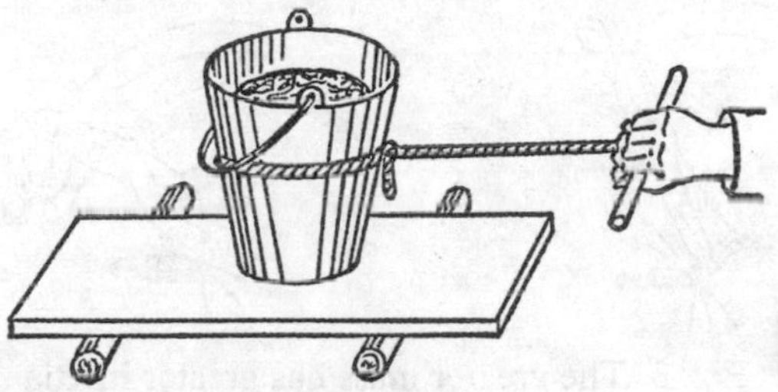

Fig. 2.

Once in motion, the weight had a tendency to keep moving, but when at rest it strongly opposed any attempt to get it into motion.

MASS AND WEIGHT

Our experience points to the fact that the heavier a body is, the more it shows this property of inertia. Now what we call the **weight** of a body is simply the amount of the pull of the earth's gravity on it. This means that a body has weight only because it happens to be near a very large object like the earth. If a standard one-pound weight is moved farther from the earth's surface it weighs less—the earth does not pull it quite so hard. But if

* This statement will be qualified to some extent later.

you think about the last experiment and others of a similar kind, you see that they would work equally well if the whole set-up were far away from the earth, so these inertia effects cannot depend directly on the *weight* of a body as such. They are found to depend only on the amount of matter in the body, and this is called its **mass.** In other words, the weight of a body depends on how near to the earth it is, while its mass would be the same anywhere in the universe, provided only that nothing is taken away from it or added to it.

For example, two bricks together have twice the mass of a single brick, but if the pair of bricks could be put on a spring scale at rest 1,600 miles above the earth's surface, their weight would be found to be only about that of a single brick at sea level.

And finally, the inertia of a body depends only on its mass, or how much material there is in it.

Fig. 3. The greater mass has greater inertia

WHAT IS ENERGY?

Besides matter, there are other things that we deal with in physics—things like electricity, light, sound, and heat. These are not kinds of matter, for they neither take up space nor have weight, in the usual sense. They are forms of **energy.** Energy is something that produces changes in matter. You saw that heat can change water from a liquid to a gas, for example. Light from the sun can fade the dye in cloth or form an image on a film in your camera. **Electrical energy** can turn a motor, put silver plating on a spoon, or send your voice over thousands of miles of space. **Chemical energy** heats your home and runs your car, and the action of atomic energy is known to everybody.

Probably the most familiar energy effects are the ones that are able to make bodies move or change their motion. This so-called **mechanical energy** has been called the "go" of things. A machine of any kind, whether it is a simple hand tool or a printing press or airplane, puts mechanical energy to work. Later you will learn how physicists measure energy exactly. But before we can measure anything as intangible as energy, we must find out how to measure some simpler things, and that is what the next chapter is about.

Practice Exercise No. 1

Put a check mark opposite the answer you believe to be correct in each case, then compare with the answers given at the back of the book.

1. The form of matter that has a definite volume but no definite shape is called a

— (A) solid. — (C) liquid.
— (B) gas. — (D) substance.

2. Of the following, the one representing a *physical* change is the

— (A) rusting of iron. — (C) burning of coal.
— (B) freezing of water. — (D) souring of cream.

3. The fact that some salt can be added to a full glass of water without causing any overflow shows that matter

— (A) is not continuous. — (C) takes up space.
— (B) has weight. — (D) has energy.

4. The inertia of an object depends only on its

— (A) bulk. — (C) shape.
— (B) physical state. — (D) mass.

5. Heat is classed as a form of energy because it

— (A) has weight. — (C) takes up space.
— (B) can change matter. — (D) exists in three different states.

SUMMARY

Instructions: Cover both columns of the following text with a card before reading further. The questions in the first column cover the main points of the chapter. Slide the card down to the solid line to uncover only the first question. When you have formulated a response, slide the card down to the next line to reveal the answer in the right-hand column. If your answer differs essentially from the one given, go back and read the part of the text referred to. When the card is moved down, a new question appears at the left. Continue as before until all questions have been answered.

1. Matter can exist in three distinct physical states; name them.	
2. What kind of change is said to be involved when ice melts?	Solid, liquid, gas.
3. What kind of change of matter produces entirely new substances?	Physical change.
4. Mention three of the most important general properties possessed by matter of all kinds.	Chemical change.
5. What does the mass of a body measure?	Permanence, the ability to occupy space, and inertia.
6. What is meant by the weight of a body?	The quantity of matter in it.
7. What term is used to describe the tendency of a body to keep its present state of rest or motion?	The pull of gravity on the body, exerted by the earth or other planet on which it is located.
8. Of the following, which is the true measure of the inertia of an object: weight, mass, bulk?	Inertia.
9. When a brick is taken from the earth to the moon, what happens to its mass? To its weight?	Mass.
10. What is the general name for the physical agency capable of producing changes in matter?	Mass unchanged, weight becomes less.
	Energy.

Chapter II

HOW WE MEASURE THINGS

Physics is known as an exact science, and this means that it is possible to make precise measurements of the things we talk about; we must not only know how to describe events and things but also be able to answer the question, "How much?" concerning them. From earliest times, people have found ways of specifying quantities such as the distance between towns, the interval of time between important events or the amount of goods bought and sold. To do this, they set up systems of measurement, based on convenient units of measure.

There are many types of measurement. Some are very direct and simple, others require great care and the use of highly complex instruments. But whatever it is that you wish to measure, you can do so only in terms of some chosen unit. And the unit must be the same *kind* of thing as the quantity that is to be measured.

MEASUREMENT OF LENGTH

For example, take the simplest kind of measuring operation—finding the *length* of an object. Before you can express the result, you must have a length **unit,** such as the inch, yard or mile. The size of the unit is arbitrary. You may choose it any way you like, but once you select it, you must stick to it as a standard. Historians are not absolutely certain how the Standard Yard was originally selected, but that is not important. In the English system of measure, which is used in civil affairs in all English-speaking countries, the Standard Yard is taken to be the distance between the end marks on a certain bronze bar kept in a vault at the Office of the Exchequer in London. It is assumed that all goods sold by length are measured by a stick or tape that has been marked off according to the Standard Yard through copies that are kept in the bureaus of standards of the various countries.

In the last paragraph, inches, yards and miles were mentioned. Why have more than one length unit? Simply for convenience in measuring things of very *different* lengths. To express the length of a pencil, the inch would be the most suitable unit; to give the distance between two cities, you would use the mile. The pencil *could* be measured in miles, but the number you would get would be ridiculously small. Similarly, expressing the distance between towns in inches would lead to an inconveniently large number. Always try to choose a unit that is not too different in order of magnitude from the thing you are measuring.

THE METRIC SYSTEM: THE METER

The sizes of the various length units in the English system do not seem to be related in any simple way. They are arbitrary, and it is necessary to remember that there are 12 inches in one foot, 3 feet in a yard, 5,280 feet in a mile, and so on. This makes it difficult to change a measurement from one unit to another; it would be much simpler if we had a system where all conversions went by *multiples of ten.* Then, in order to change units you would only have to move the decimal point the proper number of places. Such a scheme was set up about 150 years ago and is called the **Metric system.** It is now the accepted system of measure in all scientific work in all countries.

The fundamental length unit in the Metric system is the **standard meter.** It is the distance between the ends of a certain bar of platinum alloy kept at the International Bureau of Weights and Measures in France. Copies of this bar are carefully kept in other countries. The meter is a little longer than the yard—39.37 inches, to be precise.

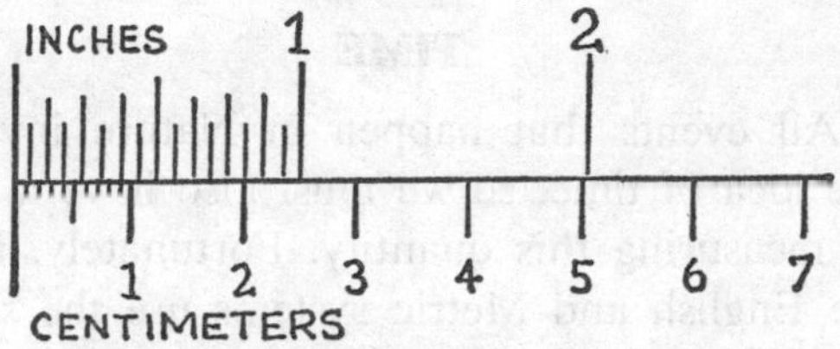

Fig. 4.

The following table gives the most commonly used Metric units of length. Notice that the name of each is formed by putting a distinguishing prefix to the word "meter." For instance, a centimeter is 0.01 meter, and a kilometer is 1,000 meters. The standard abbreviations and the relations to the English system are also given.

TABLE 1
METRIC UNITS OF LENGTH

1 kilometer (km)	= 1,000 meters
1 METER (m)	= PRIMARY UNIT
1 centimeter (cm)	= 0.01 meter
1 millimeter (mm)	= 0.001 meter

1 km = 0.621 mile; 1 m = 39.4 in.; 2.54 cm = 1 in.

EXAMPLE 1: The table shows how easy it is to change from one length unit to another in the Metric system. Suppose a rug was measured as 0.0012 km long. This is a small decimal, and it would be easier to judge the size of the result if it were written in terms of a smaller unit, say the centimeter. Since there are 100 cm in a meter and 1,000 m in a kilometer, there will be 100 × 1,000, or 100,000 cm in a kilometer. Then our 0.0012 km will amount to 0.0012 × 100,000, or (moving the decimal point five places to the right to multiply by 100,000), 120 cm. Equally well, we could write it as 1.20 m.

By comparison, see how much more arithmetical work is needed to change, say, 1.47 miles to inches: There are 12 in. to 1 ft and 5,280 ft in a mile, so we will have to multiply all three numbers together to get the result: 12 × 5280 × 1.47 = 93,100 in.

Notice, incidentally, that while actual multiplication gives us 93,139.2 we rounded off to 93,100. This is because the 1.47 is given only to 3 **significant digits,** so it would be meaningless to write the final result to any more than this number. This remark applies regardless of where the decimal point happens to come in a final result.

EXPERIMENT 4: Measure the thickness of a single page of this book by finding how many sheets are needed to extend ½ inch along the edge of a ruler. In order to count the sheets, make use of the page numbering. If you start at page 1, the last page number in the stack will be the number of sheets making up a 1-inch thickness.

Practice Exercise No. 2

1. Change 38.7 yards to inches.
2. Convert 1.34 m (meters) to inches.
3. Compute your height in meters.
4. A bolt on a French automobile has 10 threads per cm of length. How many threads per inch is this?
5. What is the cost of 3,000 m of wire if the price is quoted as 14 cents per 100 ft?

MEASUREMENT OF AREA AND VOLUME

In order to measure area (or surface) we need an arbitrary unit that is itself an area. It is simplest to choose this area to be a square, and we can avoid introducing anything really new by making the side of this square equal in length to one of our previous length units. Thus for area measurement we have square inches, square feet, square centimeters, square kilometers, etc. To write abbreviations for the area units we use *exponents* as a shorthand notation. Square centimeters is written cm^2, square inches is in^2, and so on, but these abbreviations are still to be read aloud as "square centimeters" and "square inches."

EXAMPLE 2: How many square centimeters are there in a rectangular strip of film 1⅛ in. wide and 40 in. long?

SOLUTION: The area of the film, in square inches, is $1\frac{1}{8} \times 40 = 45$ in². According to Table 1, 1 in $= 2.54$ cm, so 1 in² $= 2.54 \times 2.54 = 6.45$ cm². Multiplying 45 by 6.45 gives the result 290 cm². (Are you perfectly clear as to why the two numbers had to be *multiplied* together to get the result?)

Bulk or **volume** requires a cubical unit for its measurement. Thus there are cubic centimeters (cm³), cubic feet (ft³), etc. In all, volume measurement goes very much like length and area measurement. There is a special name given to a Metric unit of volume equal to 1,000 cm³. It is called a **liter** (pronounced "leeter"), and is just larger than a U.S. liquid quart.

MEASURING MASS AND WEIGHT

The fundamental Metric standard of mass is the **kilogram,** a cylinder of platinum alloy kept at the International Bureau of Weights and Measures. The kilogram was set up to be the mass of 1,000 cm³ of water, thus referring the standard of mass to the standard of length through the choice of a standard substance, water. As in the case of length measure, additional units are specified, differing from each other by powers of ten. Table 2 gives the commoner Metric mass units, their abbreviations, and how they are related to the English units:

TABLE 2

METRIC UNITS OF MASS

1 metric ton	= 1,000 kilograms
1 KILOGRAM (kg)	= PRIMARY UNIT
1 gram (gm)	= 0.001 kg
1 milligram (mg)	= 0.001 gm

1 kg = 2.2 lb   454 gm = 1 lb   1 oz = 28.4 gm

When we weigh an object, we balance it against copies of the standard mass units. What we are doing, fundamentally, is comparing the mass of the object with that of the standard, using the earth's attraction (weight) to do so. If we use a spring scale instead of a balance scale, both weighings must be made at the same place. Since weighing is a convenient method of comparing masses, both the weight of an object and its mass may be represented by the same number and in the same units.

TIME

All events that happen in Nature involve the idea of time, so we must also have a way of measuring this quantity. Fortunately, both the English and Metric systems use the same fundamental time unit, the **second.** Basically, time is measured by the turning of the earth, and clocks are merely devices made to keep step with this motion. The time of a complete turn, one **day,** has been divided into 24 hours, each containing 60 minutes and each minute containing 60 seconds. That is, there are $24 \times 60 \times 60 = 86{,}400$ seconds in one day. Additional units differing from the second by powers of ten are not in general use.

More recently, the second has been rigorously defined in terms of the motion of the earth in its orbit around the sun. For practical purposes, the difference can be ignored.

DERIVED UNITS; DENSITY

Up to this point you have become acquainted with units for measuring length, mass and time. These are sometimes called **fundamental units** because the great variety of other quantities that we meet in physics can be expressed as combinations of them. We already had two kinds of **derived units**—area and volume, which are both based on simple combinations of the length unit.

As a further example, let us have a look at a useful quantity called **density.** Everybody realizes that a given volume of one material has, in general, a different weight than the same volume of some other material. For instance, we ordinarily say that iron is "heavier" than wood. More exactly, we should say that *any given volume* of iron is heavier than *the* *same volume* of wood. To make the comparison exact, we can weigh a certain volume of iron, say 1 cubic foot. When this is done, the weight is found to be about 490 lb. By comparison, the weight of a cubic foot of pine wood is around 30 lb. We say that the density of iron is 490 pounds per cubic foot (written lb/ft^3), while that of the wood is 30 lb/ft^3. The density of water in these units turns out to be 62.4. In the Metric system, because one kilogram was chosen to be the mass of 1,000 cm^3 of water, the density of water is 1,000 gm per 1,000 cm^3, or simply 1 gm/cm^3. This is equivalent to 1,000 kg/m^3.

Fig. 5. The log weighs twice as much as the brick, although brick is over three times as dense as wood

In general, then, the **density** of a substance is the **weight** (or, numerically, **mass)** of any portion of it **divided by** the **volume.** Stated as a formula,

$$D=\frac{M}{V},$$

where D stands for density, M for mass and V for volume. Of course this equation may be solved for either M or V as well:

$$M=DV, \quad \text{or} \quad V=\frac{M}{D}.$$

TABLE 3

DENSITIES OF SEVERAL MATERIALS

Substance	D, *lb/ft*^{3}	D, *gm/cm*^{3}
Aluminum	170	2.7
Iron	490	7.9
Lead	700	11.3
Gold	1200	19.3
Limestone	200	3.2
Ice	57	0.92
Wood, pine	30	0.5
Gasoline	44	0.70
Water	62.4	1.00
Sea Water	64	1.03
Mercury	850	13.6
Air*	0.08	0.0013
Hydrogen*	0.0055	0.00009

EXAMPLE 3: What is the weight (mass) of a block of ice measuring 1 × 1½ × 3 ft?

SOLUTION: From these dimensions, the volume of the block is 4.5 ft^3. The table gives the density of ice as 57 lb/ft^3. Then, using $M=DV$ we get $M=57\times 4.5=256$ lb.

EXPERIMENT 5: Find the density of a stone from its weight and volume. First weigh the stone on a household scale or postal scale and record the weight in pounds. Then put some water in a straight-sided jar or glass, mark the level on the side, carefully put the stone into the water, and mark the new water level (Fig. 6). The volume of the stone will be the same as the volume of the displaced water. You can compute this, because the volume is that of a cylinder whose base is the cross-section of the jar, and whose height is the rise in water level. Measure the rise and also the inside diameter of the jar in inches. The volume, in *cubic feet,* is given by

$$\frac{\pi(\text{diameter})^2(\text{height of rise})}{4\times 12^3},$$

where $\pi=3.14$. Finally, divide the weight of the stone, in pounds, by the last result to get the density in pounds per cubic foot.

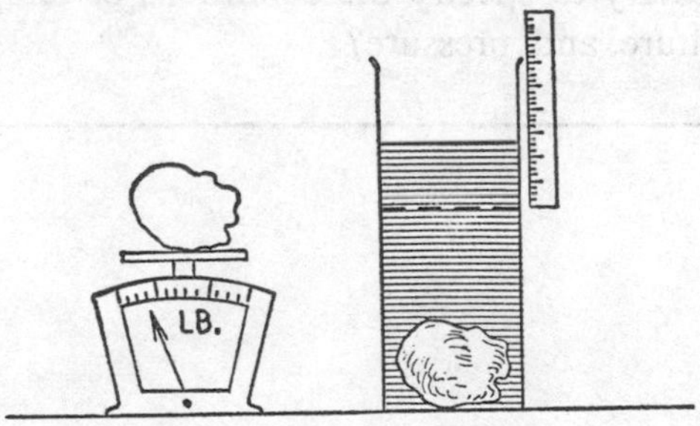

Fig. 6.

* measured at standard temperature and pressure

Practice Exercise No. 3

1. How many liters of gasoline does it take to fill the 16-gallon tank of a car? (1 gal = 231 in^3).
2. If someone offered to give you a cubic foot block of gold provided that you could carry it home, would you be able to do it? How much would it weigh?
3. Prove to yourself that the air in a room 20 × 15 × 8 ft weighs more than you do.
4. A solid metal cylinder 2 cm in diameter and 10 cm long is found to weigh 250 gm. Find the density of the metal.
5. What is the volume of a balloon that is filled with 200 lb of hydrogen at standard temperature and pressure?

SUMMARY *Instructions:* (see page 17)

1. Mention the basic steps in the process of making a physical measurement.

---

2. What is the fundamental advantage of the Metric system over most other systems of measurement?

a) Choice of a unit, b) determining how many times the unit is contained in the quantity to be measured, c) expressing the result as a number followed by the name of the unit.

---

3. Name the three primary units most commonly used in physics.

The fact that the various units of a given kind are related by powers of ten.

---

4. Define what is meant by the density of a substance.

Length, mass and time.

---

5. In giving the densities of air and hydrogen in the table on page 21, why was it necessary to specify the conditions of temperature and pressure?

The weight (or, numerically, the mass) of any sample of the substance divided by the volume it occupies.

The amount (mass) of a gas that can be packed into a given volume depends very much on these two factors. For solids and liquids, the effect is much smaller.

Chapter III

LIQUIDS

Many familiar devices and machines make use of physical principles applying to liquids. In this chapter you will find out what these facts are and how they are put to practical use.

LIQUID PRESSURE

A liquid, such as water, pushes on the sides as well as on the bottom of the container in which it rests. A wooden barrel or water tank has to be reinforced with hoops to resist the sidewise force, and the sides of a cardboard carton of milk bulge out. But it is also true that a liquid at rest presses *upward* on anything placed in it:

EXPERIMENT 6: Push the closed end of a tumbler or empty tin can beneath the surface of water in a bowl and you will actually feel the upward thrust of the water on the bottom.

Here we talk for the first time about **force.** What is a force? It is quite correct to say that a force is a push or a pull, but we want some way of measuring the *amount* of push or pull. Suppose a ten pound weight is resting on a table. Then it is reasonable to say that this object is *exerting a downward force of 10 lb* on the table top. This means that we can measure forces, at least downward ones, in *weight units,*—in pounds or grams, in kilograms or even in tons. And by means of simple arrangements such as strings and pulleys, or even liquids themselves, we can use weights to exert measured amounts of force in any direction we wish. Such devices will be described later.

The next question is, "What is pressure?" In everyday affairs, the terms "pressure" and "force" are used loosely to mean the same thing; here we must be a little more careful. **Pressure** is measured by the **force** divided by the **area** of the surface on which it acts. For example, if the ten pound weight mentioned above has a bottom area of 5 in^2 (square inches) and makes even contact with the table top all over this face, then the pressure between it and the table amounts to 10 lb/5 in^2 = 2 lb/in^2 (pounds per square inch). If the weight were standing on another one of its faces, say one that had an area of only 2.5 in^2, the pressure would then be 10 lb/2.5 in^2, or 4 lb/in^2—twice as much as before, because the same force is spread over only half the area (see Fig. 7). In general, we can say

$$p = \frac{F}{A},$$

where p is the pressure, F the force and A the area. Notice that pressure is an example of a derived quantity. It is a combination of the weight unit and the length (area) unit. Pressure can also be measured in lb/ft^2, kg/cm^2, etc.

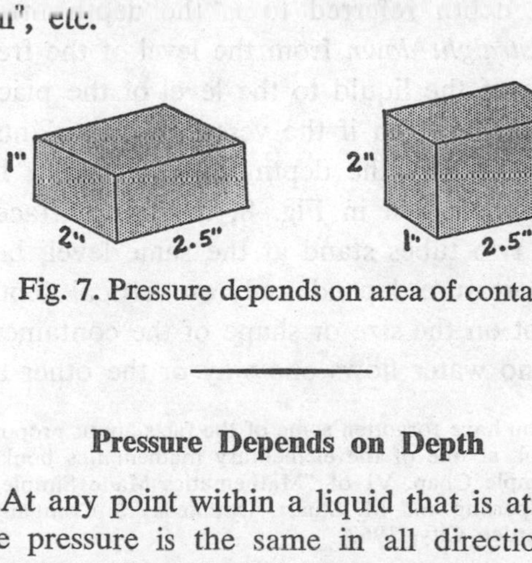

Fig. 7. Pressure depends on area of contact

Pressure Depends on Depth

At any point within a liquid that is at rest, the pressure is the same in all directions—up, down or sidewise. This is obvious, because if you think of any interior drop of liquid, it is at rest and so must be pushed equally from all sides by the surrounding liquid.

Furthermore, the amount of pressure at any point in a liquid standing in an open vessel increases with the depth of that place beneath the top surface. Prove this by an experiment:

EXPERIMENT 6a: Punch several clean nail holes at various heights along the side of a tall can or milk carton, put the container in a sink and fill it with water. A curved stream comes from each opening, but those from the lower holes extend straighter, showing that the water pressure is greater lower down.

Think of a tall, tubular jar whose cross-section area is just 1 in². If you pour a given amount of water into it, say 1 lb, the force on the bottom will be just 1 lb. Since the bottom area is 1 in², the pressure will amount to 1 lb/in². Now pour another pound of water in. The liquid is twice as deep as before. The bottom now supports 2 lb of liquid, so the pressure on it is 2 lb/in². Reasoning this way, we see that the **pressure** at any point in a free-standing liquid **is directly proportional to** the **depth** below the surface. This means that if you go twice as far beneath the surface, the pressure becomes exactly twice as great as before; if you go three times as deep it becomes three times as great, and so on.*

The depth referred to is the depth measured *straight down* from the level of the free surface of the liquid to the level of the place in question. Even if the vessel or pipe slants, this is the way the depth is to be taken. In the vessel shown in Fig. 8, the free surfaces in the two tubes stand at the same level, because pressure depends only on vertical depth and not on the size or shape of the container. Since no water flows one way or the other at the place where the tubes join, the pressure there must be the same from both sides, and so must the depth. For the same reason, the water stands at the same level in a teapot and in its spout (Fig. 1, p. 14), even though there is much greater *weight* of water in the pot than in the spout.

* If you have forgotten some of the facts about proportion, look at one of the elementary mathematics books, for example Chap. VI of "Mathematics Made Simple," by A. Sperling and M. Stuart, Doubleday & Company, Inc., Garden City, 1962.

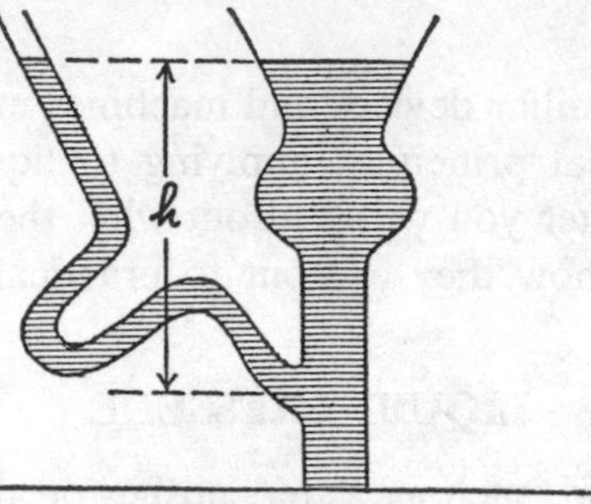

Fig. 8.

Practice Exercise No. 4

1. Explain why "water seeks its level,"—that is, why the surface of a liquid at rest is flat and horizontal.

   HINT: What would happen if the liquid were "heaped up" momentarily at one point?
2. Why are the hoops on a wooden water tank (see Fig. 10, p. 25) placed closer together near the bottom of the tank?
3. A dam or dike is made thicker toward the base (Fig. 9). Explain.

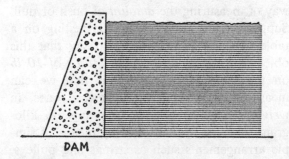

Fig. 9.

4. If there is a small hole in a dike at a point 10 ft below the water surface, does it take a greater force to keep the hole closed if the body of water is the Atlantic Ocean than it does if it were a small pond? Why?

COMPUTING THE PRESSURE

There is a simple way to get a formula for figuring the amount of pressure at any point in a liquid. You already know that the pressure is proportional to the depth. It must also be proportional to the density (p. 21) of the liquid. This is because pressure is caused by the weight of the liquid, and doubling the density would double the weight of any column of liquid. So we get the result that

$$p = hD,$$

where p is the pressure at any point in the liquid, h is the depth of that place below the surface, and D is the density of the liquid.

EXAMPLE 1: What is the pressure on the side of a dam at a point 20 ft vertically below the water surface?

SOLUTION: In the formula $p = hD$ we put $h =$ 20 ft and (from the table on p. 21), $D = 62.4$ lb/ft^3, getting $p = 20 \times 62.4 = 1{,}248$ lb/ft^2. Notice that since h was given in feet, we had to use the density in corresponding units, that is, in pounds per cubic *foot*. The result is then in pounds per square foot. Now that we have the answer, we are at liberty to change it to any other units we like. Very often, pressure in the English system is given in pounds per square *inch*. Since there are 144 square inches in a square foot, we can change our result to these units by dividing by 144. Then we have $p =$ $1{,}248/144 = 8.67$ lb/in^2.

EXAMPLE 2: What is the *total force* on the bottom of a swimming pool 80 ft long and 25 ft wide, filled to a depth of 5 ft? What is the force on one of the sides?

SOLUTION: The total force is the pressure (force per unit area) multiplied by the area on which it acts. Then $F = hDA$, or $F = 5 \times 62.4 \times 80 \times 25 = 624{,}000$ lb, or 312 tons. The pressure on a side will vary from zero at the surface to its greatest value at the bottom. To get the total force on a side, we must then use the *average* pressure, or the pressure *half way down*. In this case, we must take $h = 2.5$ ft. Then $F = 2.5 \times 62.4 \times 80 \times 5 = 62{,}400$ lb $= 31.2$ tons.

Practice Exercise No. 5

1. The water in an aquarium is 30 cm deep. What is the pressure at any point on the bottom?
2. The deck of a submarine is 100 ft below the surface of the sea (salt water). What is the pressure, and what is the total force, in tons, if the area of the deck is 1,500 ft^2?

Applications of Fluid Pressure

The water supply for a town is often pumped from a lake or reservoir to a *standpipe* (Fig. 10), from where it flows down to the water in the mains and is distributed to the houses. The height of the water in the standpipe produces the pressure that moves the water along the piping and delivers it to the places where it is used. If a building is taller than the standpipe level, there must be an auxiliary pump to supply water to the upper floors.

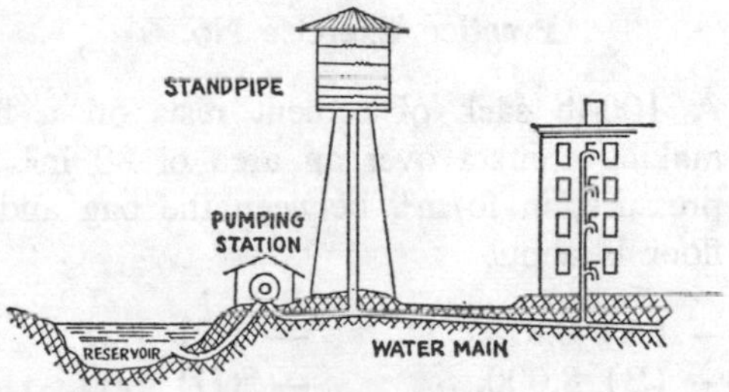

Fig. 10.

Some of the most important applications of liquid pressure use the pressure of confined liquids, rather than merely the weight of a liquid with a free surface. Any extra pressure applied to a confined liquid will be transmitted to all parts of the container. This is the principle of the **hydraulic press** (Fig. 11). Pressure is applied mechanically to a small piston, and this same amount of pressure then acts on every part of the inside surface of the system, including the large piston. But if the area of the larger piston is, say, 100 times that of the smaller one, the total force on the large one will be 100 times whatever force is applied to the small piston. Such presses are used in making bricks, glassware or metal parts and in stamping out automobile bodies. Large machines of this kind may be capable of exerting forces of 10,000 tons or more. The **car lift** used in a greasing station and the barber chair are other examples of the hydraulic press. In the car lift the pressure source is a tank of compressed air, while in the barber chair it is a small pump operated by a foot pedal.

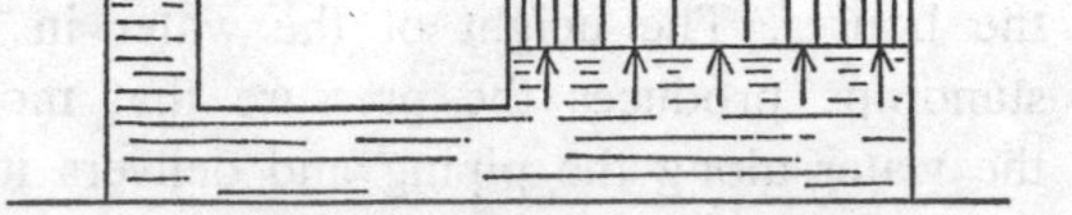

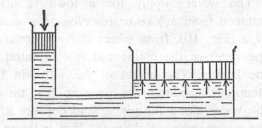

Fig. 11. Hydraulic press

Practice Exercise No. 6

1. A 100-lb sack of cement rests on a floor, making contact over an area of 80 in². The pressure, in lb/in², between the bag and the floor is about

— (A) 0.8. — (C) 1.25.
— (B) 8,000. — (D) 4.00.

2. The pressure at a point 5 ft below the surface of a pond

— (A) depends on the total depth of water in the pond.
— (C) is greater than the pressure 5 ft below the surface of a gasoline storage tank.
— (B) is less than the pressure at a depth of 4 ft.
— (D) depends on the direction in which it is measured.

3. In a city water system, the water will flow

— (A) only if the outlet is higher than the water in the standpipe.
— (C) faster from a first floor faucet than from one on the third floor.
— (B) from the mains to the standpipe.
— (D) only when the standpipe has been completely emptied.

4. An open tank is shaped like a bucket. The diameter at the top is 10 ft; at the bottom, 8 ft; the tank is 6 ft deep. When brim full of gasoline, the pressure at the bottom will be, in lb/ft², about

— (A) 7.3. — (C) 264.
— (B) 44. — (D) 302.

BUOYANCY AND FLOTATION

We saw that, at any place, a liquid exerts pressure equally in all directions, even pushing upward on the bottom of an object immersed in it. Think of a brick-like body hung in water, its sides being in a vertical position (Fig. 12). First of all, the pairs of pressure forces on the opposite sides cancel out. Also, since pressure increases with depth, the upward force on the bottom of the brick will be greater than the downward force on the top.

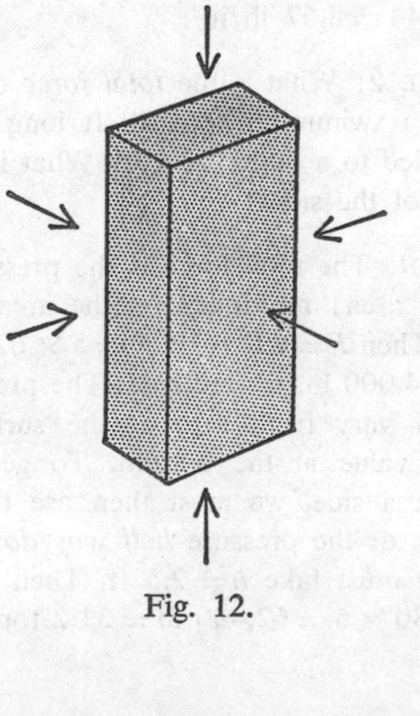

Fig. 12.

This means that there is a net *lifting* force—the brick is *lighter* when in water than it would be out in the air. This is true, of course, for an object of any shape immersed in any liquid.

The existence of such a lifting force is referred to as **buoyancy.** A large rock is easily lifted from the bottom of a pond, but becomes heavy the moment it clears the surface of the water. Sitting in a well-filled bathtub, you can support your whole weight by means of your fingertips. Nearly twenty-two centuries ago the Greek philosopher Archimedes discovered, in just this way, the scientific law governing buoyancy: **Any object immersed in a liquid appears to lose an amount of weight equal to that of the liquid it displaces,** or pushes aside. For instance, a stone having a volume of one-half cubic foot will displace 0.5 ft^3 of water, which weighs $\frac{1}{2} \times 62.4$, or 31.2 lb. Under water, then, this stone will weigh 31.2 lb less than when out of water. If a body is able to *float* in water, it means that the buoyant force is equal to the *whole* weight of the body. In this instance, the object seems to have lost its entire weight.

EXPERIMENT 7: Weigh an empty, corked bottle. Also weigh a pie tin. Put a pot in the pie tin and fill the pot brim full of water. Now lower the bottle carefully into the water, letting it float there. Remove the bottle, then the pot, and weigh the pie tin along with the water that overflowed into it. You will find the weight of water equal to the weight of the bottle, proving Archimedes' law for floating bodies.

It turns out that a body will float if its density is less than that of the liquid, otherwise it will sink. By looking at the table on p. 21, you will then understand why wood, ice and gasoline can float on water, while iron, stone and mercury sink.

EXPERIMENT 8: A fresh egg does not float in water, because its overall density is greater than that of water. Dissolve 2 tablespoonfuls of salt in a glassful of water and the egg will now float because dissolving the salt increased the density of the liquid, making it greater than that of the egg.

Long ago, the suggestion to build ships of iron was ridiculed because everybody knew that "iron is heavier than water." Actually, the overall density of a steel ship—its total weight divided by its total volume—is less than that of water, because the interior is hollow and largely empty. The total weight of a ship is called its **displacement,** because we have seen that its weight must be just equal to that of the water displaced, or pushed aside by it.

EXAMPLE 1: A ship has a volume of 230,000 ft^3 below the water line. What is its displacement?

SOLUTION: It will displace $230{,}000 \times 64 = 14{,}720{,}000$ lb, or 7,360 tons of salt water.

EXAMPLE 2: A rectangular block of wood measures $20 \times 20 \times 5$ cm. When floated flatwise, it is found that 3 cm of the short side is under water. What is the density of the wood?

SOLUTION: The block will sink until it just displaces its own weight of the liquid. The weight of water displaced will be $20 \times 20 \times 3$, or 1,200 gm, since water has a density of 1 gm/cm^3. Then the density of wood will be this weight divided by the volume of the whole block, or $1{,}200/20 \times 20 \times 5$, which comes out equal to 0.6 gm/cm^3. We sometimes use the term **specific gravity** to indicate the density of a material relative to water. Since the density of water is 1 gm/cm^3, this is numerically the same as the specific gravity; but in the English system, the density must be divided by 62.4 to get the specific gravity.

Applications of Flotation

When the lungs are filled with air, the human body has a slightly smaller overall density than water, and so can float. But, as every swimmer knows, the body must be almost completely immersed in order to displace a large enough weight of water.

A submarine can be made to descend or rise by pumping water into or out of its ballast tanks.

EXPERIMENT 9: Get a tall jar with a flexible metal screw top and fill it with water. Fill a small glass vial about two-thirds with water, close the end with the thumb, and invert into the jar of water. Adjust the amount of water in the vial very carefully, drop by drop, until it just floats. At this stage the slightest downward push should send it to the bottom momentarily. Now fill the jar to the brim and screw the cap on tightly. When you push down on the cover with your thumb, the vial will sink to the bottom: release the pressure and it comes to the top. The explanation of the action of this miniature submarine is that pressure applied to the lid is transmitted to the water, forcing slightly more water into the vial. Its overall density is then just greater than that of water, and it sinks. Releasing the pressure allows the air in the top of the vial to push the extra water out again and the vial rises.

According to an old sailors' superstition, a sinking ship will not go all the way to the bottom but will remain suspended somewhere in the depths. This is false, because when enough water has entered the hull to make the overall density of the ship greater than that of water, it keeps sinking until it hits the bottom. If it is denser than water when at the surface, it must continue to be so even at great depths, since water is practically impossible to compress. Even at the deepest spot in the ocean, where the water pressure is almost 8 tons per square inch, water is compressed by only about 3 percent of its bulk.

The depth to which a floating body immerses itself in a liquid can be used as a measure of the density of the liquid. A tall stick or tube, with one end weighted so that it floats upright, can have a scale marked on its side to read the density directly. This is a **hydrometer,** familiarly used to measure the density of the solution in car batteries (the density is a measure of the condition of charge of the battery).

Practice Exercise No. 7

1. Will aluminum, lead and gold all float in mercury? Enumerate.
2. Explain the action of a cork life-preserver in terms of Archimedes' law.
3. When a ship sails out of a river into salt water, will the position of the water line on the side of the ship change? In what way?
4. A ferry boat has a cross-section area of 5,000 ft^2 at the water line. How much lower will it ride, in fresh water, when a 20-ton trailer truck comes aboard?
5. If the overall density of an object is a certain fraction of the density of a liquid, then it will be able to float with this same fraction of the volume of the body under the surface. This being so, look up the densities of ice and of sea water on p. 21 and decide what fraction of an iceberg is under water.

SUMMARY *Instructions:* (see page 17)

1. What name is given to the force exerted on each unit area of a surface?	
2. Using the meter as a unit of length and the kilogram as a unit of force, what is the corresponding pressure unit?	Pressure.
3. How does the pressure within a uniform liquid vary with the vertical depth below the free surface?	kg/m^2.
4. How does the pressure on a surface inside a liquid depend on the angle at which the surface is inclined?	Pressure directly proportional to depth: $p = hD$.
5. State Archimedes' law.	Independent of direction.
6. What factor determines whether an object will float in a given liquid?	See p. 27.
	Whether or not its overall density (total weight divided by total volume) is less than or greater than the density of the liquid.

Chapter IV

THE AIR AND OTHER GASES

Although we are not generally aware of it, air has mass. This can be checked directly by weighing a closed bottle of air, then pumping it out and weighing again. For a 1-liter bottle, the difference amounts to more than a gram.* The fact that air has mass becomes quite evident when it is in rapid motion, as you will find out later in this chapter.

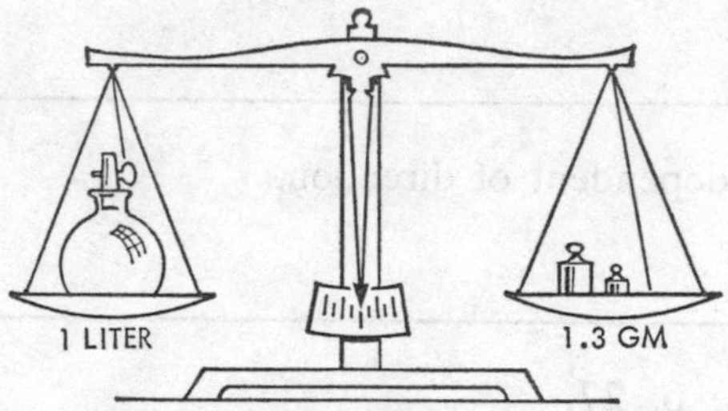

Fig. 13. Weighing air

AIR PRESSURE

Since the air weighs something, it exerts pressure on anything immersed in it, including your own body. The reason you do not feel this pressure is that it is counterbalanced by an equal pressure from the inside—there is air in the body cavities and in the tissues and fluids. At the earth's surface, air pressure amounts to about 14.7 lb/in^2 (1,034 gm/cm^2). This is over a ton per square foot.

EXPERIMENT 10: The existence of air pressure can be shown by removing the air from one side of an exposed surface. Get a tin can that has a tight-fitting cover or an opening provided with a screw cap. Put a little water in the can, stand it in a pan of water and boil it vigorously, with the cover removed, in order to drive out the air by means of the escaping steam. Weight the can down if it tends to upset. While still boiling, close the cap tightly, quickly transfer the can to a sink and run cold water over it to condense the steam inside. Outside air pressure will crush the vessel in a spectacular way.

* Can you tell why, from the Table on p. 21?

The condensing (turning to liquid) of some of the steam in the last experiment left a partial **vacuum** inside the can. A vacuum is simply a place not occupied by matter, or an empty space. For a long time, people believed that a vacuum had the mysterious power of "sucking" things into it. But how does the vacuum you create when you sip a soda succeed in getting a grip on the liquid in order to pull it up into your mouth?

THE BAROMETER

In the seventeenth century, the Duke of Tuscany decided to have a deep well dug. To his surprise, no pump was able to raise the water more than about 34 feet above the level in the well. The great scientist Galileo became interested in the question and suggested to his friend and pupil, Torricelli, that he make experiments to test "the power of a vacuum." Torricelli reasoned that if a 34-foot height of water was needed to satisfy a vacuum, a much shorter column of mercury would be sufficient. Mercury is 13.6 times as dense as water, so a height of only 34/13.6, or 2½ feet, should be enough. He tried an experiment: A glass tube about a yard long, sealed at one end, was completely filled with mercury. The other end was held closed with the thumb. Then the tube was turned over and the open end set in a large dish of mercury. When the thumb was removed, the mercury dropped away from the sealed end until its upper surface came to rest about 30 inches above the liquid in the dish (Fig. 14). The mercury, in descending from the top of the tube, left a vacuum behind it, and it seemed that this vacuum was able to hold up a 30-inch column of mercury. Torricelli concluded that the liquid is supported not by any mysterious sucking action of the vacuum, but by the outside air *pressing* on the mercury in the open dish.

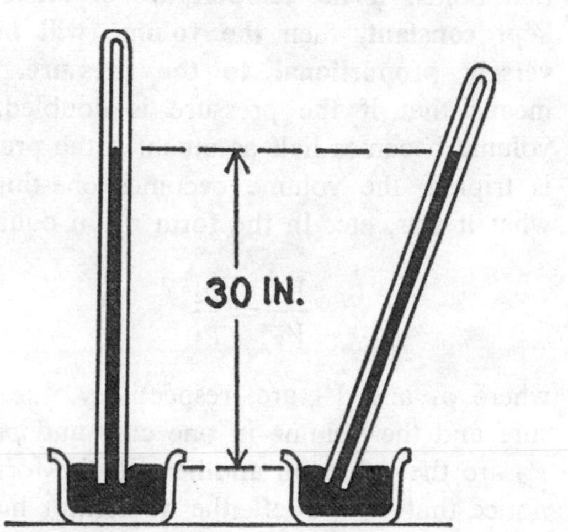

Fig. 14. Mercury tube barometer

To complete the argument, other people carried such instruments up the side of a mountain, where the air pressure is less. Surely enough, it was observed that the mercury in the tube now stood lower, but regained its former height when brought back to the valley. Here, then, is an instrument that can be used to measure changes in air pressure. It is called a **barometer.** A more compact and convenient form of this instrument is the **aneroid** barometer (Fig. 15). It consists of a sealed metal can from which most of the air has been pumped. Changes in outside air pressure make the flexible cover bend in and out very slightly, and the motion is magnified by a lever system, moving a pointer over a scale from which the air pressure can be read off directly.

One important use of the barometer is to determine altitude. Once we know how the pressure of the air depends on altitude, we can use the barometer reading to give our height. An aneroid barometer with the scale marked directly in height units forms the **altimeter** of an airplane.

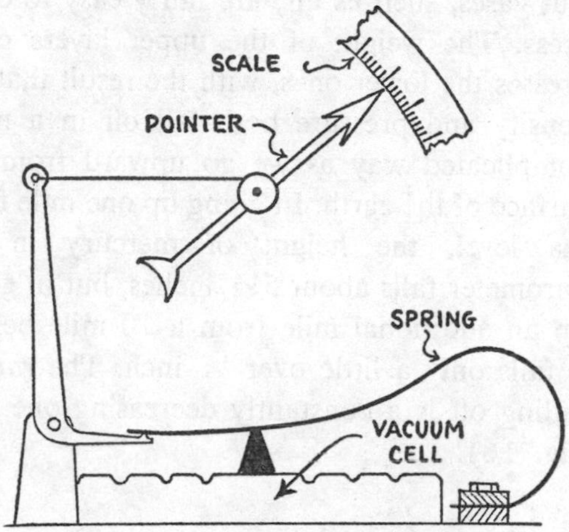

Fig. 15. Aneroid barometer

The other main use of the barometer is in forecasting weather conditions. Contrary to general belief, moist air is *less* dense than dry air, water vapor itself being only around ⅝ as dense as dry air. Since it is less dense, moist air exerts less pressure, and so in moist weather the barometer falls. This gives us a way of predicting what kind of weather we will have in the immediate future. A steady, high barometer indicates fair weather; a rising barometer means fair or clearing weather conditions; and a rapidly falling barometer means a storm is approaching. By combining information obtained at stations all over the country, the Weather Bureau is able to prepare and distribute maps from which forecasts can be made at any locality.

THE ATMOSPHERE

The **atmosphere** is the name we give to the whole body of air surrounding the earth. If it were not for the earth's gravity, this layer of gas would escape out into the vacuum of interplanetary space. As mentioned above, it is the weight of the air that causes it to exert pressure. But there is one important difference between the pressure due to the weight of a liquid, as discussed in the previous chapter, and the pressure of the air: Liquids are virtually incompressible, and this leads to the simple proportion between pressure and depth. But gases, such as air, are fairly easy to compress. The weight of the upper layers compresses the lower ones, with the result that the density and pressure both fall off in a more complicated way as we go upward from the surface of the earth. In going up one mile from sea level, the height of mercury in the barometer falls about 5½ inches, but in going up an additional mile from a 10 mile height, it falls only a little over ½ inch. The *rate* of falling off is a constantly decreasing one (see Fig. 16).

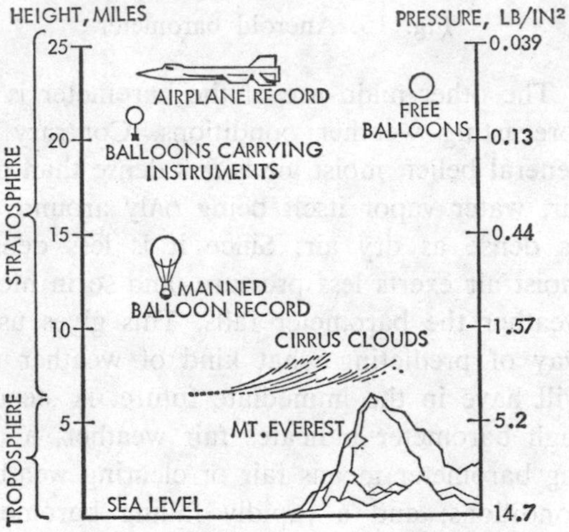

Fig. 16. The lower atmosphere

The part of the atmosphere above about 6.5 miles is called the **stratosphere.** It is a relatively cold and calm region in which no clouds form. It has been explored to some extent by free-sailing balloons carrying instruments and, more recently, by high-altitude rockets and radar. The atmosphere continues to thin out with increasing height, and apparently has no sharp boundary. Air can still be detected at heights of several hundred miles.

BOYLE'S LAW

When air is pumped into an automobile tire, a large volume of outside air is forced into the relatively small space inside the tube. All gases, including air, are compressible; and in order to force a gas into a smaller space, extra pressure must be applied to it. The greater the applied pressure, the smaller the space occupied by the gas. In the seventeenth century, Robert Boyle, an Irish scientist, discovered by experiment the exact relationship that holds: **If the temperature of the gas is kept constant,** then **the volume will be inversely proportional to the pressure.** This means that if the pressure is doubled, the volume becomes half as much; if the pressure is tripled, the volume becomes one-third of what it was, etc. In the form of an equation,

$$\frac{V_1}{V_2} = \frac{p_2}{p_1}$$

where p_1 and V_1 are, respectively, the pressure and the volume in one case and p_2 and V_2 are the values in another. In the formula, notice that on the left, the numerator has the "1" and the denominator has the "2", while on the right, it is just the other way around. This is characteristic of *inverse* proportion.

EXAMPLE 1: The air pressure in a tire is to be 30 lb/in² as read on an ordinary tire gauge, and the inside volume of the tube, assumed constant, is 0.95 ft³. What volume of outside air is needed to fill the tube to this pressure on a day when the barometric pressure is 15 lb/in²?

SOLUTION: A tire gauge reads the pressure *above* atmospheric, so the total pressure on the air in the tube is 30 + 15, or 45 lb/in². Then, if V_1 is the volume that this amount of air occupies outside, we can make the proportion

$$\frac{V_1}{0.95} = \frac{45}{15};$$

cross multiplying:

$$V_1 = \frac{0.95 \times 45}{15} = 2.85 \text{ ft}^3.$$

Buoyancy in Gases

Archimedes' law of buoyancy, described on p. 27 for liquids, also holds for gases. In making very accurate weighings, the difference in the weight of air displaced by the object and by the metal weights must be taken into account. But air has such low density compared with solids, this effect can usually be neglected. A large, hollow body, such as a balloon, can displace more than its own weight of air, and so can float in air. Since the air is less dense higher up, a balloon will rise only to the level where the weight of the displaced air becomes equal to its own weight. Balloons are usually filled with hydrogen or helium. These gases are the lightest known, and provide a large lifting force.

Uses of Air Pressure

There are many uses for compressed air: It is utilized in inflating tires, in operating air brakes and tools such as the riveting hammer, and in keeping water out of underwater workings (see Experiment 1, p. 15).

Low pressures have their uses, too. The vacuum cleaner is a familiar example. In making electric lamps, radio and television tubes and X-ray tubes it is extremely important to be able to remove as much air as possible. Modern pumps can reduce the air pressure in a tube to less than one-billionth of normal atmospheric pressure. Special methods can attain a billionth of this.

Practice Exercise No. 8

1. Knowing that normal atmospheric pressure can hold up a column of mercury 30 in. high, use the relation $p = hD$ (p. 25) to prove that the pressure amounts to 14.7 lb/in^2. (The density of mercury as given in the Table on p. 21 must be changed to pounds per cubic *inch* by dividing by 1,728).
2. If the pressure inside a can of "vacuum-packed" coffee is 5 lb/in^2, what is the total force pressing down on the lid, whose diameter is 5 in?
3. What pressure is needed to compress 100 ft^3 of air at normal pressure into a volume of 7.35 ft^3?
4. A weather balloon filled with hydrogen has a volume of 4,000 ft^3 when on the ground. The bag itself weighs 50 lb. What weight of instruments can it carry and just get off the ground?

AIR RESISTANCE

So far, the discussion has been about air at rest. When air moves, even with moderate speed, important new forces come into play. These forces are responsible for the operation of sailboats, atomizers, parachutes, airplanes, etc. The most evident effect is the resistance that the air offers to the movement of objects through it. Hold your hand out the window of a moving car and you feel the resistance force directly. The car itself experiences such a force. At usual driving speeds, more than half the power delivered by the engine may be used up in working against air resistance.

The actual resistance force increases with the *cross-section area* of the moving body and especially with its *speed* of motion. In addition, the *shape* of the object is of great importance. What we call **streamlining** a body means giving it a suitable shape so that it will offer a minimum of opposition to the flow of air past it. This means eliminating all sharp corners and projections, approaching the general "tear-drop" shape shown in Fig. 17a. Contrary to what you might expect, the front of the body is broader than the rear. But if the body is to be a high-speed jet plane or rocket traveling faster than sound, a sharp-nosed shape gives best performance (Fig. 17b).

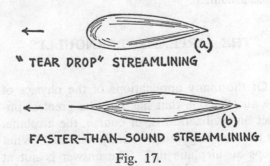

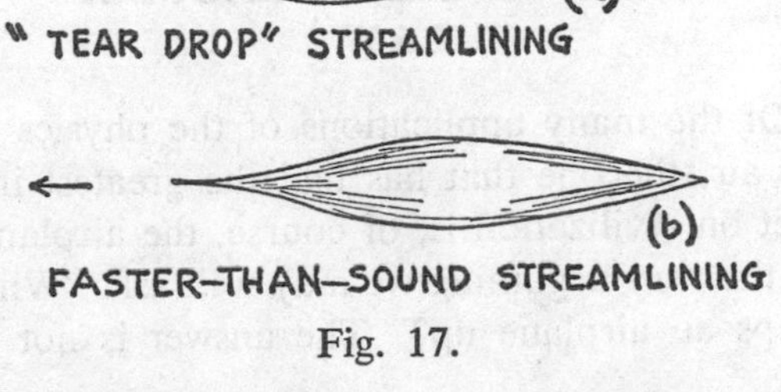

Fig. 17.

Fig. 18 shows the comparative resistance, of (a) a streamlined rod, (b) a round rod and (c) a flat plate of the same cross-section and all moving at a given speed. The air flow around each is also pictured. Behind the round and flat objects, the stream lines break up into whirls, whose effect is to retard the movement of the body. The tapered tail of (a) fills in this region, allowing the flow to join smoothly at the rear.

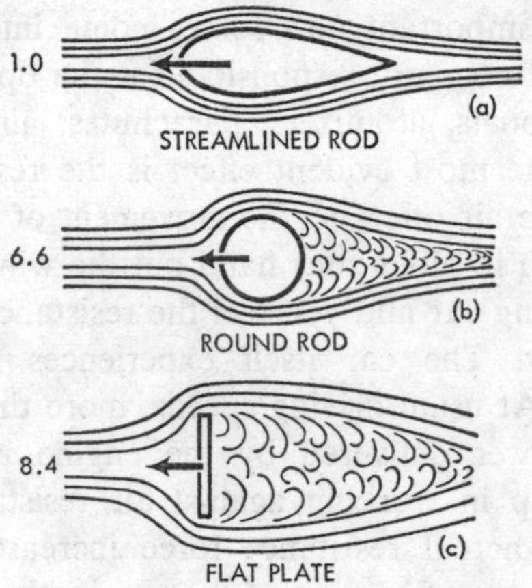

Fig. 18. Relative resistance

Bodies falling through the air are retarded by air resistance. If not for this effect, all objects, regardless of difference in weight, would fall at the same rate (p. 46).

EXPERIMENT 11: Drop a coin and a sheet of paper from shoulder height at the same instant. The coin quickly reaches the floor, while the paper flutters down slowly. To show that this result is not due to their difference in weight but only to the difference in air resistance, repeat the trial after first wadding the paper up into a small ball. This time both will be seen to hit at the same instant.

THE AIRPLANE; BERNOULLI'S LAW

Of the many applications of the physics of the air, the one that has had the greatest impact on civilization is, of course, the airplane. At the very beginning we may well ask, "What keeps an airplane up?" The answer is not at all obvious. We know that a plane must be moved rapidly through the air in order to sustain itself, and that it must have a large, slightly inclined surface—a wing—to furnish the supporting force. Seen from the moving airplane, the surrounding air streams backward, over and around it. The tilted wing surface deflects some air downward, and as a result the plane is literally "knocked" upward. But this is responsible for only a small effect. Actually, it is the flow of air around the curved *upper* surface of the wing that accounts for most of the lift. To see how this works, try an experiment:

EXPERIMENT 12: Hold one edge of a piece of letter paper against your chin, just below your lower lip, with the paper hanging over and down (Fig. 19). If you now blow above the paper, it will rise to a horizontal position as if pulled upward into the air stream.

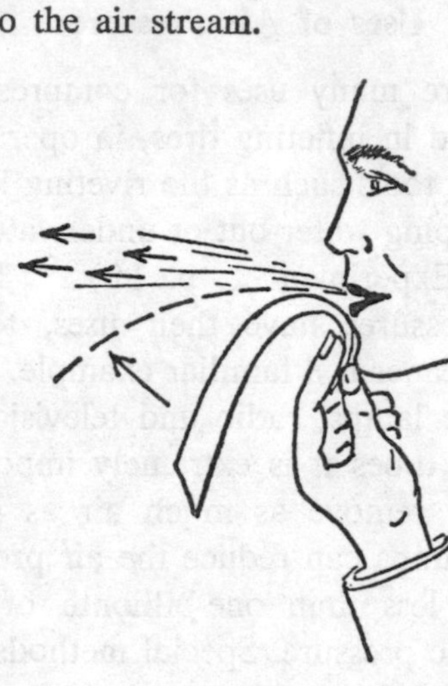

Fig. 19.

This action is an instance of a general law discovered by the eighteenth century Swiss scientist Daniel Bernoulli: A moving stream of gas or liquid exerts less sidewise pressure than if it were at rest. The result is that things seem to be drawn into such a stream; they are really *pushed* in by the greater pressure from outside.

Bernoulli's principle gives us a way of understanding the action of air on a wing. In a properly designed wing, the airstream separates at the front of the wing and rejoins smoothly at the rear (Fig. 20). Since the air that flows over the upper surface has to travel a greater distance its average speed must be greater than that below, and so the decrease in pressure is greater on the top side, resulting in a lifting force on the entire wing. The forces on the upper side of a wing may account for over four-fifths of the whole lift.

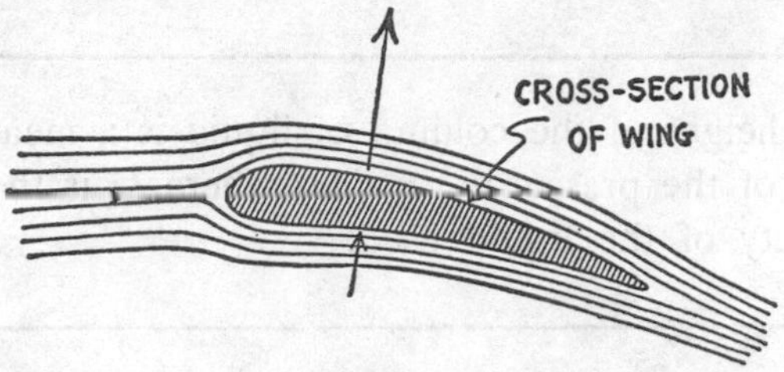

Fig. 20. Airplane wing

The control surfaces of the airplane, as well as the propeller that moves it through the air, operate on this same principle. In the **helicopter** the airflow over the wing surfaces is produced by whirling the rotating wings, rather than by rapid motion of the whole plane through the air. As a result, a helicopter can hover over one spot on the ground, or even move in the backward direction.

Other Applications

A number of familiar observations and devices can be described in terms of Bernoulli's law. In an **atomizer** (spray gun), a stream of air is blown across the end of a small tube that dips into the liquid (Fig. 21). The decreased pressure at the side of the air stream allows normal air pressure, acting on the surface of the liquid in the bottle, to push the liquid up the tube. Here the moving air breaks it up into small drops and drives it forward. The **carburetor** of an auto works in the same way.

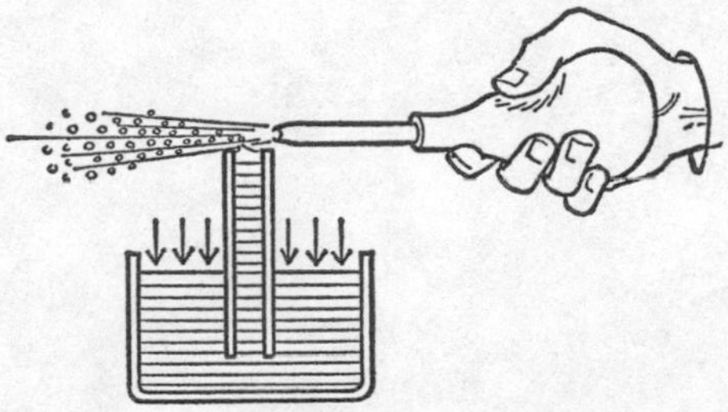

Fig. 21. Atomizer (spray gun)

Two cars, passing each other at high speed, are in danger of sideswiping because of the decrease in air pressure in the space between them. A strong gale is capable of lifting the roof off a house. An amusing experiment shows the same effect:

EXPERIMENT 13: Lay a dime about half an inch from the edge of a table and place a saucer a few inches beyond. With your mouth at the level of the table top, blow a sudden strong breath across the top of the dime (as if whistling) and it will jump into the dish.

The curving of a baseball or of a "sliced" golf ball is explained by Bernoulli's principle. Some air is dragged around by the spin of the ball (Fig. 22). At "A" this air is moving *with* the stream of air caused by the ball's moving along, while at "B" the two *oppose* each other. The greater relative air speed at "A" makes the ball veer to that side.

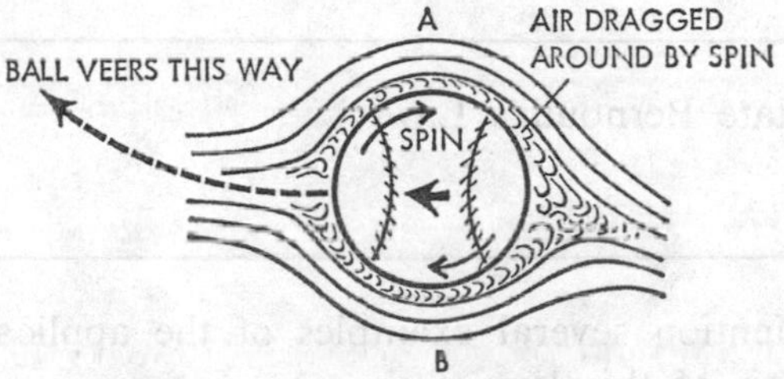

Fig. 22. Curving of a baseball

Practice Exercise No. 9

1. When you inhale, do you "suck" air into your lungs? Explain.
2. Explain the action of the rubber suction cups used for fastening objects to a smooth surface.
3. Does the height at which the mercury stands in a barometer depend on the cross-section of the barometer tube? Give a reason for your answer.
4. A toy balloon, partly filled with air, is clamped shut at the neck and put into a closed jar. If the air is now pumped from the jar, what will happen?
5. Explain the action of a parachute in slowing down the motion of a body falling in air.
6. Explain why two motor boats, moving side by side, will tend to drift together.

SUMMARY *Instructions:* (see page 17)

1. Define a vacuum.	
2. How can the air pressure be measured by means of a liquid barometer?	A region not occupied by matter—an empty space.
3. What is meant by the stratosphere?	The height of the column of liquid is a measure of the pressure: $p = hD$, where D is the density of the liquid used.
4. State Boyle's Law.	The cold, relatively calm region of the atmosphere extending upward from about 6.5 miles.
5. What is the main cause of the retarding (drag) force acting on an object that moves rapidly through a fluid?	If the temperature of a gas is held constant, the volume will be inversely proportional to the pressure: $V_1/V_2 = p_2/p_1$.
6. State Bernoulli's Law.	The eddies or whirls that form behind the object.
7. Mention several examples of the application of this law.	There is a decrease of pressure at the side of a moving stream of fluid.
	Lift of an airplane wing, operation of a spray gun, curving of a baseball, lifting effect of a wind on the roof of a house.

SECTION TWO

FORCE, MOTION AND ENERGY

Chapter V

FORCES

On p. 23 a force was described as a push or a pull—something that would produce the same effect as the direct action of your muscles. It was also pointed out that forces can be measured in ordinary weight units, such as grams, pounds, etc. In this chapter we shall have a closer look at forces and find out how, under certain conditions, they are capable of holding an object in balance.

REPRESENTATION OF FORCES; VECTORS

In most of the practical situations we deal with, not one but a number of forces act on the body in question. There is a simple and convenient way of representing the forces and of finding their net effect. In the first place, in order to describe a force completely, we must specify not only its *amount* (say, in pounds) but its *direction* in space; obviously it makes a difference whether a force acts to the left or to the right, or whether it acts upward or downward.

A force acting at a given point is pictured by a line drawn outward from that point in the given direction, and the *length* of the line is made to represent the *strength* of the force.

Besides forces, there are other physical quantities, to be discussed later, that have both magnitude and direction. Such a quantity is called a **vector.** Any vector may be represented by a directed line segment.

In Fig. 23 *A* stands for a force of 5 lb acting toward the northeast. The scale chosen for this drawing is "¼ in = 1 lb," and so the line, drawn in the proper direction, is made 5 quarter-inches long. An arrow is placed at the end of the line to give its sense of direction. In the same way, *B* is an eastward force of 9 lb acting at the same point. Any convenient scale may be used in these drawings, as long as we stick to the same scale throughout the problem.

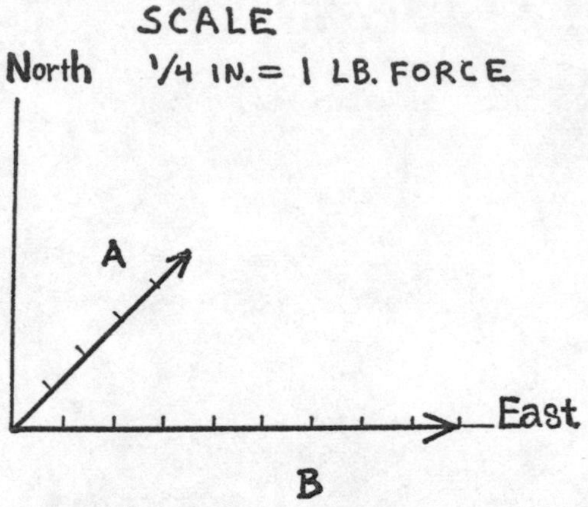

Fig. 23. Representing force vectors

RESULTANT OF A SET OF FORCES

It is found by experience that when a number of forces act on a body they can always be replaced by a single force having a definite amount and direction. This single force, which replaces the effect of all the others, is called their **resultant.** There is a simple way of finding it by means of a drawing: Draw all the forces, end to end, until they have all been put down (the order in which you pick them off from the original drawing does not matter). Then, if you draw a line out from the starting point to the end of the last force, this line will correctly represent the resultant as to direction and amount.

EXAMPLE 1: Three forces act at a point. One is 4 lb straight down, another is 11 lb to the right and the third is 9 lb upward and to the left at an angle of 45 degrees. Find their resultant.

SOLUTION: Fig. 24 shows these forces, drawn to scale. Now, keeping the same length and direction for each force, lay them off end to end, as in (b). Then the resultant is gotten by drawing a line from the starting point out to the end of the last force. This line, when measured, turns out to be 11/16 in. long. Therefore the resultant amounts to 11/16 divided by ⅛, or 5.5 lb, and has the direction shown. In (c) the forces have been laid off in a different order, but the resultant has the same size and direction as before.

Notice that the size (length) of the resultant is, in general, *not* equal to the sum of the magnitudes of the separate vectors. The actual value will depend on their relative positions.

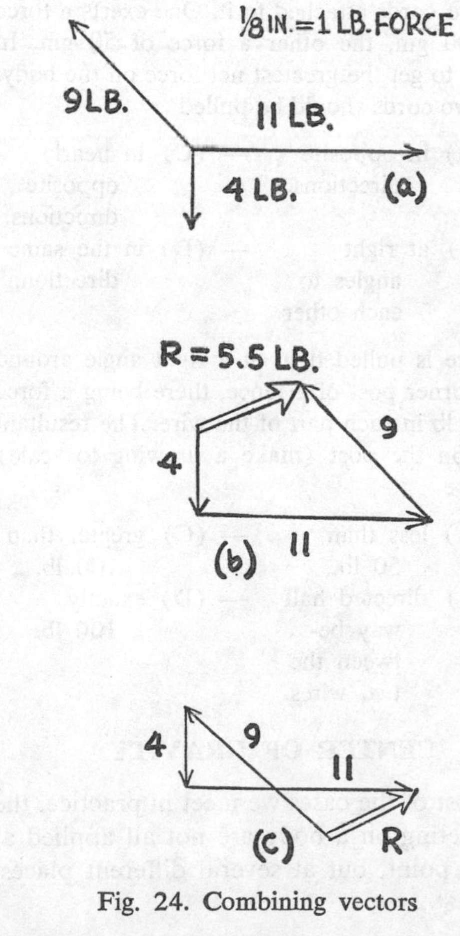

Fig. 24. Combining vectors

If all the acting forces are in a single line (such as east-west), the magnitude of the resultant is simply the sum of all those acting to one side less the sum of all those acting toward the other. As an example, suppose a man can pull with a force of 100 lb, while a boy can pull only 70 lb. If they both pull toward the east, the combined effect is 170 lb force; if the man pulls westward and the boy eastward, the resultant is a 30 lb force toward the west (the direction of the larger force).

Another case where the resultant can easily be calculated rather than measured from a scale drawing is that of two forces at right angles to each other (Fig. 25). The resultant is the hypotenuse of a right triangle and its amount may be computed by the right triangle rule.

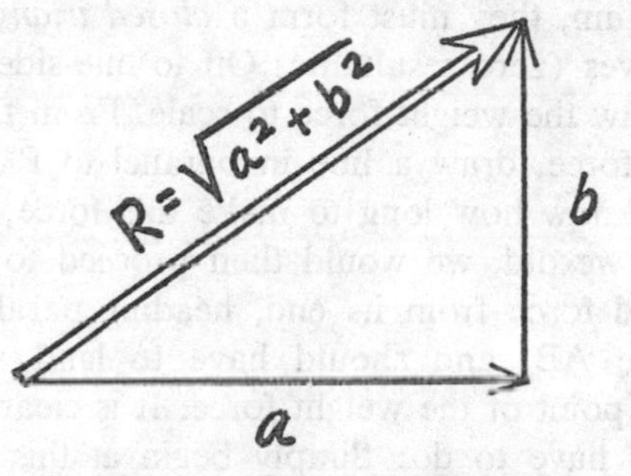

Fig. 25. Forces at right angles

EQUILIBRIUM OF FORCES

One of the most important mechanical situations that engineers and designers must deal with is that in which all the forces acting on a body just hold it at rest. This balancing-out of the applied forces will occur if the **resultant** of all of them **is zero.** When this happens, the body is said to be in **equilibrium.** Conversely, if a body is observed to remain at rest, we know that the resultant of all the acting forces must be zero. This fact can be used to find the values of some of the forces. An example will show how:

EXAMPLE 2: A wire-walker at the circus weighs 160 lb. When at the position shown in Fig. 26, what is the stretching force in each part of the wire?

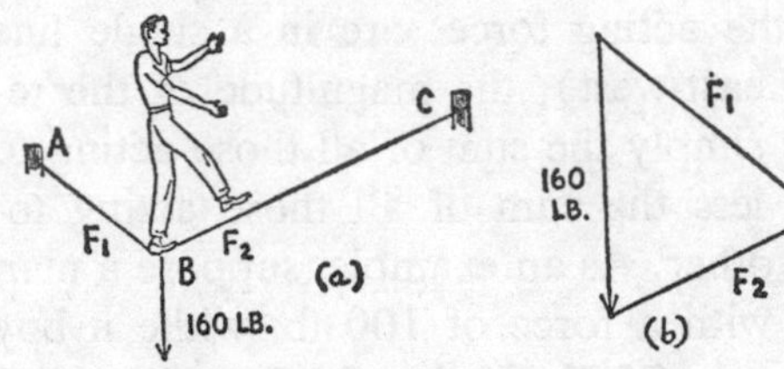

Fig. 26. Tensions in a wire

SOLUTION: First we note that the point *B* is the place where the forces in question meet. One of them is the man's weight. We sketch it in the downward direction from *B* as shown and label it "160 lb." Acting from *B* along the left-hand portion of the wire is some force—call it F_1—whose value is still unknown. As yet, we can only sketch it in, but do not know how long to make it. Likewise, F_2 is the force in the other part of the wire. In general F_1 and F_2 will be different.

Since the three forces hold the point *B* in equilibrium, they must form a *closed triangle* by themselves (zero resultant). Off to one side, Fig. 26b, draw the weight force to scale. From the tip of this force, draw a line in parallel to BC. We do not know how long to make this force; however, if we did, we would then proceed to draw the third force from its end, heading parallel to the wire AB, and should have to land at the starting point of the weight force. It is clear what we now have to do: Simply begin at this point and draw a line back in the proper direction until it crosses the line of F_2. This crossing point fixed the lengths (or amounts) of the two forces. The force lines can now be measured, using the same scale that was employed in drawing the 160-lb weight, and so the magnitudes of F_1 and F_2 can be found. In this example they turn out to be about 165 lb and 135 lb, respectively. Try a construction like this yourself, using a weight and direction of your own choosing.

Practice Exercise No. 10

1. A force acting at a point may be completely described by stating

— (A) its amount, in lb.
— (B) all the other forces that act.
— (C) its amount and direction.
— (D) its direction in space.

2. The resultant of a number of forces acting at a point is

— (A) the single force that produces the same effect.
— (B) not fixed in direction, but has a definite magnitude.
— (C) dependent on the order in which the forces are taken.
— (D) zero under all circumstances.

3. A body is said to be in equilibrium if all the forces acting on it

— (A) have the same direction.
— (B) are of equal magnitude.
— (C) have zero resultant.
— (D) are arranged in opposite pairs.

4. A block of wood resting on a table is pulled by two cords attached to it. One exerts a force of 100 gm, the other a force of 50 gm. In order to get the greatest net force on the body, the two cords should be pulled

— (A) in opposite directions.
— (B) at right angles to each other.
— (C) in nearly opposite directions.
— (D) in the same direction.

5. A wire is pulled tight at a right angle around the corner post of a fence, there being a force of 50 lb in each part of the wire. The resultant pull on the post (make a drawing to scale) will be

— (A) less than 50 lb.
— (B) directed half way between the two wires.
— (C) greater than 100 lb.
— (D) exactly 100 lb.

CENTER OF GRAVITY

In most of the cases we meet in practice, the forces acting on a body are not all applied at a single point, but at several different places.

The weight of a body is a good example. The earth's gravity pulls downward on every particle of a material body with a force equal to the weight of that particle, as pictured in Fig. 27. However, we can replace all these separate

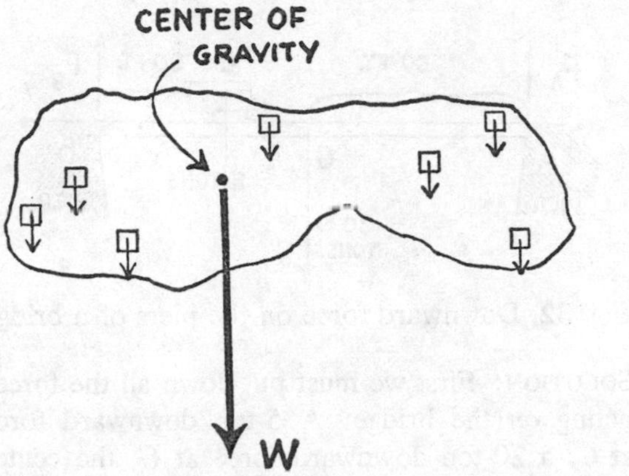

Fig. 27.

forces by a single one, equal to the entire weight of the object. This force must be considered to act at a given place called the **center of gravity** of the body. There is such a point for every object. If the body is made of uniform material and has a simple shape, such as a sphere, cube, straight rod, etc., the location of the center of gravity is obvious (Fig. 28a). The position of the center of gravity of an irregular object may be found by trial, by seeing where it will balance without any tendency to rotate in any direction (Fig. 28b).

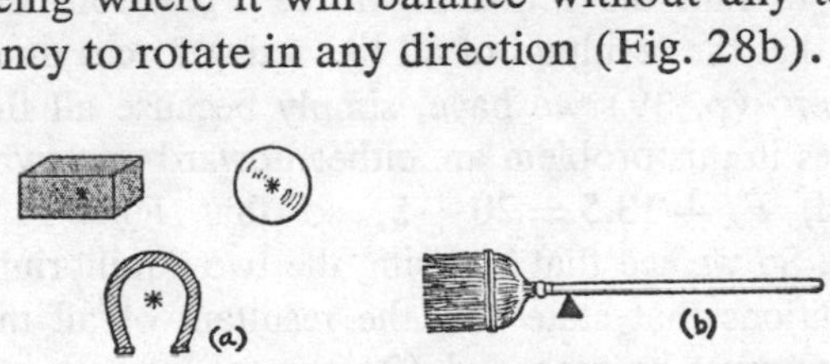

Fig. 28. Locating the center of gravity

If a body is supported at any point other than its center of gravity, it will try to move until its center of gravity is as low as possible. This explains, for instance, why it is impossible to balance a pencil on its point.

EXPERIMENT 14: Fasten a weight to the inner edge of a flat cylindrical box (Fig. 29). Placed on a sloping board, it will mysteriously roll *up* the slope when released. Notice that the center of gravity is very near the position of the concealed weight, and that while the box goes up the hill, the center of gravity goes *down,* as it must.

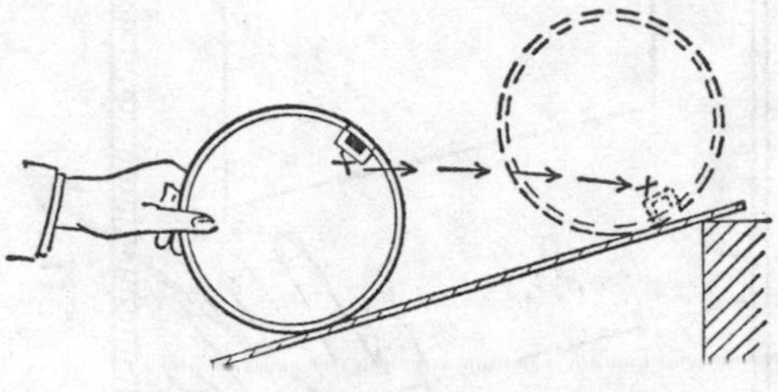

Fig. 29. The mystery cylinder

TORQUE AND ROTATION

In general, if the forces applied to a body do not all act at a single point, there is the possibility that the body will rotate. How can we measure the ability of a force to produce rotation? Think of the example of pushing a revolving door (Fig. 30). If you want to turn the door most effectively, you push with your hand near the edge of the door rather than near the hinge. It is found that the **turning effect** of any force is given by multiplying the **amount of the force** by the **distance from the pivot** point to the line of the force. This turning effect of a force is called the **torque,** and the distance mentioned is the **torque arm.** In symbols,

$$T = Fh$$

where T is the torque, F the force and h the torque arm. Notice what the units are for T: If F is in pounds and h is in feet, the units for T will be **foot pounds.** Here again we have an example of a derived quantity (p. 20).

If the body in question is not to rotate, then the net torque must be zero, that is, **the sum of all torques that tend to turn the body in one direction must be equal to the sum of all those tending to turn it in the opposite direction.** The word "direction" here refers to the sense of rotation—**clockwise** (in the direction turned by the hands of a clock), or **counterclockwise.**

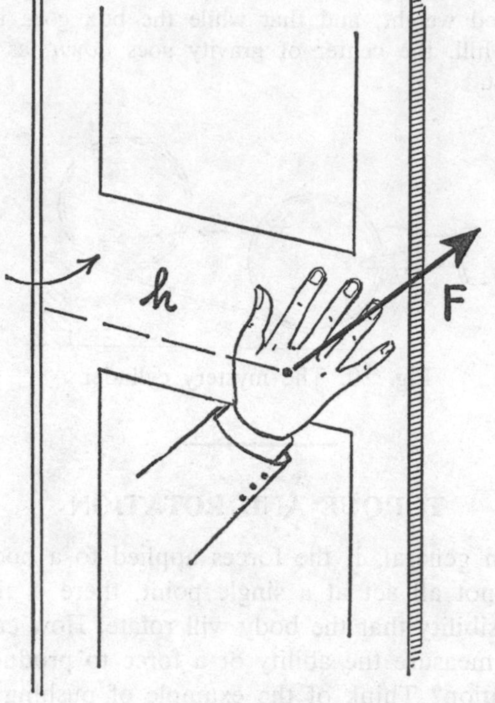

Fig. 30. Revolving door

In figuring the torques, we may take any point as a prospective center of turning—it need not be the place where the actual pivot or axle is located.

EXAMPLE 2: How big a downward force must be applied to the end of the crowbar shown in Fig. 31 in order just to lift the 200-lb weight? Neglect the weight of the bar itself.

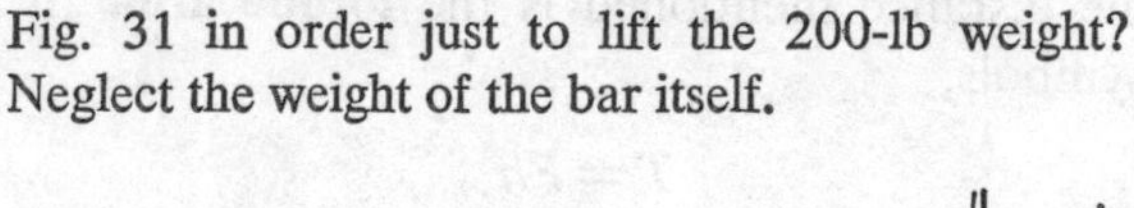

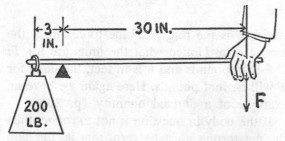

Fig. 31. Lifting by means of a crowbar

SOLUTION: Taking the torques about the pivot point, the one due to the weight will be 200×3, or 600 in.lb. If we call the applied force F, in pounds, it will have a torque around this point of amount $30F$ in.lb. These two torques are in opposite directions: The latter one is clockwise, the other is counterclockwise. Setting the two equal, $200 \times 3 = 30F$, or $F = 20$ lb force.

EXAMPLE 3: A 5-ton truck stands 30 ft from one pier of a uniform bridge 100 ft long weighing 20 tons (Fig. 32). Find the downward force on each pier.

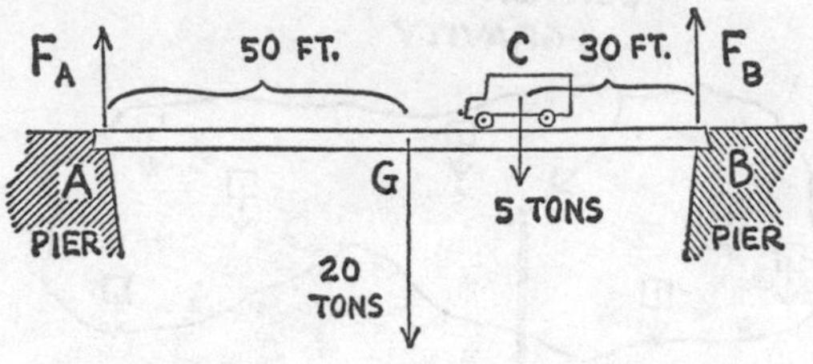

Fig. 32. Downward force on the piers of a bridge

SOLUTION: First we must put down all the forces acting *on* the bridge: A 5-ton downward force at *C;* a 20-ton downward force at *G,* the center of gravity of the bridge structure; and at the piers, upward forces F_A and F_B whose values are to be found. Take torques around *A*. The two weight forces tend to turn the bridge clockwise about *A*, and their torques amount to $20 \times 50 + 5 \times 70$, or 1,350 ft-tons. The only counter-clockwise torque is that of F_B, amounting to $100\,F_B$. Notice that F_A does not contribute any torque, since it has no torque arm around *A*. Setting the torques in the two directions equal, $100\ F_B = 1{,}350$, $F_B = 13.5$ tons force. We could now repeat the process, taking torques around, say, the point *B;* but there is a simpler way to find the remaining force F_A: From the fact that the resultant of all the acting forces must be zero (p. 39) we have, simply because all the forces in this problem are either upward or downward, $F_A + 13.5 = 20 + 5$, so that $F_A = 11.5$ tons. So we see that by using the two equilibrium conditions that state (1) the resultant of all the forces must be zero and (2) the torques around any point must balance, we can work out any equilibrium problem.

GRAVITATION

One of the greatest scientific achievements of all time was Newton's discovery of gravitation, around the middle of the seventeenth century. Earlier, the astronomer Kepler had found certain regularities about the motion of the planets around the sun. Newton, trying to explain these rules, decided that the planets must move in the observed way because they are pulled by a force exerted by the sun. He concluded that this force of gravitation exists not only between the sun and the planets but between *any* two objects in the universe, and he worked out the factors on which the amount of force depends. This is stated by his **Law of Gravitation: Any two bodies in the universe attract each other with a force that is directly proportional to their masses and inversely proportional to the square of their distance apart.**

This may be stated as a formula:

$$F = \frac{Gm_1m_2}{d^2}$$

where F is the force of attraction, m_1 and m_2 are the two masses, and d is their distance apart. G is a constant, whose value is fixed once we have chosen our units for F, m and d. If F and m are measured in pounds and d in feet, the value of G is 0.000 000 000 033. Because G is so small, the attraction between ordinary objects is very weak, but when the bodies concerned are very massive, the force may be extremely large. Thus, the attractive force between the earth and the moon amounts to about 15 million trillion tons.

The gravitational force of the earth for objects on it—what we have been calling **gravity**—is responsible for their weight. The attraction of the moon for the waters of the ocean is the main cause of the **tides.**

Notice that while Newton's law allows us to calculate the amount of the attraction in any case, it does not tell us what gravitation is, nor why such a force exists. These are philosophical rather than scientific questions!

Practice Exercise No. 11

1. In terms of the idea of center of gravity, explain why a ship is less stable when empty than when loaded.
2. Two men carry a 150-lb load hung from a lightweight pole resting on their shoulders. If the load is attached at a point 4 ft from one man and 5 ft from the other, how much of the weight does each carry?
   HINT: Follow the method of Example 3, in this chapter.
3. A uniform brick whose dimensions are 8½ × 4 × 2 inches weighs 5.4 lb. It rests with its largest face on the floor. How big an upward force, applied at the center of the smallest face, will just lift one end off the floor?
4. If the earth were 3 times as far from the sun as it is now, how would the gravitational attraction compare with its present value?
5. Compute the force of attraction between two 15,000-ton ships whose centers of gravity are effectively 150 ft apart.

SUMMARY *Instructions:* (see page 17)

1. Define a vector quantity.	
2. What is meant by the resultant of a set of vectors?	A physical quantity whose direction as well as magnitude must be specified. Force is an example of a vector.
3. What is true of the resultant of a set of vectors that is said to be in equilibrium?	A single vector that would produce the same effect as all the given vectors acting together.
4. Define the center of gravity of a body.	The resultant is zero.
5. What is meant by the torque of a given force, about a given axis?	The place where the entire weight (force) of the object may be considered to act.
6. If a body is in *rotational* equilibrium, what must be true of all the forces that act on it?	The turning, or rotation-producing effect. It is measured by the force multiplied by the perpendicular distance from the axis to the line of the force.
7. State Newton's Law of Gravitation.	The sum of all the torques tending to produce clockwise rotation must equal the sum of all those tending to produce counter-clockwise rotation (about any axis).
	Any two bodies in the universe attract each other with a force that is directly proportional to their masses and inversely proportional to the square of their distance apart: $F = Gm_1m_2/d^2$

Chapter VI

MOTION

In the world about us, everything moves. This may seem to contradict the discussion in the last chapter where we talked about bodies at rest. But a body at rest on the ground is really moving with the rotation of the whole earth, and the earth in turn moves in its path around the sun, and so on. Rest and motion are relative terms. In this chapter you will find out how to measure the motions of bodies, and how the forces acting on them determine the way in which they move.

SPEED AND VELOCITY

In any kind of motion—for example, in making a trip—two things are of interest: What is the *rate* of motion and in what *direction* does it take place? Rate of motion is what we call **speed.** It is measured by the distance covered divided by the elapsed time. In symbols,

$$v = \frac{d}{t},$$

where d stands for the distance, t is the time required and v is the speed. Speed is a derived unit, and we are at liberty to use any distance unit and any time unit for this purpose. Table 4 gives convenient factors for changing from one common speed unit to another.

TABLE 4

CONVERSION FACTORS FOR SPEED UNITS

To change from a unit given at the side to one given at the top, multiply by the factor in the appropriate square. Thus 100 cm/sec = 100 $\times$ 0.0328 = 3.28 ft/sec.

	mi/hr	ft/sec	cm/sec	knots*
mi/hr	—	1.47	44.7	0.868
ft/sec	0.682	—	30.5	0.592
cm/sec	0.0224	0.0328	—	0.0194
knots*	1.15	1.69	51.5	—

* 1 knot = 1 nautical mile per hour.

Even where the rate of motion is not constant over the whole journey, the above formula has a meaning: it gives the **average speed** for the entire trip. For instance, if a car travels to a city 90 miles away in a total time of 3 hours, the average speed will be 90 mi/3 hr = 30 mi/hr. But no trip of this kind is made at constant speed; there may have been times when the car was going much faster or much slower than this, as indicated by the speedometer.

When the directional aspect is combined with the speed we have the **velocity** of motion. Velocity, like force, is a vector (p. 38), and so an arrowed line can be used to stand for a velocity. A body can have several velocities at the same time. A ball rolled across the floor of a moving railroad car (Fig. 33) has the common forward velocity of everything in the train, plus the crosswise velocity with which the ball is rolled. The **resultant**

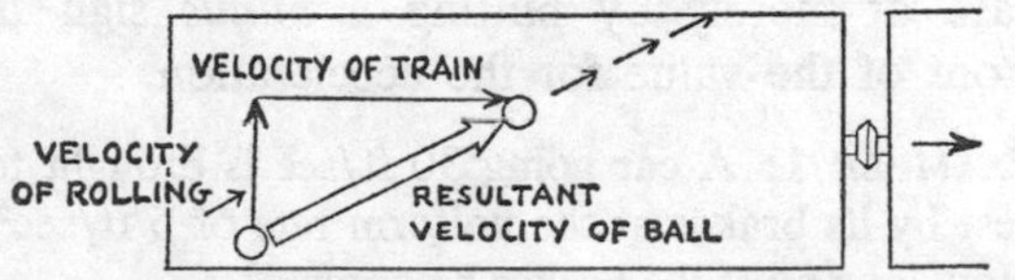

Fig. 33. Combination of velocities

velocity—how the ball would appear to move as seen by someone on an overhead bridge—is given by the same construction we used before (p. 39). The actual path is the straight line indicated.

ACCELERATION

In most of the motions we commonly observe, the speed is not at all constant, whether it is the flight of a bird, the swinging of a pendulum or the fall of a stone. Any motion in which the speed or direction are variable is called **accelerated motion.** The **acceleration** is defined as the **rate of change** of the **velocity,** that is, the change in velocity divided by the time it takes to make that change. For instance, if a car going 25 ft/sec picks up speed until, 5 sec later, it is going 60 ft/sec, its rate of pick-up will be 60—25, or 35 ft/sec in 5 sec. Dividing, this amounts to 7 ft/sec/sec ("feet per second per second"). This means only that the car increased its speed at an average rate of 7 ft/sec *each second.* Instead of writing "ft/sec/sec," we recognize that the time unit comes in *twice* as a factor in this derived unit, and we write "ft/sec²" and read it "feet per second squared."

Motion with Constant Acceleration

One kind of motion that is readily described and computed is that where the amount of the acceleration is *constant.* This holds, for a limited time at least, when a train is gathering speed, or when it is being brought to rest by the brakes. In the latter case, the speed is *decreasing,* and this is sometimes called decelerated motion. However, no special name is really needed; this can be taken care of merely by putting a *minus* sign in front of the value for the acceleration.

EXAMPLE 1: A car going 30 ft/sec is brought to rest by its brakes at the uniform rate of 5 ft/sec². How long must the brakes be applied?

SOLUTION: Saying that the braking acceleration amounts to —5 ft/sec² means that the car will lose speed at the rate of 5 ft/sec each second. To take away all the initial speed of 30 ft/sec will then require 30/5 or 6 sec.

How *far* will a constantly-accelerating object move in a given time? To answer such a question, you must remember that the speed of motion is changing all the while. But we can find out what is happening by making use of the *average* speed; and here, since the speed changes at a uniform rate, the average speed will be half way between the speed at the beginning and the speed at the end of the interval. The next example will show how we can compute the distance in a specific case:

EXAMPLE 2: A car going 26 ft/sec begins to accelerate at the rate of 2 ft/sec². How fast will it be going after 8 sec, and how far will it go in this time?

SOLUTION: In 8 sec, the total gain in speed will be $8 \times 2 = 16$ ft/sec, so the final speed will be $26 + 16$, or 42 ft/sec. To find the distance traveled, we note that the speed at the beginning of the acceleration period was 26 and at the end was 42 ft/sec, so that the average speed over this interval is $\frac{1}{2}(26 + 42) = 34$ ft/sec. Going, in effect, 34 ft/sec for 8 sec, the car would cover a distance of 34×8, or 272 ft.

Falling Motion; Projectiles

The ancient Greek philosopher Aristotle described the motion of a freely falling body by saying that the heavier the body, the faster it would fall. This does, at first thought, seem true, but you have already performed an experiment (p. 34) that throws some doubt on this conclusion. In the latter part of the sixteenth century, the great Italian scientist Galileo tried some experiments that convinced him that it is merely the disturbing effect of air resistance that ordinarily make a light object fall more slowly than a heavy one. In a vacuum, all bodies fall at the same rate.

Galileo went on to find just how a falling body moves. He found that, when the effects of the surrounding air can be neglected, a falling body has a constant acceleration—the kind of motion we have been discussing above. This acceleration is called the **acceleration due to gravity,** and is denoted by the symbol *g*. Its value changes slightly from place to place on earth, and especially with height, but the standard value is close to

$$32 \text{ ft/sec}^2, \text{ or } 980 \text{ cm/sec}^2.$$

Knowing the value of *g*, it is not difficult to calculate the motion of a falling body. The results will be quite accurate for compact solid objects falling moderate distances. The case of a body falling great distances in air is, in general, too complicated for computation.

EXAMPLE 3: A small stone is dropped from the roof of a tall building and is seen to hit the ground 7.0 sec later. Neglecting air resistance, find the height from which the stone fell and how fast it was going when it hit the ground.

SOLUTION: In the stated time, the stone, starting from rest, picks up a speed of $7 \times 32 = 224$ ft/sec, which is its speed just before hitting the ground. Its *average* speed for the whole trip is half the sum of the speed at the start and at the finish, or $\frac{1}{2}\ (0 + 224) = 112$ ft/sec. Going at this speed for 7 sec, a body would cover a distance of $112 \times 7 = 784$ ft, which is the distance of fall.

A **projectile**—a thrown stone or a bullet—is really a falling body. If shot upward at an angle (Fig. 34), it immediately begins to *fall* short of the direction of fire, just like any falling object. It continues to fall in this way while moving forward, and so follows the observed curved path. Since bullets travel at high speed, the results may be somewhat altered by air resistance.

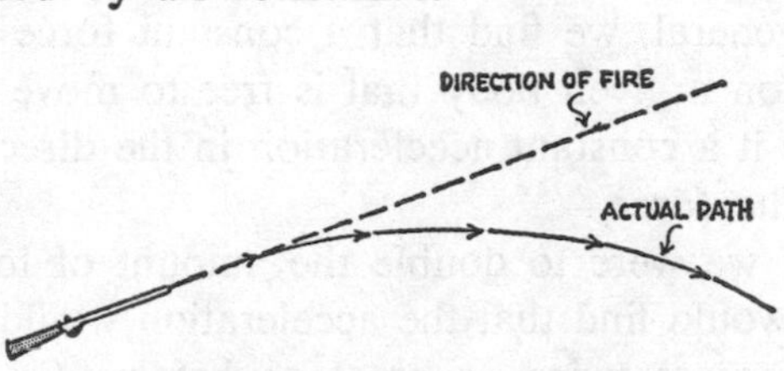

Fig. 34. Path of a projectile

EXPERIMENT 15: Place two coins at the very edge of a table, one on top of the other. A sharp blow with a knife blade held flat against the table will send the lower coin off like a projectile, while the upper one will fall almost straight down. In spite of this difference in path, both will be heard to strike the floor at the same time, since both really *fall* the same distance.

Practice Exercise No. 12

1. A delivery truck covers 2 miles of its route at a speed of 24 mi/hr, makes a stop for 15 min, and then takes 6 min to go the remaining 1½ mi. What is the average speed for the whole trip?
2. If the acceleration due to gravity on the moon is ⅙ the value on earth, how fast will a freely-falling stone be moving on the moon 2 sec after it is dropped?
3. Compare the distance a stone falls in the first second after being dropped with the distance it falls during the second second.
4. If the stone in the preceding example were *thrown* downward instead of being dropped from rest, how would this affect its average speed for the whole trip? How would this affect the time required to fall the whole distance?
5. Considering Fig. 34, must one aim high or low in order to hit a distant target? Explain.

FORCE AND MOTION

In the preceding pages you learned how to describe certain types of motion, such as motion with constant speed or motion with constant acceleration, and how to figure out times, distances, etc. Now we take up the more involved question of what *causes* and *maintains* the motion of an object—that is, the relation of force to the motion it produces.

NEWTON'S LAWS

The general answer to such questions was given by the brilliant work of Newton in the form of his **Three Laws of Motion.** These principles form the basis of the whole subject of Mechanics.

Law of Inertia

The First Law is called the **Law of Inertia.** In Chapter I, p. 15, inertia was described as one of the fundamental properties of matter.* Although the general idea was anticipated by Galileo, Newton succeeded in putting it into precise form:

Every body remains in a state of rest or of uniform motion in a straight line unless acted upon by forces from the outside.

This law states that motion is as natural a condition as rest. A car going along a straight, level road at constant speed is in equilibrium: The weight of the car is balanced by the supporting force of the pavement, and the forward pull of the engine counterbalances the retarding forces of friction and air resistance. The resultant force is zero, and the car is in equilibrium just as truly as if it were at rest.

Centripetal Force; Satellites

If the car comes to a curve, the pavement must furnish, through friction with the tires, an additional force to swerve the car from its

Fig. 35. Not enough centripetal force; the car continues along its "natural" straight path

natural straight path and enable it to round the curve. If the road is slippery, this force will be lacking and the car will continue straight ahead, tending to skid off the road.

The force required to hold a moving object in a circular path is called **centripetal**** force.

Many situations arise in practice where centripetal force must be taken into account. The curves on a road or on a bicycle racetrack are "banked," or raised at the outer edge to furnish such a force. Mud flying from the wheel of a car leaves the wheel in a straight line—it "flies off on a tangent." Laundries make use of centrifugal ("away from the center") dryers in which the wet clothes are whirled in a wire basket. Chemists and biologists use a **centrifuge** to separate suspended solid matter from a liquid. When the mixture is whirled rapidly, the difference in centripetal force on the solid material and on the less dense liquid causes the solids to collect at the outer rim. Using special arrangements, the centripetal force on a particle can be made to exceed 100 million times its weight.

A satellite following an orbit around a planet or a planet going around the sun is held in orbit by the centripetal force furnished by gravitational attraction.

The Second Law

Newton's First Law is limited in its usefulness, since it tells what happens only in the case where there is *no* resultant force. In the majority of actual situations, outside forces do act; the Second Law tells what can be expected under such circumstances.

In order to see what is involved, consider the particular case of a hand truck which can be pushed along on a level floor. If the truck is standing still to begin with and nobody pushes on it, it will remain at rest (First Law). What happens, now, if it is pushed in such a way that the force acting on it is kept constant? An actual trial shows that the truck will move forward with *constant acceleration*. In general, we find that a constant force acting on a given body that is free to move will give it a constant acceleration in the direction of the force.

If we were to double the amount of force, we would find that the acceleration would become just twice as great as before. On the other hand, if the mass of the car were doubled and the same force used as before, the acceleration would be just half of its earlier value. From experiments such as these, we

* This section should be looked at again before going on.

** The word means "toward the center."

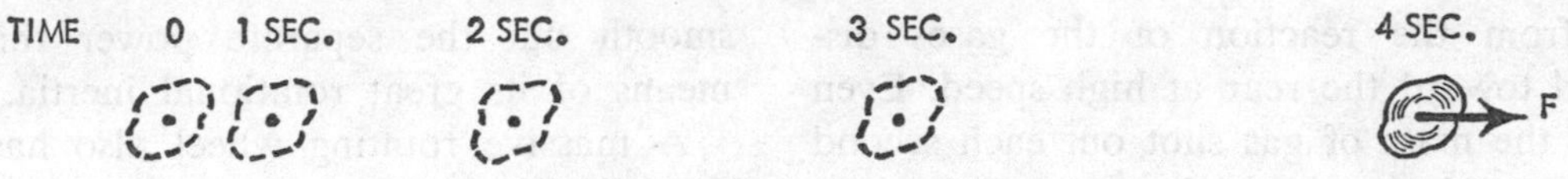

Fig. 36. A constant force produces a constant acceleration

conclude that the acceleration is proportional to the force divided by the mass (Fig. 36).

We are now able to state the **Second Law: A body acted upon by a constant force will move with constant acceleration in the direction of the force; the amount of the acceleration will be directly proportional to the acting force and inversely proportional to the mass of the body.**

Newton's Second Law can be put into a useful form by remembering what happens to any given object when it falls under gravity: Here the acting force is equal to the weight of the body, and the acceleration is, in every case, that of gravity, *g*. Making a direct proportion between force and acceleration, we can write

$$\frac{F}{W} = \frac{a}{g}$$

where W is the weight of the body, F is any applied force and a is the acceleration that this force will give to the body. F and W are to be measured in the same units, and a and g are to be measured in the same units.

EXAMPLE 4: A car weighing 3,200 lb accelerates at the rate of 5 ft/sec^2. Neglecting friction, what is the effective forward force exerted by the engine?

SOLUTION: The proportion gives $F = W\ (a/g)$. Substituting the numbers, $F = 3200 \times 5/32 =$ 500 lb force.

The Third Law; Action and Reaction

Newton's Third Law deals with the observed fact that it is not possible to exert a force on a body without exerting a force in the opposite direction on some other body or bodies. There are many common illustrations of this: If you jump from a rowboat to a pier, the boat is thereby shoved backward. A gun "kicks" when the bullet goes forward. A ship's propeller can drive it forward only because it continually throws water backward.

Newton defined what is called the **momentum** of a body. It is the **mass multiplied by the velocity.** In symbols

$$M = mv,$$

where M is the momentum, m is the mass and v the velocity of the body. M is a derived quantity and any appropriate units may be used for m and v. The **Third Law** makes a simple statement about momentum. It says that **when any object is given a certain momentum in a given direction, some other body or bodies will get an equal momentum in the opposite direction.**

EXAMPLE 5: A gun has a mass of 2,500 gm and the bullets each have a mass of 100 gm. If a bullet leaves the gun with a speed of 800 meters/sec, with what speed will the gun start back?

SOLUTION: The momentum of the bullet will be 100×800 gm m/sec (gram meters per second). Calling the recoil speed of the gun V, its momentum just after firing will be $2500V$. Setting the two momenta equal, $2500V = 100 \times 800$, so that $V = 32$ m/sec. V comes out in m/sec because the speed of the bullet was given in these units.

If the gun and bullet were subject to no other forces after firing, the two would go in opposite directions, each continuing to move with its own constant speed forever (First Law). This would nearly be the case, for example, if the gun were fired far out in space where friction and gravitational forces are negligible. If the gun were fixed in the ground rather than free to recoil, the reaction would be transmitted to the whole earth instead of to the gun alone. Because of the earth's enormous mass, its resulting motion would be far too small to be detectable.

A jet engine or rocket gets its propelling

force from the reaction of the gases discharged toward the rear at high speed. Even though the mass of gas shot out each second is not very large, its high speed makes the product *mv* very large. The jet plane or rocket gets an equal momentum in the forward direction. A rocket will work perfectly well in the vacuum existing in interplanetary space, provided it carries its own fuel and the oxygen needed to burn it.

EXPERIMENT 16: The reaction principle can be demonstrated by making a rubber-band slingshot on a board resting on rollers (Fig. 37). Tie the band back by means of a string and place a fairly massive stone in firing position. Release the stretched band by burning the thread and observe the recoil of the board as the stone goes forward.

Fig. 37. Recoil

ROTATIONAL INERTIA

Newton's laws apply to rotation as well as to the forward motion of an object as a whole. A body that is set spinning has a tendency to keep spinning—**rotational inertia.** The purpose of a heavy flywheel on an engine is to smooth out the separate power thrusts by means of its great rotational inertia.

A massive rotating wheel also has a tendency to keep its axis in a constant direction in space. This is the principle of the **gyroscope,** a rapidly rotating wheel mounted in a pivoted frame, so that the axis may hold its direction in spite of any motion of the mounting. The ability to keep its direction constant makes the gyroscope useful in the construction of several aircraft instruments, such as the turn indicator, artificial horizon, gyrocompass and automatic pilot.

Practice Exercise No. 13

1. Collisions usually involve very sudden changes in speed or direction of motion on the part of the bodies involved. How does this explain the destructiveness of an automobile collision at high speed?
2. Explain how it is possible to exert a blow of several hundred pounds of force by means of a hammer weighing only a few pounds.
3. If the gun and bullet get equal amounts of momentum, why is it not as dangerous to take the "kick" of the gun as to be hit by the bullet?
4. In walking, we push back on the ground; the reaction is the ground pushing forward on us. Why is it difficult to walk on ice?
5. Why is it harder to stop a ferry boat than a canoe going at the same speed?
6. In the absence of a breeze, would it be possible to propel a sailboat by blowing on the sail with an engine-driven fan mounted on the boat? Explain.
7. What is the effect of the rotation of the earth on the apparent weight of a body?

SUMMARY *Instructions:* (see page 17)

1. What is meant by the average speed of a body over a given interval?	
2. Define velocity.	The average speed is the total distance covered divided by the total elapsed time: $v = d/t$.
3. Define acceleration.	Velocity is a vector embodying the speed and direction of motion.
4. What type of motion does a body have when falling freely under gravity, in a vacuum?	The rate of change of velocity.
5. What is the numerical value of the acceleration due to gravity at the surface of the earth?	Motion with constant acceleration.
6. State Newton's Laws of Motion.	About 32 ft/sec^2, or 980 cm/sec^2.
7. Define centripetal force.	See text, page 48.
8. What is meant by the momentum of a moving body?	The centrally-directed force needed to hold a body in a curved path.
9. Explain the term "rotational inertia."	Its mass multiplied by its speed: $M = mv$.
	The tendency of a spinning body to keep rotating.

Chapter VII

WORK, ENERGY AND MACHINES

In the first chapter of this book, energy was briefly described as something capable of producing changes in matter. In the present chapter we take a closer look at this quantity, especially at the form known as **mechanical energy—**the kind that is utilized in the great variety of machines on which our present industrial civilization is built.

WORK

In learning about science, the beginner occasionally has the impression that altogether too many formal definitions and new quantities are introduced. The scientist, like anybody else, is not interested in making things more difficult for himself or for others; he defines what he talks about with great care in order to avoid misunderstandings and he brings in new ideas only because he wants to simplify the structure of the subject. In the first place, science uses language for its description. Sometimes this language is mathematical, and this goes according to definite rules. More troublesome is ordinary language, for words change their meaning slightly according to how, why and where they are used. In science, a word must have one definite meaning all the time.

The word "work" is a good example of what has been said. As the term is commonly understood, a laborer who holds up one end of a plank or tugs at a heavy stone which fails to move would feel that he is working. So would a soldier standing guard or an inspector watching canned goods go by on a moving belt. But in the sense in which the word is used in mechanics, **work is done only when a force succeeds in moving the body it acts upon.** The quantity of work done is the amount of the **force multiplied by the distance moved** in the direction in which the force acts. If we call the force F, the distance d and the work W, we can put this definition in general terms by saying

$$W = Fd.$$

Work may be expressed as any force unit times any distance unit, such as foot-pounds, kilogram-meters, and so on. There is a special Metric unit of work, useful in some instances, called one **erg.** It is equal to 1/980 of a gram centimeter. This unit is too small for many practical purposes, so another unit, called one **joule,*** is introduced. It is simply 10,000,000 ergs, and is equivalent to just under ¾ of a foot-pound.

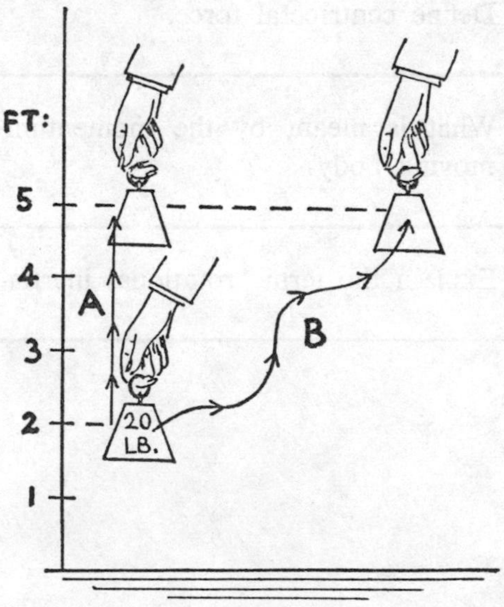

Fig. 38. Work done in raising a weight

* Pronounced "jōōl," and named for J. P. Joule, a nineteenth century physicist.

EXAMPLE 1: (a) A man holds a 20-lb weight at rest at a height of 2.0 ft from the floor. How much work does he do? (b) How much work is done when he then lifts it straight up to a height of 5.0 ft from the floor? (c) When he lifts it by the crooked path "B" in Fig. 38.

SOLUTION: (a) None, since no movement is involved. (b) Just to lift the weight slowly and steadily requires an upward force of 20 lb. This force moves through a distance of 3.0 ft in the direction of the force, so the work done amounts to $20 \times 3 = 60$ ft lb. (c) The only thing that matters is the distance moved *in the direction of the force*. Here again the weight is moved only 3 ft vertically, so the work done is the same as in (b).

THE ENERGY PRINCIPLE

With the idea of work before us, we can now sharpen up the meaning of mechanical energy: **Mechanical energy is measured by the amount of work a body can do.** A raised weight, such as the one in the example, evidently possesses energy, because in letting it come back to its former level we can get it to do work. For example, in coming back down, it can be made to raise another weight, to stretch a spring, etc. While at its higher level, the body is said to have **potential energy**—energy of position. In particular, we might call the energy of a raised weight **gravitational potential energy.** The abbreviation for potential energy in general is PE; for gravitational potential energy, GPE.

There are many kinds of PE. When a watch is wound, work is done in coiling the spring tighter. This work is stored in the spring as elastic potential energy. Similarly, steam under pressure in a boiler has PE. A stick of dynamite has chemical potential energy; so has a lump of coal or a charged storage battery.

Suppose that a lifted weight, instead of being allowed to come back slowly to its former level, is let fall. In falling it acquires speed and if it is allowed to hit the floor, it can do work—demolish something, drive a nail into the floor, compress a spring, etc. So, just before hitting, it must have had energy. What kind of energy? Obviously not what we have been calling potential energy because it is back at the original level from which we agreed to measure GPE. On the contrary, its energy is due to its motion. **The energy of a moving body is called kinetic energy,** abbreviated KE.

When at the point of release, the falling body had only PE, and just before striking the floor it had only KE. While falling, the PE was gradually changed into KE. It got this KE at the expense of its original PE, which came in turn from the work done in raising the body to that height to begin with. If we measure the KE properly, we can say that if no work is wasted along the way against friction, air resistance, etc., the total mechanical energy, PE + KE, stays constant; a gain in one means an equal loss in the other.

The general proposition that, in the absence of friction or other dissipative forces, **the total mechanical energy (PE + KE) of a system remains constant,** is called the **Conservation of Mechanical Energy.** It enables us to answer many questions about mechanical systems.

A **pendulum** (Fig. 39) is another example of conversion between GPE and KE. In pulling the pendulum aside prior to letting it go, work is done against gravity because the bob is effectively raised to a distance h. At the position A it possesses an amount Wh of potential energy. If released, the pendulum

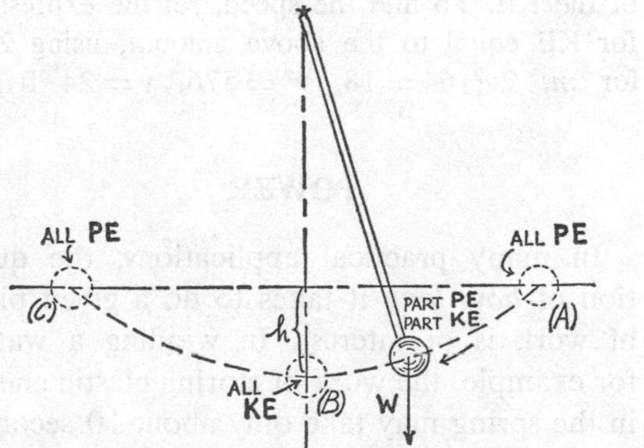

Fig. 39. Pendulum

swings down and the GPE changes to KE. After passing the bottom point, this KE begins to change back to GPE, and in the absence of air resistance, the bob climbs up to the original level. Then everything repeats.

It turns out that the measure of the KE of a body of mass m moving with a speed v is $mv^2/2g$:

If m is in lb and v is in ft/sec then KE will be given in ft lb by

$$KE_{ft\,lb} = \frac{mv^2}{2\times 32} = \frac{mv^2}{64};$$

If m is in gm and v is in cm/sec then KE will be given in gm cm by

$$KE_{gm\,cm} = \frac{mv^2}{2\times 980} = \frac{mv^2}{1960}$$

EXAMPLE 2: How much KE is possessed by a 3,000-lb car moving at a speed of 60 mi/hr?

SOLUTION: Using the table on p. 45, 60 mi/hr is equivalent to 88 ft/sec; and so, from the first of the above relations, $KE = 3000 \times (88)^2/64 = 363{,}000$ ft lb.

EXAMPLE 3: A 2-lb rock is released from a height of 9.0 ft above the ground. Neglecting air resistance, find its KE just before it strikes the ground, and its speed at that time.

SOLUTION: To raise the rock to its original position required an amount of work $W = 2 \times 9 = 18$ ft lb, and this is the amount of its original GPE. By the time it reaches ground level, all the PE has become KE, and so this is also the magnitude of the KE. To find the speed, set the expression for KE equal to the above amount, using 2 lb for m: $2v^2/64 = 18$, $v^2 = 576$, $v = 24$ ft/sec.

POWER

In many practical applications, the question of *how long* it takes to do a given piece of work is of interest. In winding a watch, for example, the work of storing elastic energy in the spring may take only about 10 seconds, while the same amount of energy is returned to the surroundings over a period of perhaps 30 hours as the watch runs down. The chemical energy stored in a tree by sunlight over a period of years may be released in a few minutes as heat when the wood is burned.

The **rate of doing work** is called **power;** it is work divided by time, or

$$P = \frac{W}{t},$$

where W is the amount of work (or energy) expended, t is the time interval during which this is done, and P is the power. James Watt, who improved the steam engine, measured the rate at which a horse could work and found it to be about 550 ft lb/sec. This has become the definition of a standard unit, the **horsepower.** Thus, for instance, a horse should be able to raise a 275-lb weight at the rate of 2 ft/sec. In symbols, we can write the general relation

$$P_{hp} = \frac{W_{ft\,lb}}{550 \times t_{sec}}.$$

One of the Metric units of power has a special name: A rate of working of **one joule per second** is called **one watt.** A larger unit, used especially by electrical engineers, is the **kilowatt** (kw), equal to 1,000 watts. One hp is about ¾ kw.

EXAMPLE 4: The car described in Example 2, above, attained full speed 15.0 sec after starting out from rest. What power was the engine exerting?

SOLUTION: We found that the KE of the car amounted to 363,000 ft lb. This work was done in 15 sec, so the power developed was $P_{hp} = 363{,}000/550 \times 15 = 44$ hp.

EXPERIMENT 17: A horse can presumably go on expending energy at about 1 hp for extended periods of time. A human being can exert surprisingly large amounts of power but only for short intervals. Determine your power output in running up a flight of stairs. You will have to know your weight, the height of the stairs (vertical distance) and the time. If possible, use a stopwatch for timing yourself.

Practice Exercise No. 14

1. When a block of wood acted upon by a force of 48 lb moves 10 ft in the direction of the force, the work done amounts to

— (A) 4.8 ft lb. — (C) 58 ft lb.
— (B) 480 ft lb. — (D) 0.21 ft lb.

2. Of the following, all are possible units of mechanical energy *except*

— (A) ft sec. — (C) joules.
— (B) gm cm. — (D) in-lb.

3. Of the following, the one possessing KE is

— (A) a stretched rubber band. — (C) the air in a bicycle tire.
— (B) a firecracker. — (D) a bullet in flight.

4. Energy is

— (A) work divided by time. — (C) measurable in horsepower.
— (B) the ability to do work. — (D) force divided by distance.

5. If the car in Example 2 (p. 54) has a collision when going full speed and is brought to rest in a distance of 11 ft, the average retarding force acting on it in this time will be

— (A) 273 lb. — (C) 33,000 lb.
— (B) 660 lb. — (D) 36,300 lb.

MACHINES

In trying to adapt our environment to serve our needs, we meet many tasks that require greater forces or more speed than our muscles alone can furnish. To overcome these limitations, man has invented **machines.** These machines enable him to transfer energy from one place to another and to transform energy from one form to another.

The Conservation of Mechanical Energy (p. 53) can easily be extended to describe an important general proposition governing the performance of any machine. In the operation of a machine, some outside agency—a motor, a battery, animal muscle, etc.—does work on the machine. In turn, the machine delivers work to something on which it acts. These two amounts of work are related in a simple way: As long as any energy stored up in the machine itself remains constant, and in the absence of friction, **the work done *by* the machine is just equal to the work done *on* it.**

This work-energy principle, applying as it does to every machine we can devise, shows the impossibility of devising a **perpetual motion machine**—a device that, without continued input of work, would furnish unlimited energy or even keep itself running indefinitely. Any actual mechanism that we can build necessarily involves friction or other energy-wasting forces to some degree. No matter how small we are able to make this waste, any energy supplied to the device will eventually drain away in the form of heat, and the machine must stop unless more energy is supplied from outside sources.

Misguided inventors have, in many cases, designed clever-looking devices intended to furnish power "for nothing," but in every instance an analysis shows that the work-energy principle is violated. The best way to disprove the claims of such an inventor is to persuade him to build an operating model of his machine.

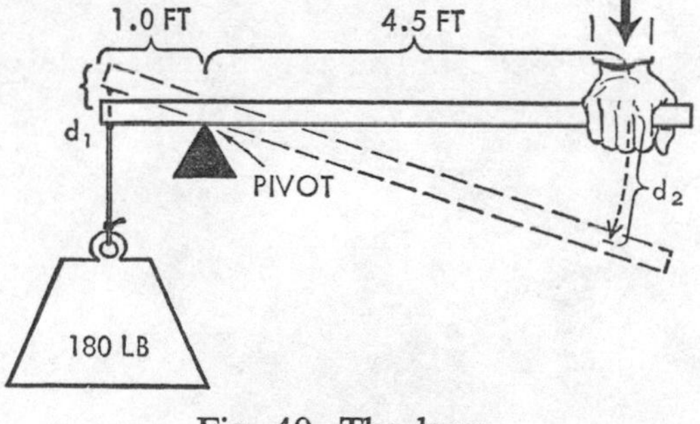

Fig. 40. The lever

Practice Exercise No. 15

1. *Principle of the Lever.* In the arrangement shown in Fig. 40, how large a downward push is needed to raise the load, friction being negligible?

HINT: Use the work principle and notice that

the distances moved by the applied force and the weight force are directly proportional to the distances from the pivot.

2. A man rolls a 200-lb keg up a sloping board to a loading platform 4.0 ft high. The board is 10 ft long, and rolling friction can be neglected. How hard must the man push if the force he exerts is parallel to the incline at all times?

   HINT: The amount of work required will be the same as that needed to raise the keg straight up through a distance equal to the height of the platform.

3. A downward force of 10 lb is applied to the smaller piston of the hydraulic press described on p. 25. Under ideal conditions, what load can then be lifted by the larger piston?

4. When a lever (crowbar) is used under the conditions specified in Problem 1, how does the *power* exerted by the applied force compare with the power expended on the load?

SUMMARY *Instructions:* (see page 17)

1. Under what conditions is a force said to do mechanical work?	
2. How is the work that is done measured?	When it succeeds in moving the point to which it is applied.
3. Define potential energy.	By the product of the magnitude of the force and the distance moved in the direction of the force. $W = Fd$
4. Define kinetic energy.	Energy of position, or of the relative positions of parts of a system.
5. On what factors does the magnitude of the KE of a moving body depend?	Mechanical energy possessed by a body because of its motion.
6. What is meant by Conservation of Mechanical Energy?	KE is proportional to mv^2. The numerical factor to be applied to this product will depend on the system of units used (see p. 54).
7. Define power.	For an isolated, non-dissipative mechanical system, the total mechanical energy (KE + PE) remains constant.
8. Name a work (energy) unit of practical size in a) the English system and b) the Metric system.	The rate of doing work, or expending energy. $P = W/t$.
9. Name and define a practical unit of power in each system of units.	Foot-pound; joule.
10. What is the work principle as applied to machines?	a) 1 hp = 550 ft-lb/sec; b) 1 w = 1 j/sec.
	In any mechanism that does not store up energy and in which dissipative forces are negligible, the work done *on* the machine and the work done *by* the machine in a given interval of time are equal.

Chapter VIII

MOLECULES

From very early times, people wondered about the nature of matter and looked for ways of thinking about it that would enable them to understand how substances behave under various conditions. Some found it hard to believe that if a piece of matter is cut up into smaller and smaller bits, one could go on this way indefinitely. It seemed reasonable to assume that by such means one would eventually come to the smallest indivisible particles of which the material is made. They called these particles **atoms.** In what follows you will get to know how this idea was developed and how it succeeded in explaining the things we know about matter through our experience.

ATOMS AND MOLECULES

The Greek philosopher Democritus, who lived about 400 B.C., is generally believed to be the one who first proposed the atomic idea. While the early scientists usually did not test their findings by experiment, the atom concept at least proved to be a lucky "hunch" that paid off later. But already in ancient times, many observations could be explained—at least in a general way—by the assumption that matter is not the continuous stuff it appears to be, but really consists of separate particles. These particles must be assumed to be very small and exceedingly numerous. It turns out that the smallest speck that can be seen in a high-powered microscope may consist of a million **molecules.***

There are many observations that suggest also the fact that **the molecules of a substance are in rapid motion:** Place a drop of perfume on a dish and in a short time the odor will be noticed in all parts of the room. Drop a few grains of sugar into a glassful of water and the sugar soon disappears, but after some time the sweet taste is found to be distributed all through the water. It must be that the molecules are in rapid motion, and are capable of wandering off from their source.

A little over a century ago a botanist named Robert Brown first observed a direct effect of the movement of molecules. He was looking through the microscope at a drop of water in which some very small solid particles were suspended, and noticed that these particles had a continual, haphazard, trembling motion—something like that shown in Fig. 41; he rightly concluded that this was because they were buffeted about by their random collisions with water molecules. This so-called **Brownian motion** is also shown by smoke particles suspended in air. We see the rebound of the bigger particles, but not the molecules that hit them. It is like a hockey game in which the puck is visible but the players are not.

THE KINETIC THEORY

From a wide variety of other observations, science has come to the conclusion that **all matter is made of molecules,** and that **these molecules are in a continual state of rapid,**

* Nowadays we ordinarily use the term *molecule* for the smallest particle of a substance that can have an independent existence, reserving the word *atom* for the smallest unit in the case of the chemical elements (p. 14). Chemists find, for example, that a molecule of ordinary table salt, sodium chloride, can be broken up into an atom of the element sodium and an atom of the element chlorine; but then we no longer have salt—the original substance has lost its identity.

Fig. 41. Brownian movement

random motion. These assumptions form the basis of what is called the **Kinetic Theory of Matter.**

It turns out that this theory can readily explain the great mass of information we have gathered about matter in general. Starting with a solid substance, we know that the molecules are held in relatively fixed positions in a regular array—what we call the **crystalline structure** of the solid. But even in this state, they have slight random movements around their positions of equilibrium. If heat is supplied, their energy of motion is increased. At a given temperature they gain enough energy to break way from the forces holding them in place, and the solid is said to **melt.**

We now have the liquid state, in which the molecules are free to move about, sliding over each other but still remaining close together. Because they collide with each other all the time, some of them will happen to get considerably greater speeds than the average. If one of these faster molecules happens to find itself near the surface and moving upward, it may escape from the liquid. We call this **evaporation,** and the individual molecules that have left the liquid form the vapor, which has the properties of a gas.

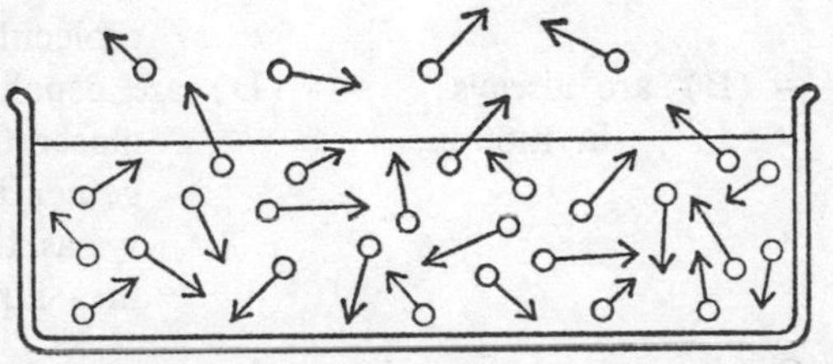

Fig. 42. Evaporation of a liquid

Even solids evaporate to some extent. A mothball, for example, gradually disappears in this way, and the odor is evidence of its evaporation.

The diffusion of one kind of molecules through another kind, as in the spreading of an odorous substance through the air or by sugar molecules through water, is readily explained by the Kinetic Theory. The molecules in question have, as you will see later, very high speeds, yet it takes a little while before they get some distance from their source. The reason is that they are continually encountering other molecules. For instance, a sugar molecule that succeeds in darting away from a sugar crystal in water will have to "elbow" its way among the myriad of water molecules surrounding it; instead of going straight away, it will have a path something like the one in Fig. 41.

GAS PRESSURE

The fact that a confined gas exerts pressure also finds a ready explanation in terms of moving molecules. Tremendous numbers of molecules are hitting the sides of the container each second, and this continual bombardment has the effect of a steady push. If the molecules are forced into a smaller volume, they hit the sides more often and the pressure is increased. This at once gives us Boyle's Law (p. 32). Later you will find out that warming a gas speeds up its molecules, and so this, too, operates to increase the pressure.

The Kinetic Theory, then, pictures a gas as a swarm of swiftly moving molecules, con-

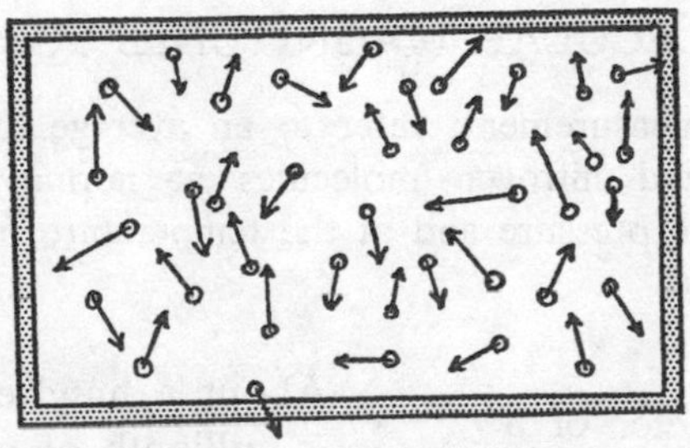

Fig. 43. A gas is a collection by flying molecules

tinually colliding with each other and with the sides of their container. The molecules themselves turn out to be very small compared with their average distance apart, and they "occupy" the container only in the sense that their rapid movement keeps other things out. In spite of their frequent collisions, the molecules of a gas never "settle out" on the bottom of the vessel, so the impacts must involve no loss of energy. Instead of thinking of such collisions as the actual bumping together of matter, they should be looked upon as a close approach against a strong force that tends to push the molecules apart as they come nearer together. This kind of repulsion need not involve any net loss in energy (Fig. 44).

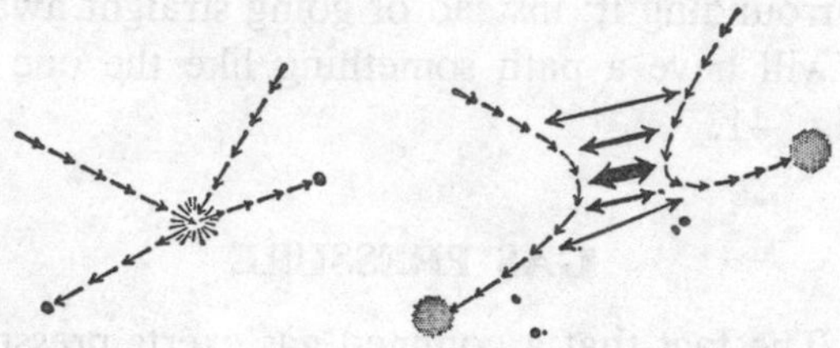

Fig. 44.

What appears to be a collision . . . . . . may be only a "close approach" against a repelling force

The great success of the Kinetic Theory is due to the fact that by applying mathematics to its ideas, physicists have been able to compute such things as the size, mass, number and speed of the molecules. Here, in tabular form, are some of the results:

TABLE 5

MOLECULAR MAGNITUDES FOR AIR

The measurements refer to an average for oxygen and nitrogen molecules at normal atmospheric pressure and at the temperature of melting ice.

Diameter of a molecule	About a hundred millionth of an inch
Mass of a single molecule	0.000 000 000 000 000 000 000 000 1 lb
Number of molecules per cubic inch	400,000,000,000,000,000,000
Average speed	⅓ mi/sec.
Average distance each travels between collisions	Four millionths of an inch
Average number of collisions per second made by each	Five billion

Practice Exercise No. 16

1. The ancient Greeks originated the idea that

— (A) matter and energy are the same thing.
— (B) perpetual motion is not possible.
— (C) matter is discontinuous.
— (D) matter does not exist in different forms.

2. In the Brownian motion, we observe directly the movement of

— (A) water molecules.
— (B) the atoms of a chemical element.
— (C) small particles of matter.
— (D) a cloud of vapor.

3. In addition to the idea that matter consists of molecules, the Kinetic Theory of matter assumes that these molecules

— (A) are perfectly stationary in solids.
— (B) are always in motion.
— (C) move only when struck by other molecules.
— (D) are usually closer together in a gas than in a liquid.

4. Outdoors in winter, ice and snow gradually disappear even though the temperature re-

mains below the freezing point. This is because ice can

— (A) evaporate. — (C) liquefy.
— (B) solidify. — (D) crystallize.

5. If "air molecules" could be arranged in a row in contact with each other, the number required to stretch across the period at the end of a sentence (about 1/50 inch) would be about

— (A) 50,000. — (C) 100,000,000.
— (B) 2,000,000. — (D) 50.

MOLECULAR FORCES IN SOLIDS

The special uses to which we put different kinds of matter are dependent, in the last analysis, on the forces between molecules. The continual motion of the molecules tends to drive them farther apart, and this accounts for the fact that gases diffuse, as already explained. But when molecules are brought quite close together, as in liquids and solids, we observe that they tend to stick together. These forces of **cohesion** that show up when the distance between molecules is very small, are especially strong in solids. They are responsible for many of the useful properties of materials we use in industry and in everyday life.

One of the most obvious attributes of solid matter is its resistance to being pulled apart. We call this **tenacity,** or **tensile strength.** It takes a force of over 200 tons to pull apart a good quality steel rod of 1 in^2 cross-section. This is what makes steel so useful in structural engineering. If the two pieces of a broken specimen are pressed together again they no longer stick together, because we cannot get the molecules on both sides of the break close enough together to make the cohesive forces effective. However, by heating the pieces and pounding them together, they can be welded into one.

Some solids have low tensile strength, but have strong resistance to crushing. This makes stone useful for building arches and piers, where it bears compressive stresses only.

Another widely used property of solids is **elasticity.** This is the ability of substances to return to their previous form after deformation. If a strip of steel or bronze is given a moderate twist or bend or stretch, it returns very perfectly to its former shape afterward. This property makes such metals useful for springs. Compare this behavior with that of grease or putty; they show no tendency to recover their shape after being deformed, and are said to be highly **plastic.** But even steel, if stressed more than a certain amount, will fail to return completely. Structural materials should never be required to work as far as these limits.

Solids, liquids and gases all have elasticity of compression. The fact that the molecules of solids and liquids are already almost in contact makes these forms of matter very hard to compress, but gases are much more compressible, as you already know.

OTHER PROPERTIES OF SOLIDS

There are several other useful molecular properties of solids. Certain metals, such as gold, copper and tin, are highly **malleable,**—that is, they can be pounded or rolled into very thin sheets. Gold can be beaten into sheets that are about 1/50,000 inch thick. Other metals, such as copper, platinum and silver, can be drawn out into very fine wires. They are said to be **ductile.** Wires less than one-hundredth the thickness of a hair can be made out of platinum. The **hardness** of a material is measured by its ability to scratch other substances. Diamond is the hardest known substance; alloys such as carborundum and carboloy are nearly as hard. Diamond-tipped tools are used in drilling and cutting hard rock and metal.

EXPERIMENT 18: Make tests to enable you to arrange several materials in their order of decreasing hardness: You will find you can scratch a piece of chalk with your fingernail, not the other way around. Your nail, in turn, is unable to scratch a copper penny, but the coin can abrade your nail. A piece of glass scratches the coin, but is not scratched by it. Try to place other available materials in such a series.

SURFACE TENSION

The cohesive forces in a liquid make any free liquid surface act as if it were covered with a tightly-stretched membrane. This behavior is attributed to what we call **surface tension.** A little water spilled on a very clean plate wets it and spreads over the bottom because the plate attracts the water molecules strongly. But in a dirty dish, even the thinnest film of grease is enough to weaken the attraction of the dish, and the cohesion of the water molecules (their attraction for each other) makes them collect in separate drops (Fig. 45). Falling water, being free of the deforming effect of nearby things, tends to break up into round drops. A soap bubble blown on a pipe or tube will contract when the tube is left open. These and many other observations show that **a liquid surface acts like a stretched, flexible skin.**

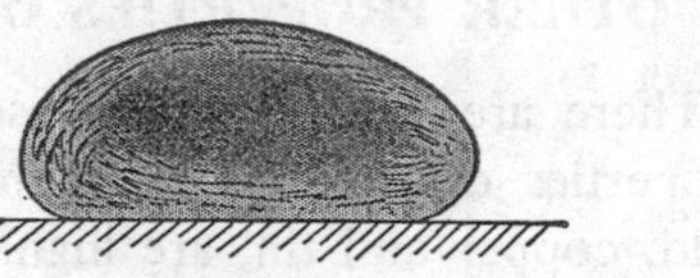

Fig. 45. A drop of water on a glass plate

EXPERIMENT 19: Float a razor blade or a paper clip on water by laying it across the prongs of a dinner fork and lowering it carefully onto the liquid surface. Steel cannot float by its own buoyancy (Archimedes' law, p. 27), but here it is not floating *in* the water but *on top* of the surface film. Look closely at the surface of the water and you will notice that it curves up all around the edge of the object. Once you push the blade or clip down through the surface, it goes clear to the bottom.

Fig. 46. Cross-section of a razor blade floating on water

EXPERIMENT 20: Dissolving a substance like soap in water will weaken the surface forces very noticeably. Put some water in a clean dish and sprinkle talcum powder evenly over it to make the surface easy to see. Touch the corner of a wet bar of soap to the water surface near one side of the dish. Instantly, the surface film will snap over to the opposite side, where the pull of the film has not been weakened by dissolved soap.

CAPILLARITY

If one end of a very narrow glass tube is dipped in water, the liquid will rise inside the tube until it stands at some height above the level in the dish. This seems to contradict the principle that the level should be the same everywhere (p. 24). But in fine tubes, the forces of surface tension get the upper hand. They become more important than the weight forces, which usually dominate. Since water molecules are attracted by the glass and wet it, the water curves upward along the glass, making a concave surface (Fig. 47). This surface tends to make itself smaller, pulling the water up the tube. The climbing goes on until the surface effect is balanced by the weight of the column of water. This elevation of water in narrow tubes is called **capillarity.** The smaller the tube, the higher the liquid rises. In a tube 1/32 inch in diameter, water will rise nearly 4 inches.

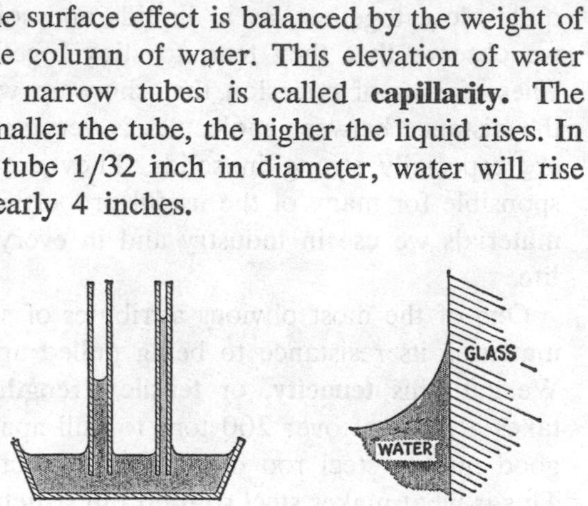

Fig. 47. Capillary action

Capillary action is responsible for the soaking-up of water by a towel, or of ink by a blotter. It causes the rise of subsurface water in the soil and, to some extent, in the roots and stems of plants.

Practice Exercise No. 17

1. There are cohesive forces between the molecules of a gas, although they are much weaker than for liquids or solids. Under what circum-

stances would you expect the former to show up at all?

2. From the information in Table 5, compute how many times its own diameter a molecule of the air travels, on the average, between impacts with other molecules.
3. Could a steel wire, hanging straight down, support the weight of a mile of its own length? HINT: Consult Table 3, p. 21 and compute the weight of a wire one mile long and of cross-section 1 in^2.
4. In view of the result of Experiment 20, why will a small speck of soap, thrown onto a water surface, dart about on a zig-zag path? Try it.
5. When a glassblower holds a sharp-edged piece of glass in a flame, the edges become rounded as the glass softens. Explain this.

SUMMARY *Instructions:* (see page 17)

1. What is the Brownian motion, and what does it show about the structure of matter?	
2. State the basic assumptions of the kinetic theory of matter.	The continual, random motion of small particles suspended in a liquid or gas. It shows that the molecules are in unceasing motion.
3. According to the theory, what is the cause of the pressure exerted by a gas on the sides of its container?	a) Matter is made of molecules, and b) These molecules are in a continual state of rapid motion.
4. What is meant by cohesive forces?	The many impacts of the moving molecules.
5. Name some properties of solid materials that depend on these forces.	Forces of strong attraction between the molecules of a substance when they are not too far apart.
6. How do cohesive forces manifest themselves in a liquid?	Tensile strength (tenacity), elasticity, plasticity, hardness.
7. Define surface tension.	Through surface tension, for which these forces are responsible.
8. What is capillarity?	The property which makes a free liquid surface act like a stretched skin.
	The rise of liquids in small-bore tubes and pores, caused by surface tension forces.

SECTION THREE

HEAT

Chapter IX

THE NATURE OF HEAT

Heat, besides being necessary to all living things, is one of our most valuable tools. It cooks our food, frees metals from their ores, refines petroleum, runs trains and automobiles and finds countless other uses in industry and commerce.

A little over a century ago heat was believed to be an invisible, weightless substance that passed from a hot to a cold object. You will find below that heat is now known to be a form of energy—the energy of motion of molecules.

TEMPERATURE AND ITS MEASUREMENT

Temperature is something we perceive by means of a special set of nerve endings in the skin, but our judgment of hot and cold is influenced by many other factors, and so some more "impersonal" way of measuring temperature must be found. An experiment shows how unreliable our temperature sense can be:

EXPERIMENT 21: Place three bowls in a row—the first containing cold water, the second lukewarm water, the third hot water. Put your left hand in the cold water, your right hand in the hot. After a few seconds, remove and plunge them at once into the middle bowl. The lukewarm water in it will seem hot to your left hand and, at the same time, cold to your right, although you know it to be the same temperature all through.

Generally, when the temperature of a piece of matter is changed, other things happen to it. Its size, its electrical, magnetic, or optical behavior may become different, and any such change could be used to detect and measure its change of temperature. The simplest to use, in most cases, is the change in size: Nearly all **materials expand when their temperature is raised and shrink when it is lowered.**

The common mercury thermometer makes use of the expansion and contraction of the liquid mercury to measure temperature. The very slight changes in bulk are made more evident by attaching a very fine tube to the bulb (Fig. 48). In order to specify a scale for the instrument, two fixed points are chosen. It is found that the position of the mercury thread on any given thermometer is always the same when it is placed in a mixture of ice and water. This temperature level is called the **ice point** ("freezing point"), and is one of the fixed points that is used. Again, when the instrument is held in the steam rising from boiling water it always comes to another fixed indication, called the **steam point** ("boiling point"). In the **Celsius*** system, which is universally used for all scientific work, the ice point is marked 0° C (zero degrees **Celsius)** and the steam point is marked 100° C, and the space between is divided into 100 equal parts. The same-sized divisions may be carried above and below this range, completing the calibration of the thermometer.

For the **Fahrenheit** scale, which is still in everyday use in English-speaking countries, the fixed points are chosen in a different way, being originally based on the temperature of a mixture of ice and salt and the temperature of the human body. The ice point happens to come at 32° F, the steam point at 212° F (see Fig. 48). The relation between any temperature reading C on the Celsius scale and the

* Formerly called the Centigrade system.

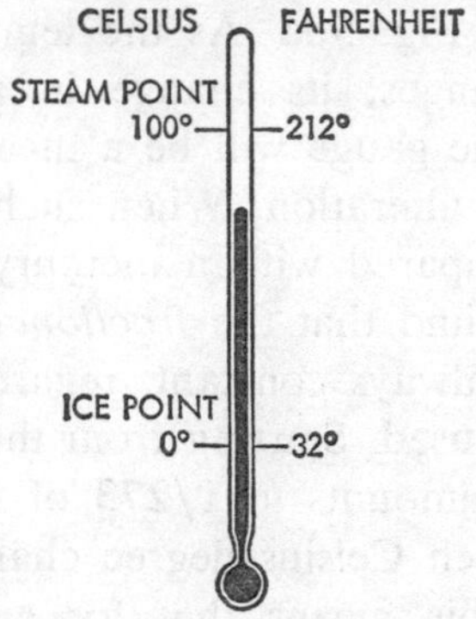

Fig. 48. Liquid-in-glass thermometer

corresponding value F on the Fahrenheit scale is given by

$$F = \frac{9}{5}C + 32.$$

If a temperature is below zero on either scale, a minus sign must be placed in front of its number when using this equation.

EXAMPLE 1: The temperature of solid carbon dioxide ("dry ice") is about −80° C. What is this on the Fahrenheit scale?

SOLUTION: Putting −80 for C in the above formula gives

$$F = \frac{9}{5}(-80) + 32 = -144 + 32 = -112° \text{ F},$$

or 112 degrees below zero Fahrenheit.

Notice that in taking up the measurement of temperature, an additional unit—the degree—has been introduced into our systems of measure.

EXPANSION OF SOLIDS AND LIQUIDS

Different substances expand at different rates when warmed. An iron bar one foot long increases in length about 1/70 in. when heated from the ice point to the steam point. A brass bar expands about 1½ times as much, while a glass rod expands only ½ as much as the iron. It is found that a solid object increases in length by a certain fraction for each degree rise in temperature. This result, which is accurate over a fairly large range of temperature, can be used for calculating how much an object will expand for a given change in temperature, once we have measured the extent of the expansion of the material of which it is made. This is given for each substance by a number called its **coefficient of linear expansion.** Values for some common solids are found in the table:

TABLE 6

COEFFICIENTS OF LINEAR EXPANSION FOR SOLIDS

Substance	*Fractional change in length for each degree C change in temperature*
Aluminum	0.000024
Brass	0.000019
Iron or steel	0.000011
Ordinary glass	0.000009
Pyrex glass	0.000004
Invar (an alloy)	0.0000009

EXAMPLE 2: How much will a 1,000-ft long steel bridge expand between a winter temperature of −10° C and a summer temperature of +40° C?

SOLUTION: The temperature goes from 10 below zero to 40 above, or a difference of 50°. According to the table, the *fractional* increase in length for each degree will be 0.000011, so for 50° it will be 0.000011 × 50. If the original length is 1,000 ft, the *actual* increase in length will be $0.000011 \times 50 \times 1{,}000 = 0.55$ ft.

Linear expansion must be allowed for in structures and machines of all kinds. Long steel bridges are provided with rollers or rockers at the ends; expansion joints are provided between the concrete slabs of a road; the aluminum pistons of an automobile engine are made enough smaller in diameter than the steel cylinders to allow for the much greater expansion coefficient of aluminum.

The very slight increase in length of a moderate-sized object may be magnified by using a device called a **bimetal** (Fig. 49). It consists of a strip of iron and a strip of brass welded or riveted together along their length. The difference in their amounts of expansion shows up easily because the double strip bends into a curve when its temperature changes. The movement may be used to turn a pointer, to regulate a valve or to close a switch. A bimetal forms the main element of a **thermostat** (see figure).

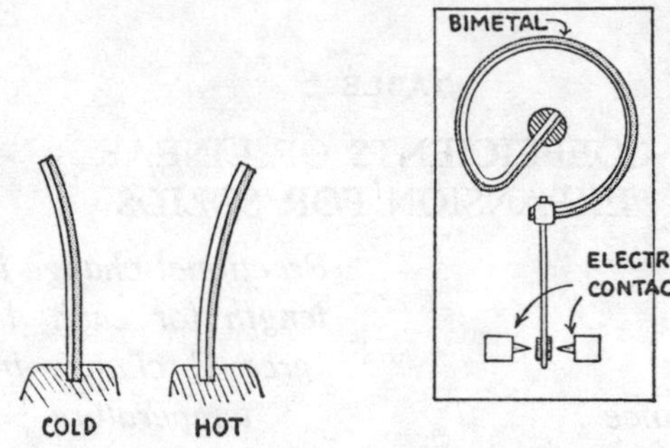

Fig. 49.

Bimetallic strip — The essential parts of a thermostat

Most liquids behave like mercury in that they expand with increased temperature. Water is an exception: Between the ice point and about +4° C it *contracts* very slightly, then with further increase of temperature it expands. This property, together with the fact that it freezes at a moderate temperature, makes water unsuitable for use in a thermometer.

The fact that water reaches its maximum density at a temperature above its freezing point has important consequences. In winter, the water at the surface of a pond is in contact with the cold air. On cooling, it becomes denser and sinks. In this way the water circulates until it is all at 4° C before the top layers can get any colder and freeze. The circulation process takes a long time, giving fish and other aquatic life a better chance to survive.

EXPANSION OF GASES; ABSOLUTE TEMPERATURE

While mercury is the most convenient substance to use in a thermometer, the use of a gas gives us a better understanding of what goes on. One way to make a **gas thermometer** is shown in Fig. 50a. As the temperature of the gas changes, its change in pressure as shown by the gauge will be a measure of the temperature alteration. When such an instrument is compared with a mercury thermometer, it is found that the *fractional* change in pressure is always constant, regardless of the kind of gas used. Starting from the ice point, the change amounts to 1/273 of the original value for each Celsius degree change in temperature. This means that for every degree that the temperature is lowered, the pressure decreases by 1/273 of its value at 0° C, and suggests that—provided the gas does not first liquefy or solidify—if the temperature were lowered 273° below the ice point, the gas would no longer exert any pressure at all!

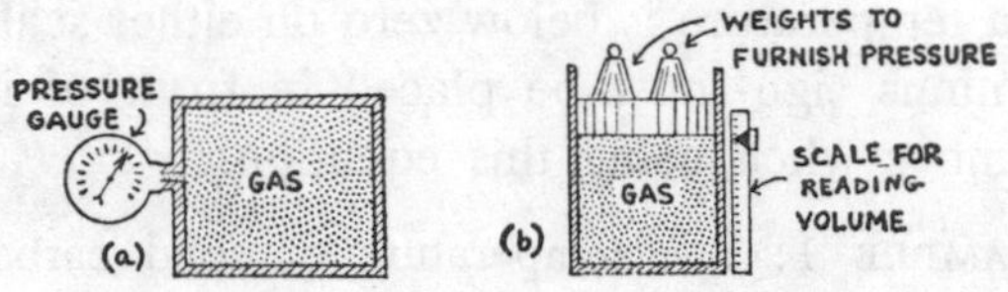

Fig. 50. Two forms of gas thermometer

Another way of making a gas thermometer is shown in Fig. 50b. Here the pressure on the piston is held constant, and the changes in volume of the gas are measured. Starting again from the ice point, it is found that the *fractional* change in volume is always 1/273 the original volume—the same fraction we found above. Here it means that if the temperature could be lowered to 273° below the ice point, a gas would no longer occupy any space.

Both experiments point to the existence of a lowest possible temperature of −273° C, where a gas would no longer exert pressure on its container or take up any space. This temperature is called the **absolute zero.** In the laboratory, physicists have been able to come within a few thousandths of a degree of this point.

The Kinetic Theory makes all of this understandable. We saw that a gas exerts pressure because its ever-moving molecules have kinetic energy, and when they strike the sides of the container they push on it. Lowering the temperature of a gas takes away some of this KE.

If all of it could be taken away, the gas would no longer press on the walls and would no longer take up any space (except the negligible space occupied by the molecules themselves). The absolute zero is, then, the lowest possible temperature in the universe. In principle, there is no *upper* limit.

TABLE 7

TEMPERATURES OF VARIOUS OBJECTS

Center of a hot star	over 1,000,000,000° K
Hydrogen bomb	100,000,000
Center of the sun	20,000,000
Surface of a hot star	50,000
Surface of the sun	6,000
Carbon-arc lamp	4,000
Melting iron	1,800
Boiling water	373
Melting ice	273
Dry ice (solid carbon dioxide)	200
Liquid air, boiling	88
Liquid helium, boiling rapidly	0.7

For all theoretical purposes, scientists measure temperatures upward from the absolute zero as a starting point, using the Celsius degree as the unit. This scheme is called the **absolute,** or **Kelvin scale,** and has the advantages of being based on the fundamental idea of molecular energy and of involving no negative temperatures. To change from a Celsius reading to Kelvin, simply add 273. For example, a summer temperature of 27° C is equivalent to $27 + 273 = 300°$ K.

Practice Exercise No. 18

1. Which is larger, a Fahrenheit degree or a Celsius degree? What is the ratio of their sizes?
2. The normal temperature of the human body is taken to be 98.6° F. How much is this on the Celsius scale? On the absolute scale?
3. Examine the table on p. 67 and explain why a pyrex dish can be taken direct from the oven and plunged into cold water without cracking.
4. Why is an automobile engine noisy until it has warmed up to running temperature?
5. Find out how the pendulum of a clock and the balance wheel of a watch are compensated for temperature changes. (Consult an encyclopedia.)
6. When a piece of iron with a cavity inside it is heated, does the hole become larger or smaller? Explain.
7. An aluminum piston in a car engine is 2¾ in. in diameter. How much does its diameter increase when warmed from 10° C to its normal operating temperature of 170° C?

CONDUCTION OF HEAT

Heat is always observed to pass of its own accord from a hot body to a cold one. According to the Kinetic Theory, heat is a form of energy—the kinetic energy of the random motion of the molecules. When you warm up an object you merely supply more energy to the molecules. This means that when two bodies at different temperatures are put in contact, the faster-moving molecules of the warmer one, colliding with the slower molecules of the cooler one, transfer some of their motion to the latter. The warmer object loses energy (drops in temperature), while the cooler one gains energy (rises in temperature). The transfer process stops when the two reach the same temperature. It reminds one of what happens when two vessels containing water at different levels are connected together (Fig. 51) and suggests one reason why heat was once thought of as a fluid.

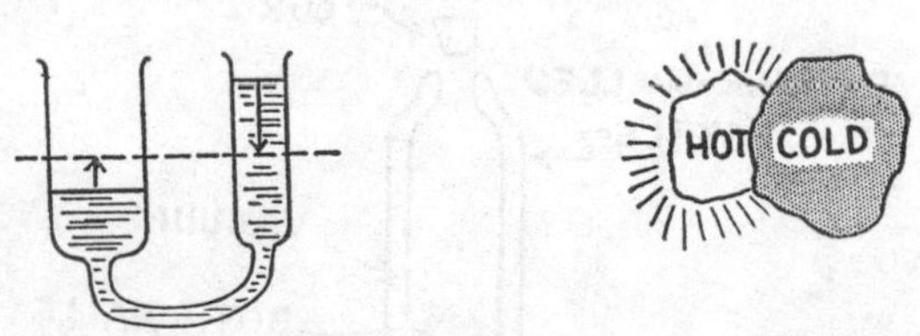

Fig. 51. The liquids come finally to the same level—the hot and cold bodies to the same temperature

One way in which heat passes from one place to another is by the handing-on of molecular motion through a substance. This is called heat **conduction.** Materials differ in how fast they let this transfer go on. Metals are good conductors; stone is moderately good; wood, paper, cloth and air are poor conductors of heat. If one end of an iron rod is held in the fire, the other end soon becomes hot because iron is a good conductor; but you can comfortably hold the rod by means of a wooden handle—a poor conductor.

EXPERIMENT 22: Bring a piece of wire screen down onto a candle flame. The flame will be cut off above the screen, since the heat is conducted away before the vaporized wax there can be ignited.

Early in the last century, there were many disastrous explosions in the British coal mines, caused by ignition of mine gases by the open flames of the miners' lamps. The great chemist, Sir Humphry Davy, suggested surrounding each lamp with a fine wire screen. It worked.

Poor conductors of heat are often called heat **insulators.** Air, when trapped in small pores or spaces, is an excellent heat insulator (see Table 8). Most of the warmth of woolens and furs is attributable to the poor conduction by the air held between the fibers. The walls of refrigerators are filled with a porous insulating material such as mineral wool for a similar reason. The best heat insulator of all is a good vacuum. A **vacuum bottle** consists of a double-walled glass flask with the space between pumped clear of air (Fig. 52).

Fig. 52. The inner flask of a "Thermos" bottle

TABLE 8

HEAT CONDUCTION COEFFICIENTS

The numbers give the relative rates of heat transfer in the materials listed. Silver is arbitrarily given the rating 100.

Material	*Coefficient*
Silver	100
Copper	92
Aluminum	50
Iron	11
Glass	0.20
Water	0.12
Wood	0.03
Air	0.006
Perfect vacuum	0

CONVECTION

Most liquids and all gases are poor conductors of heat as seen from the examples of water and air given in the table. But there is another way in which liquids and gases can transport heat. The air just above a bonfire becomes warmed and expands considerably. Being less dense than the surrounding air, it rises in the manner of a balloon. Cool air then flows in from all sides to take its place, and soon a continuous circulation is set up. A similar circulation takes place in a pot of water set on the stove to warm. This mass movement of a heated liquid or gas is called **convection.** It is responsible for the operation of hot air (Fig. 53) or hot water house heating systems. Winds are the result of rapid convec-

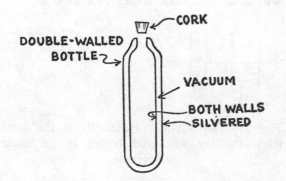

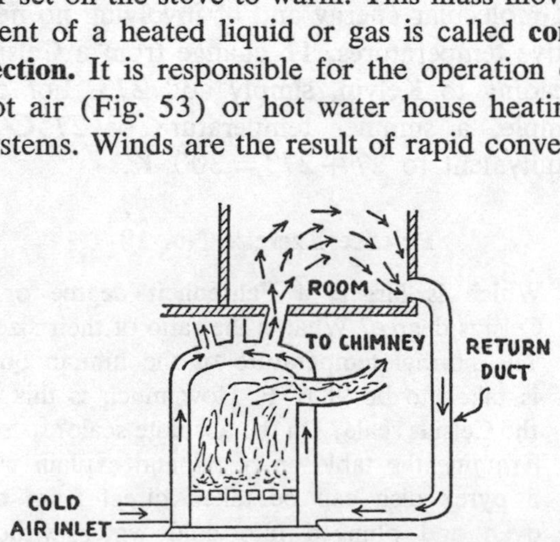

Fig. 53. Convection in a hot-air heating system

tion currents in the atmosphere. Near the equator, the intense heat of the sun causes a general rising of the warmed air, while cooler air flows toward the equator to replace it. Many other factors operate to modify this effect. Ocean currents, such as the Gulf Stream, are produced by convection.

EXPERIMENT 23: Hold some small pieces of ice in place at the bottom of a vial or test tube containing water by pushing in a tuft of steel wool on top of them (Fig. 54). Heat the water near the top of the tube by means of a candle or gas flame. Soon the water will start to boil, yet the ice will not melt. The warmed water is already at the top, so no convection takes place, and the conduction by water is very small; altogether, then, very little heat is transferred to the ice.

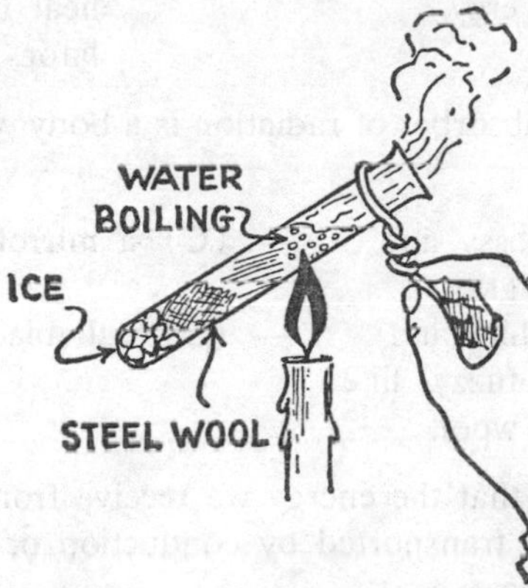

Fig. 54. Hot above, cold below

RADIATION

Sitting before an open fireplace, you get a definite sensation of warmth despite the fact that heat is not reaching you by convection (the flow is actually in the opposite direction), and conduction by the air is negligible. The heat reaches you by a third process, called **radiation.** This means that the source is sending out waves of the same general nature as light waves. Some of these rays may be invisible, as in the radiation from a hot stove. Like ordinary visible light, these radiations can travel through empty space. You already know that heat transfer by the other methods (conduction and convection) requires *direct contact* between substances.

Almost all the energy available on earth comes to us from the sun in the form of radiation. When coal is burned it merely releases chemical potential energy which the sun stored up in plants millions of years ago. The falling water that turns a power-plant turbine has energy only because the sun maintains the great cycle of evaporation by which water is continually lifted from the lakes and oceans, later to condense as rain that feeds streams and waterfalls. The energy of the wind is the result of convection caused by the sun's rays.

Not only very hot bodies, such as the sun, but all things send out radiation to their surroundings. As you would expect, the higher the temperature of the body, the more intense its radiation. Even a cake of ice sends out radiant energy. It feels cool when you place your hand near it only because the ice, being at a lower temperature, sends back to your hand less energy than it gets from it. There is no such thing as "transferring cold," since cold is merely the absence of heat.

The amount of energy sent out by a radiating object depends not only on its temperature but on the nature of its surface as well. Dark, rough surfaces send out more radiation than smooth, light-colored ones at the same temperature. The reverse is also true: Dark, rough surfaces are better **absorbers** of radiation. In the tropical sun, a dark-colored jacket feels warmer than a light-colored one of the same weight. The inside surfaces of a vacuum flask (Fig. 52) are silvered in order to reflect, rather than transmit or absorb, radiation. In sunshine, dirty snow melts faster than clean snow.

EXPERIMENT 24: Cut out the ends of a tin can and paint one with flat black paint or coat it with soot from a candle flame. Set both disks out in the sun and, after several minutes, feel each one and notice how much hotter the blackened one is, due to its greater rate of heat absorption.

Ordinary glass is transparent to visible light, but not to the longer, invisible waves given off, say, by soil that has been warmed by the sun. This fact is made use of in a **greenhouse** or hot frame (Fig. 55). The sun's rays pass readily through the glass roof and are absorbed in the soil within. This, being warmed, then emits rays of its own. But these are mainly long waves which cannot get out through the glass, and so the greenhouse acts like a heat trap. In localities where there is enough sunshine in winter, it is found possible to heat houses by the same principle.

Fig. 55. Greenhouse principle

Practice Exercise No. 19

1. A silver spoon and a book are both at room temperature. The spoon feels colder to the touch because

— (A) it is made of a denser material.
— (B) silver is a very good heat conductor.
— (C) silver is an almost pure material.
— (D) the book has the greater weight.

2. Ice is placed in the *upper* part of an ice chest because

— (A) it is easier to reach there.
— (B) the water formed in melting can run out more readily.
— (C) convection will distribute the cooled air.
— (D) it will come in direct contact with the food.

3. Every object at a temperature above absolute zero

— (A) must receive heat by convection.
— (B) radiates energy.
— (C) occupies less space than it would at absolute zero.
— (D) is a good heat insulator.

4. The best absorber of radiation is a body whose surface is

— (A) glossy and gray.
— (B) white and fuzzy, like wool.
— (C) a mirror.
— (D) dull black.

5. We know that the energy we receive from the sun is not transported by conduction or convection because

— (A) interplanetary space is a good vacuum.
— (B) air is less dense at high altitudes.
— (C) the sun is gradually cooling off.
— (D) there are always some clouds in the atmosphere.

SUMMARY *Instructions:* (see page 17)

1. What is understood by the term "temperature"?	
2. In the commonest and simplest forms of thermometer, how is the temperature measured?	The property of a body that determines the sensation of warmness or coldness obtained from it.
3. How is the Celsius scale of temperature specified?	By the expansion or contraction of some thermometric substance.
4. Define the coefficient of linear expansion of a substance.	By the use of two fixed points—the ice point and the steam point—called 0° C and 100° C, respectively.
5. How is the absolute zero of temperature determined from the behavior of a gas under ideal conditions?	A number that gives the fractional change in length of a sample of the material for each degree change in temperature.
6. What is meant by the absolute (or Kelvin) scale of temperature?	The absolute zero is the temperature at which the gas would no longer occupy space or exert pressure.
7. Define heat conduction.	The temperature measured upward from the absolute zero (−273° C). The size of the degree is the same as the Celsius degree; only the starting-point of the scale is different.
8. What is meant by convection?	The handing-on of motion from molecule to molecule, constituting a transfer of heat energy.
9. What is the relation of radiation to heat?	The transfer of heat (energy) by the bodily movement of a warmed portion of a fluid.
10. How hot must a body be in order to send out radiation?	When radiation (radiant energy) is absorbed in a substance, the energy is converted into heat (molecular motion).
	At all temperatures above absolute zero, all bodies emit radiation.

Chapter X

HEAT ENERGY

The earlier idea that heat is a fluid that can be transferred from a hot to a cold object failed to explain the unlimited production of heat by friction and other processes. Science was forced to recognize heat as a form of energy, and it was seen that mechanical energy could be transformed into heat energy by such means as friction. The opposite process—transforming heat into mechanical work—is also possible and underlies the operation of the steam, diesel, gasoline and other heat engines widely used today. The development of the concept of heat energy and its applications form the subject matter of this chapter.

QUANTITY OF HEAT

A thermometer can tell us something about the heat contained in a body, but it does not tell the whole story. A cup of boiling water has a higher temperature than a tub full of warm water, but the tubful contains more heat energy. For instance, you would find that a large block of ice could be completely melted by putting it in the tub of lukewarm water, but only a small part of it could be melted by the cupful of hot water.

Experience shows also that the nature of the material determines the amount of heat transferred to or from a body when its temperature is changed by a given amount. Imagine an experiment in which you take an iron ball and a lead ball of the same size, heat them both to the temperature of boiling water and then lay them on a block of wax. You would find that the iron ball melts a considerable amount of wax, while the lead ball, in spite of its greater mass, melts hardly any. It would seem that different materials, in cooling through the same temperature range, give up different amounts of heat.

From experiments of many kinds we find that the quantity of heat energy given up or taken on when a body changes its temperature is proportional to the mass of the object, to the amount that its temperature changes, and to a characteristic number called the **specific heat** of the substance of which the body is made. In the language of algebra we can put

$$Q = smt,$$

where Q is the quantity of heat, s is the specific heat of the material, m is the mass of the body and t is its temperature change.

About units: We agree to call the specific heat of water 1, and measure the values for other materials in terms of this standard. Some typical values are given in the following table. No special unit need be attached to s; it is merely a ratio, and so is an ordinary fraction.

TABLE 9

SPECIFIC HEATS
OF COMMON MATERIALS

Substance	*Specific Heat,* s
Water	1.00
Alcohol	0.65
Aluminum	0.22
Glass	0.20
Iron	0.11
Copper, Brass	0.09
Silver	0.06
Lead	0.03

Heat Units

Heat quantity, Q, is of the nature of energy, but it is convenient to have a special unit for it, based on the above relation. In the Metric system, the unit is one **calorie,** the amount of heat entering or leaving one gram of water when its temperature changes by one Celsius degree.*

In the English system, one **British Thermal Unit** (Btu) is defined as the amount of heat needed to change the temperature of 1 lb of water 1 Fahrenheit degree. 1 Btu is equivalent to 252 cal.

If we put hot and cold substances in contact and take care to avoid heat transfer with the surroundings, everything will finally come to a common temperature. Then, provided there is no conversion of heat to other forms of energy (or vice versa), it will be true that the

Total heat given up by hot bodies = Total heat taken on by cold bodies.

If we know all the other circumstances, we can use this statement to find the final temperature.

EXAMPLE 1: A 200-gm brass ball is heated to 80° C and plunged into 150 gm of water at 20° C. What will be the final equilibrium temperature of both?

SOLUTION: Call the final temperature t° C. It must lie somewhere between 20° and 80° C. Using $Q = smt$, the heat given up by the brass in cooling from 80° to t° will be (use the table for finding s): $0.09 \times 200 \times (80 - t)$. Similarly, the quantity of heat taken on by the water will be $1 \times 150 \times (t - 20)$. Setting these two heat quantities equal, we can solve for t: $0.09 \times 200 \times 80 - 0.09 \times 200 \times t = 1 \times 150 \times t - 1 \times 150 \times 20$; finally, $t = 26.4$° C.

The fact that the specific heat of water is considerably larger than that of most other substances makes water act as a sort of storehouse for heat. For example, this reduces the daily and seasonal temperature variations of islands and of places on the seacoast. When the sun is strong, the ocean takes up a great deal of heat but does not go up much in temperature while doing so. When the sun is weak, or at night, this heat is given up to the surroundings, thus preventing the temperature from going as low as it otherwise might.

* Not to be confused with the *kilocalorie* (= 1,000 calories), the unit used in specifying food values. When a dietitian says that a slice of bread has a food value of 80 (kilo) calories, he means that in the process of digestion it furnishes that amount of heat energy. The average worker needs between 3,000 and 5,000 kilocalories per day.

FUSION OF A SOLID

If a material has its temperature changed considerably it may also change its physical state. It is found that when a crystalline substance is heated, the temperature at which the solid form melts is the same as the temperature at which the liquid freezes when cooled. For water we call this single temperature the **ice point** (p. 66). Materials such as wax or glass are non-crystalline and have no definite melting (or solidifying) point—for example, butter gradually softens as the temperature is raised.

It requires heat to melt ice. A beverage is cooled when ice cubes are put in it because the heat used to melt the ice is taken from the surrounding liquid. If ice is put into water at room temperature, the temperature of the mixture will finally come to the ice point (0° C) as long as any ice remains. Putting in more ice or more water will not alter the final temperature. Only when the ice has all melted will the water temperature begin to rise.

The quantity of heat required to melt one gram of a given substance (without producing any change in temperature) is found to be constant, and is called the **heat of fusion** of the substance. For water, this amounts to about 80 cal/gm, or 144 Btu/lb. Because energy cannot be destroyed, this same amount of heat must be *given off* when one gram of the material solidifies. For instance, we find that when a gallon of water freezes, it *gives up* as much heat as would be produced by burning an ounce and half of good coal. In winter, the air temperature is somewhat moderated by the heat given off by the formation of snow and ice. Large tubs of water, placed in a cellar, may prevent vegetables stored there from freezing. If the temperature should go below the ice point, the water would freeze before the fluids inside the vegetables (impure water), and the heat given off may be enough to prevent the cellar temperature from going much lower.

Crystalline materials generally *increase* sharply in volume when the liquid freezes. We know that this is true for water because ice floats. It is also a matter of experience that the force of expansion of freezing water can burst water pipes or auto radiators and can split rocks. Type metal is an alloy that expands on solidifying, and so produces sharp, clear castings.

VAPORIZATION OF A LIQUID

Earlier (p. 59) you found out that the evaporation of a liquid consists of the escape of molecules from its surface. Since only the faster, more energetic molecules can get away from the attraction of the others, the average speed of the molecules of the liquid is thereby reduced, and this means that the temperature gets lower. Thus **evaporation produces a cooling effect,** as common experience shows.

Evaporation at the free surface of a liquid goes on at all temperatures, but when bubbles of the vapor form all through the liquid, we say it is **boiling.** This happens as soon as the pressure exerted by the vapor becomes equal to the pressure of the surrounding air. If the liquid was made to boil by heating it, the continued application of heat will not make it any hotter, but will merely make it boil away faster. The energy supplied is used to separate the molecules from each other.

It is found that a given amount of heat is carried away for each gram of liquid that vaporizes. This is called the **heat of vaporization** of the substance. For water, at the normal steam point, it amounts to about 540 cal/gm, or 970 Btu/lb. Again, we can say that this same quantity of heat is *given off* whenever a

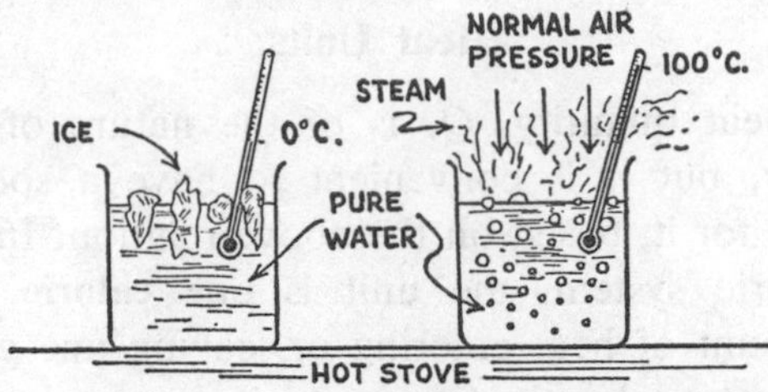

Fig. 56.

Stays at 0° C as long as any ice is left.	Stays at 100° C as long as any water is left.

gram of steam condenses at the normal steam point.*

If the air pressure acting on the surface of water is less than the normal value of 14.7 lb/in², boiling will begin at some temperature lower than 100° C. For instance, at the summit of Pike's Peak, the vapor pressure of steam becomes equal to the reduced air pressure at that altitude (14,000 ft) when the water temperature is only 85° C (185° F), and the water boils. The cooking of food in an open vessel becomes difficult under such conditions. If a closed vessel is used, the pressure of the vapor can build up inside, and the steam point will then be raised. This is the principle of the **pressure cooker.** If the valve is set for a pressure of, say, 10 lb/in² (above normal atmospheric) the steam temperature inside the cooker will be about 115° C (239° F), and the contents will cook in a short time.

EXPERIMENT 25: Half fill a thin-walled glass flask or bottle with water and bring to a boil. Holding the flask with a towel, remove from the heat and cork it tightly. The boiling stops, because the pressure builds up inside, but each time you pour some cold water over the bottle the contained water starts to boil again. The cooling condenses some of the steam inside the vessel; this lowers the pressure, permitting the hot water to boil even though its temperature may be far below the normal boiling point.

* The value of the heat of vaporization (or condensation) is slightly different at other temperatures than the steam point.

Moisture in the Air

The great play of evaporation and condensation of water in the atmosphere is one of the most important factors affecting the weather. Indoors, too, we are concerned with the humidity of the air. One of the functions of **air conditioning** is to regulate the amount of moisture in the air, keeping it to a healthful and comfortable amount at all times.

When moist air is cooled, the vapor may condense into a **fog** of tiny, slowly-settling droplets. If this takes place at some distance above the ground we have **clouds,** and when the drops become large enough, they fall as **rain.** Quickly taking the cap off a cold bottle of soda-water often causes a fog to form in the neck of the bottle. Fogs produced by sudden expansion of moist air are used in a **cloud chamber** to show up the paths of particles produced in atomic disintegration experiments.

In winter, moisture in the air may go directly into the solid state, depositing on a chilled surface in the form of **frost.** If this happens in the air itself we have individual crystals that fall as **snow. Hail** consists of frozen raindrops, formed when the drops pass through cold layers of air on their way down to the ground.

Practice Exercise No. 20

1. The sparks from the flint of a cigarette lighter are red hot, yet they do not burn the skin of your hand. Why?
2. How many Btu does it take to heat a 5-lb iron from 65° to 330° F?
3. How many Btu does it take to change 1 lb of ice at 32° F to steam at 212° F?
4. It may be said that a) boiling is a cooling process and, b) freezing is a warming process. Explain.
5. Why is a burn by live steam at 100° C worse than one by boiling water at 100° C?
6. Can you cool a perfectly dry object by fanning it?
7. A glass of cold milk is observed to "sweat" on a warm, moist day. Where does the water come from?
8. Wet clothes hung out on a line in winter are often observed to "freeze dry." Explain.

CONSERVATION OF ENERGY

In Chapter VII you saw that the operation of any practical machine or mechanical process involves the unavoidable wasting away (dissipation) of mechanical energy in the form of heat. The bearings of a machine become warm; a pump for compressing air is hotter than can be accounted for through friction alone; a nail is warmed by the blows of a hammer. There is always something to show for the dissipated work: The mechanical energy that seems to be lost appears again in the form of heat energy.

Careful experiments in which mechanical work is all converted into heat and the quantity of heat measured show that whenever a given amount of mechanical energy disappears, a fixed quantity of heat appears in its place, regardless of whether the change is brought about by friction, by the stirring of liquids, by the compression of a gas, etc. This fixed "rate of exchange" may be called the **heat-work equivalent.** The experimental value is 4.18 joules* per calorie, or 778 ft-lb per Btu.

The experiments mentioned in the last paragraph involve the transformation of work into heat, but we know that the reverse process is also possible. In fact, any heat engine, such as the ones to be described below, is a device for changing heat energy into mechanical work. Measurements show that in all such processes the relation between heat and work is numerically the same as the one given above—the same ratio as when work is changed into heat. This is in agreement with a general principle first announced by J. R. Mayer a little over a century ago. It is called the **Conservation of Energy,** and says that **it is impossible to create or destroy energy—what disappears in one form must reappear in another.** This principle is broader than the

* Recall that a joule was defined as ten million ergs (p. 52).

Conservation of Mechanical Energy (p. 53), for it includes *all* forms of energy—mechanical, thermal, chemical, electrical, etc. The rule, which is one of the most far-reaching in all of science, effectively denies the possibility of building a perpetual motion machine (p. 55).

HEAT ENGINES

The human body has often been likened to an engine; indeed, in some respects, the two are quite similar. In your body, part of the chemical energy of the food you eat is converted into useful muscular work, part into heat, and the rest into nutrition and repair of the tissues. The fraction converted into work is only around 25–30%.

Heat engines have been responsible for significant changes in our civilization. The invention of the steam engine early in the eighteenth century led directly to the Industrial Revolution; later, the gas engine, the steam turbine, the diesel engine and the jet engine produced equally great upheavals in power plant operation, transportation, manufacturing, etc.

Jet- and **rocket-propulsion engines** make direct use of the reaction principle (p. 50). The burning of the fuel produces a large volume of gas which streams from openings at the rear of the unit, and the mechanical reaction on the unit itself drives it forward. A rocket carries its own supply of oxygen to burn the fuel, while a jet takes in air and compresses it beforehand. In the jet, the outstreaming gases deliver part of their energy to a gas turbine.

There is a limit to the speed and height attainable by a propeller-driven airplane

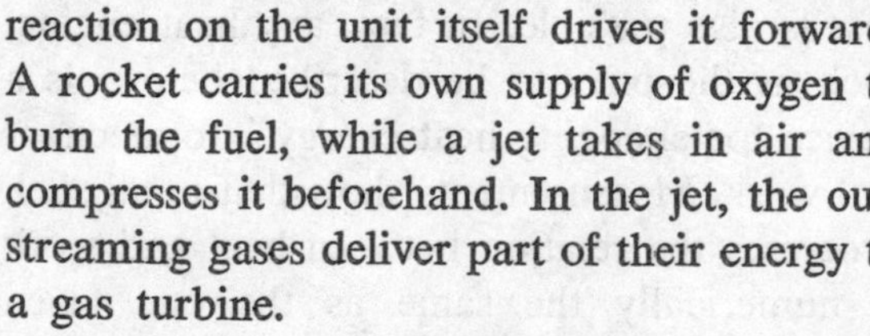

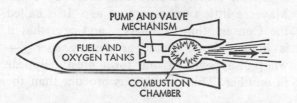

Fig. 57. Rocket propulsion

powered by piston engines. Rocket units can go beyond these limitations, and are also more efficient at high speeds and high altitudes. Their role in the exploration of the upper atmosphere and in space navigation has become well known in recent years.

REFRIGERATION

A **refrigerator** is really a heat engine in reverse: Mechanical work, supplied to a pump, is made to produce a difference in temperature. The pump (Fig. 58) compresses an easily liquefied gas, such as ammonia, methyl chloride, Freon, etc. The compressed gas is then passed through coils cooled by air or water, where it becomes a liquid. This liquid is pumped into the cooling unit in the upper part of the refrigerated chamber. The cooling unit is a coil where the pressure is reduced to make the liquid evaporate. In the process, heat is taken from the surroundings, cooling the air and other contents of the box. The vaporized fluid goes back to the pump, and the cycle is repeated. In the **gas refrigerator,** the function of the pump is taken over by a small gas flame.

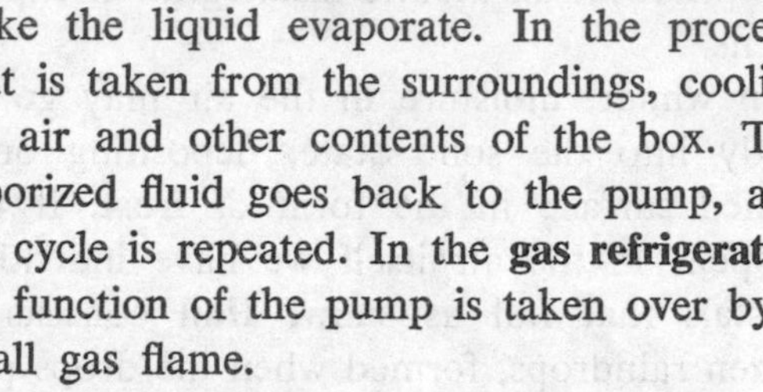

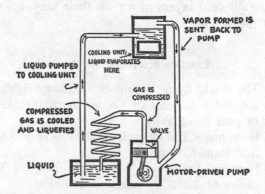

Fig. 58. The mechanical refrigerator

EXPERIMENT 26: Put some water on a large cork and set a watch crystal or a piece of tinfoil shaped into a small dish on it. Into this dish pour a little alcohol or ether (keep away from open flames) and make it evaporate rapidly by vigorous fanning. Enough heat will be carried away to turn the water into snow, or even to freeze the dish firmly to the cork.

Practice Exercise No. 21

1. What becomes of the KE of an automobile when it is brought to a stop by the brakes?
2. How much heat energy, in Btu, is used by a 160-lb man when he climbs a mountain 3,900 ft high?
3. In level flight, a certain rocket motor has a thrust of 3,000 lb force. If a pound of rocket fuel can furnish 30,000 Btu when burned, how far will 1 lb of fuel drive the rocket, assuming that ¼ the energy of this fuel is changed to mechanical work?
4. Is the temperature of the steam under pressure in the boiler of a steam engine higher or lower than 100° C?
5. Does a refrigerator, operated with the door open, produce any net change in the temperature of the room? If so, in what direction?

SUMMARY *Instructions:* (see page 17)

1. Upon what factors does the quantity of heat energy taken up by a body depend?	
2. Define the calorie.	The temperature change, the mass of the body and the specific heat of the material: $Q = smt$.
3. What can be said of an isolated system in which heat exchanges take place between hot and cold bodies?	The amount of heat energy entering or leaving 1 gm of water when its temperature changes by 1 C°.
4. What is meant by the heat of fusion of a substance?	Total heat given up by the hot bodies equals total heat taken on by the cold bodies.
5. Distinguish between boiling of a liquid and evaporation.	The quantity of heat required to melt 1 gm of a substance (without producing any change in temperature).
6. Define heat of vaporization of a liquid.	Evaporation is the escape of molecules at the free surface of a liquid; it goes on at all temperatures. Boiling is the formation of vapor bubbles all through a liquid at a particular temperature called the boiling point.
7. What is meant by the heat-work equivalent?	The amount of heat carried away from the liquid when 1 gm evaporates.
8. State the Principle of the Conservation of Energy.	The numerical relationship between heat energy and mechanical energy: 4.18 joules = 1 calorie.
9. What is a heat engine?	It is impossible to create or destroy energy.
	A device for converting heat energy into mechanical energy.

SECTION FOUR

SOUND

Chapter XI

THE NATURE OF SOUND

When a stone is dropped into a quiet pond, a set of **waves** spreads outward from the point of impact in ever-widening circles. The size of each circular ripple grows at a constant rate. A floating chip of wood does not move forward with the waves that strike it but merely bobs up and down, scarcely moving from its place.

Besides waves on water, there are other types: Light, X rays and radio are all forms of wave motion, as are the sound waves to be described in this and the following chapter.

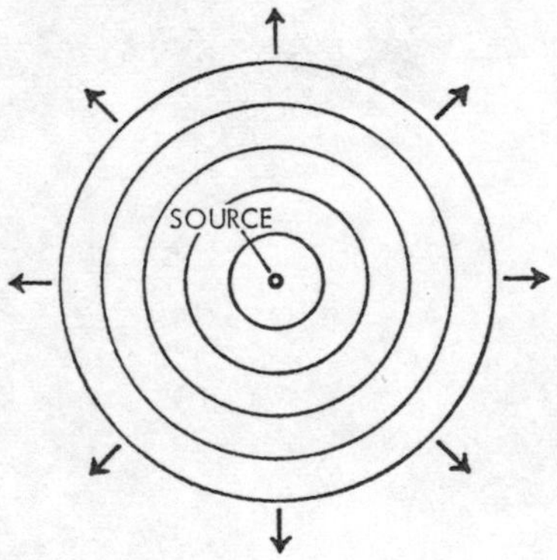

Fig. 59. Spreading of waves

SOUND WAVES

Suppose that instead of tossing a stone into a pond we explode a firecracker outdoors. The sudden explosion compresses the air nearby. Air, being highly elastic, expands outward and in doing so, compresses the layer of air just beyond. In this way the state of compression is handed on and spreads rapidly outward in much the same way as the ripples spread out over the surface of the pond in the previous experiment. Here, however, we have a **wave of compression,** for that is exactly what a sound wave is. As it passes, the molecules of the air crowd together, then draw apart. The sensation of hearing results when such waves strike the ear.

Compressional waves (sound waves) can travel through solids and liquids as well as through gases such as air, since all substances are elastic to some extent; but always some material is needed as a carrier. Experiments show that sound does not travel in a vacuum. The following table gives the approximate speeds of sound waves in some common substances:

TABLE 10

SPEED OF COMPRESSIONAL WAVES IN VARIOUS MATERIALS

Values are for room temperature (20° C)

Substance	*Speed V, ft/sec*
Air	1,126
Hydrogen	4,315
Carbon Dioxide	877
Water	4,820
Iron (Steel)	16,800
Brass	11,500
Granite	12,960

Notice that the speed in air amounts to almost 770 mi/hr, and that in water sound travels over 4 times as fast, in iron nearly 15 times as fast as in air.

EXPERIMENT 27: Observe the delay between the time you see a puff of steam from a distant whistle and the time the sound arrives. You can estimate how far away a thunderstorm is by counting the number of seconds between the lightning flash and the thunder clap which accompanies it. The flash is seen almost instantly because it is carried by light waves that travel about 900,000 times as fast as the sound waves that bring you the noise of thunder. Since sound waves take about 5 sec to go a mile, simply divide the number of seconds' delay by 5 in order to get the distance in miles.

EXAMPLE 1: An observer hears the report of a gunshot 3.5 sec after he sees the flash of the burning powder charge. How far is he from the gun?

SOLUTION: Taking the speed of sound in air to be roughly 1,100 ft/sec, the distance sound goes in 3.5 sec will be 1100×3.5, or about 3,900 ft.

Temperature Effects

The speed of sound depends in general on the temperature of the substance through which it is passing. For solids and liquids the change is small and usually can be neglected, but for gases the change is large, the speed increasing with temperature. For moderate temperature differences, this increase may be taken to be about 2 ft/sec for each degree C. For example, if the speed of sound in air at 20° C is 1126 ft/sec (as given in the table), the speed at 39° will be

$$1126 + 19 \times 2 = 1164 \text{ ft/sec.}$$

If the air were at rest and the same temperature throughout, sound would travel uniformly in all directions. This condition rarely exists. On a hot summer day the air next to the ground is hotter than the layers above. Since the speed of sound increases with temperature, sound will travel faster near the ground, with the result that the waves are bent away from the surface, as shown in Fig. 60. These waves will not reach an observer at P, and so sound does not seem to travel far under such conditions. On a clear night the ground cools more rapidly than the air above, and sound travels faster some distance above the earth than in the cooled layer of air next to the surface. This has the effect of bending the waves down toward the earth (Fig. 60), making the sound appear to carry farther than usual. Winds can cause similar effects.

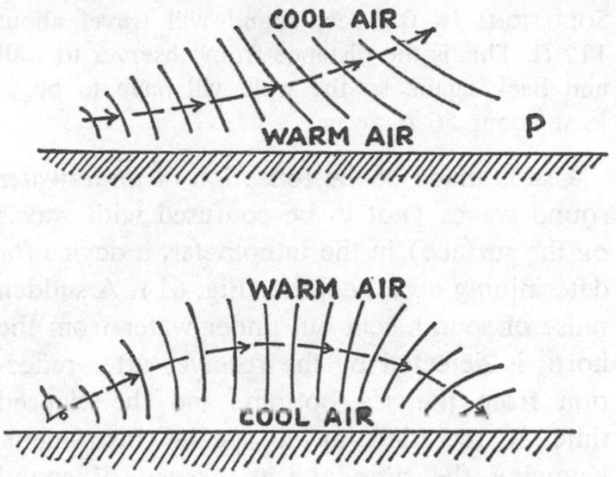

Fig. 60. Bending of sound waves

Reflection of Waves

When ripples traveling on water strike a wide obstacle, such as a floating board, a new set of ripples is observed to start back from the obstacle. The waves are said to be **reflected** from it. In a similar way, sound waves may be reflected from walls, mountains, the ground, etc. The prolonged "rolling" of thunder is usually due to successive reflections from clouds and ground surfaces.

EXPERIMENT 28: Make a mechanical model of the reflection of sound by tying one end of a heavy cord or rope to a doorknob. Holding the other end in your hand, pull the rope fairly taut and give your hand a sudden downward jerk. A "hump" will travel down the rope and be reflected from the fixed end, returning to your hand in the form of a "hollow." Several back and forth reflections may be noted before the wave dies out.

The human ear can distinguish two sounds as separate only if they reach it at least 0.1 sec apart; otherwise, they blend in the hearing mechanism to give the impression of a single sound. If a short, sharp sound is reflected back to the observer after more than about 0.1 sec, he hears it as an **echo**—a repetition of the original sound.

EXAMPLE 2: How far from a wall must an observer be in order to hear an echo when he shouts?

SOLUTION: In 0.1 sec, sound will travel about 112 ft. This is the distance from observer to wall and back again, so the wall will have to be at least about 56 ft away.

Use is made of the reflection of *underwater* sound waves (not to be confused with waves on the surface) in the **fathometer,** a device for determining ocean depths (Fig. 61). A sudden pulse of sound, sent out under water from the horn, is detected by the receiver after reflection from the sea bottom, and the elapsed time is recorded by a special instrument. Knowing the time and the speed of sound waves in water, the depth of the sea at any point may be computed, often to the nearest foot. Measurements may be made almost continuously as the ship moves along. A similar method, using radar waves (Fig. 105, p. 120), is sometimes used instead.

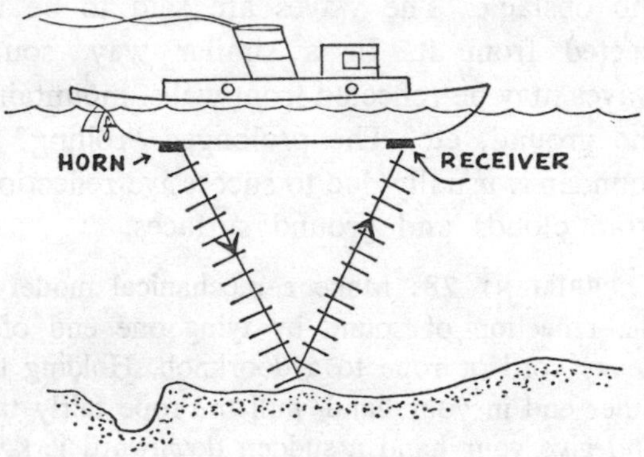

Fig. 61. The fathometer

Sound waves, like light, may be reflected from hollow (concave) surfaces in order to increase the intensity in certain directions. In Statuary Hall in the Capitol at Washington, a person standing a few feet from the wall can hear the whispering of another person who stands facing the wall at the opposite side, about 50 feet away. At intermediate points the sound is not heard. Other famous "whispering galleries" are the auditorium of the Mormon Tabernacle at Salt Lake City and the dome of St. Paul's Cathedral in London. In a similar way, a large horn may be used to collect sound waves and concentrate them at the ear, or other detector.

Practice Exercise No. 22

1. Explain why soldiers marching near the end of a long column are observed to be out of step with the music of a band marching at the head of the column.
2. Give a reason for believing that sounds of different pitch, such as those coming from various instruments of an orchestra, all travel at about the same speed in air.
3. In the polar regions, on a day when there is little wind, the air temperature is found to increase fairly regularly with distance above the ground. Explain why, under such conditions, ordinary speech can sometimes be heard nearly a mile away.
4. A sounding device on a ship shows an echo coming back after 3.5 sec. How deep is the water if the speed of sound waves in sea water at the existing temperature is 4700 ft/sec?
5. When an open umbrella is placed with its handle in a horizontal position and a pocket watch is tied to the end of the handle, the ticking of the watch can be heard at the opposite side of a large room. Explain.

Continuous Waves

The disturbance produced by dropping a stone into water consists of only a few crests and hollows. If *continuous* waves are to be formed, a steadily **oscillating** or **vibrating** body must be allowed to dip into the water. Exactly the same thing is true of sound waves. Sustained sounds come from sources such as vibrating bells, violin strings, drum heads.

Suppose a small rubber balloon is partly inflated and attached to a hand pump (Fig. 62). If the handle is quickly pushed down a short distance, the balloon expands and the outside air in contact with it is suddenly compressed. This layer of air will, in turn, compress the layer beyond it, and so on. The compression that was started by the swelling of the balloon will thus travel away from the balloon in all directions. Similarly, if the handle is quickly pulled up a short distance the balloon contracts and the adjoining air suddenly expands. This time, a region of *low* pressure spreads outward in all directions.

Moving the handle up and down at regular intervals makes a succession of compressions and expansions travel out from the source. Such a regular train of disturbances constitutes *continuous wave motion.* If the up-and-down motion of the piston could be made rapid enough, a nearby observer would hear a sound as these compressional waves reach his ear. A more practical source of sound waves would be a vibrating violin string, bell, drumhead, etc.

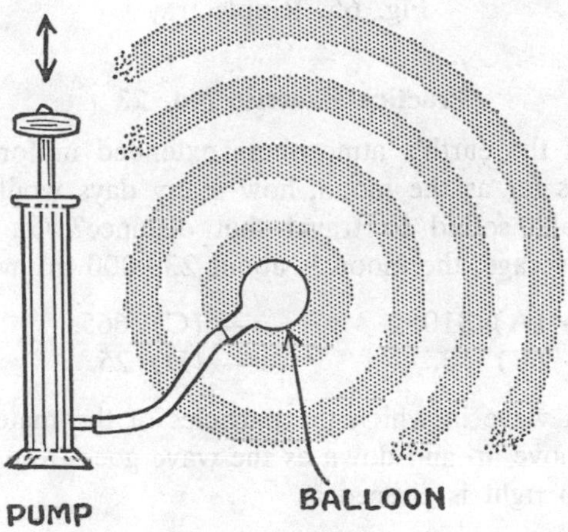

Fig. 62. Producing compressional waves in air

In any wave motion, no particle of the material that is carrying the waves ever moves very far from its normal place, but is merely displaced a short distance, first one way and then the other. In compressional (sound) waves, the particles oscillate *along* the line in which the waves are moving, and so these are also known as **longitudinal waves.** In other types of waves the individual particles may move, instead, in a direction *perpendicular* to the line of advance of the waves. These are called **transverse waves.** Waves in a rope or stretched string are of this kind. Still other waves are combinations of longitudinal and transverse—for example, waves on the surface of water. The floating chip of wood referred to on p. 82 is observed to move slightly forward and upward as the crest of a wave meets it, then moves back and downward again as the next trough comes by.

FREQUENCY AND WAVELENGTH

When waves are sent out by a vibrating body, the number of waves produced in one second is the same as the number of vibrations per second, or **frequency** of vibration, of the source. The **wavelength** is defined as the distance between two successive places in the wave train that are in the same state of compression. In Fig. 63, the strip across the top represents a sound wave, and the wavy line below is a graph of the way the pressure in this wave changes—that is, the height of the curve at any point gives the pressure, above or below normal air pressure, at that place in the wave train. The distance l on this graph is one **wavelength.** In particular, it might be measured from one crest to the next, or from one trough to the next. There is a simple relation between the frequency n, the wavelength l and the wave speed V: Suppose the source vibrates for exactly one second. In this time, just n complete waves will be sent out (Fig.

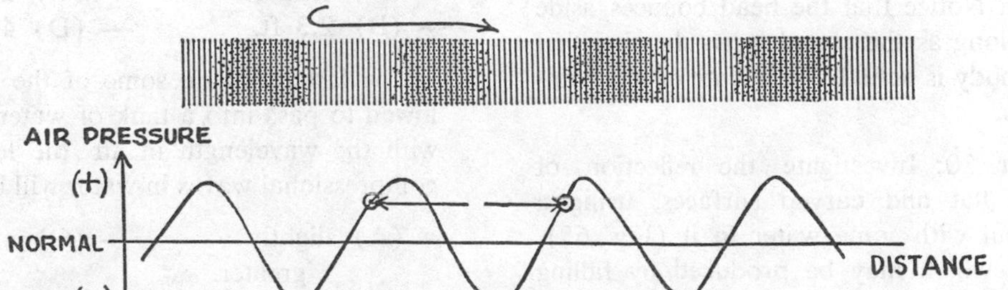

Fig. 63. Graph of change of pressure in sound wave

64). Each of these waves has a length l, so the first wave will be at a distance nl from the source. But in one second's time, the first wave will have traveled a distance equal to V, the wave speed, so we have

$$nl = V,$$

or **the frequency times the wavelength is equal to the wave speed.** This wave equation holds for continuous wave motion of any kind.

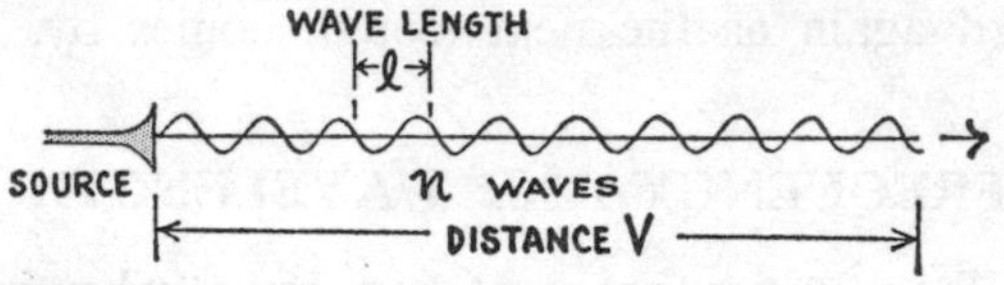

Fig. 64. Why $V = nl$

EXAMPLE 3: In air at ordinary temperature, the sound waves coming from a certain whistle are found to be 27 in. long. What is the frequency of the sound?

SOLUTION: In applying the wave equation, the same kind of length unit must be used throughout. The speed of sound is usually given in *feet* per second, so we must change the wavelength from 27 in. to $27/12 = 9/4$ ft before substituting. Then

$$n = \frac{V}{l} = \frac{1126}{9/4} = 500 \text{ vibrations per second.}$$

EXPERIMENT 29: Hang a bead or small button from a piece of silk thread about 2 ft long, so that the bead just touches the lip of a large, thin drinking glass. Holding the glass firmly at its base, set it into vibration with a sharp snap of the finger. Notice that the bead bounces aside violently as long as the sound lasts, showing that a sounding body is actually in a state of mechanical vibration.

EXPERIMENT 30: Investigate the reflection of waves from flat and curved surfaces, using a large, flat pan with some water in it (Fig. 65). The ripples, which may be produced by falling drops of water, are easily seen if lighted by an unshaded lamp placed some distance above the pan.

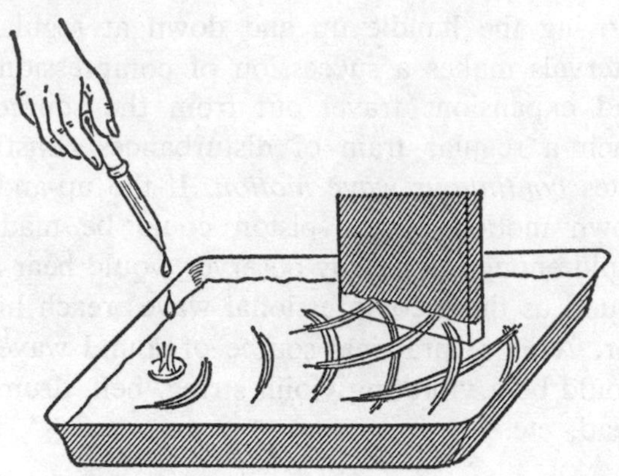

Fig. 65. Ripple tray

Practice Exercise No. 23

1. If the earth's atmosphere extended uniformly as far as the moon, how many days would it take sound to travel that distance? On the average, the moon is about 239,000 mi away.

— (A) 310. — (C) 665.
— (B) 13. — (D) 25.

2. A wave in which the particles of the material move up and down as the wave goes from left to right is classed as

— (A) longitudinal. — (C) compressional.
— (B) transverse. — (D) sound.

3. On a certain day, sound is found to travel 1.00 mi in 4.80 sec. What is the temperature of the air through which the sound is passing?

— (A) 7.0° C. — (C) 26° C.
— (B) 27° C. — (D) −6.0° C.

4. How long are the sound waves produced in the air when middle "C" is struck on a piano, the frequency of vibration being 256 vib/sec?

— (A) 0.23 ft. — (C) 288 ft.
— (B) 2.3 ft. — (D) 4.3 ft.

5. In the last problem, some of the sound is allowed to pass into a tank of water. Compared with the wavelength in air, the length of the compressional waves in water will be

— (A) slightly greater. — (C) about 4 times as large.
— (B) the same. — (D) considerably less.

SUMMARY *Instructions:* (see page 17)

1. What is another word for a sound wave?	
2. How does the speed of sound waves in air change when the temperature is changed?	Compressional wave.
3. What is meant by the reflection of waves?	Speed increases when temperature increases.
4. How must a source move if it is to give rise to a continuous train of waves?	The throwing-back of waves from an obstacle.
5. Distinguish between longitudinal and transverse waves.	It must oscillate, or vibrate.
6. What is meant by the frequency of waves or of the source that produces them?	In longitudinal waves, the vibrations are *in* the direction of wave travel; for transverse waves, the vibrations are perpendicular to the direction of wave travel.
7. What is meant by wavelength?	The number of complete waves produced, or the number of vibrations of the source that occur, each second.
8. State the expression relating wave speed, wavelength and frequency.	The distance between two successive places in a wave train that are in the same state of vibration.
	The wave equation $nl = V$.

Chapter XII

ACOUSTICS

Since sound waves are always present in our surroundings, it is of interest to find out something about their behavior. There are useful and acceptable sounds, such as those of speech or music, and unwanted sounds such as noise. What physical characteristics make them so? How does sound behave indoors? Are there sounds that do not affect the ear at all? What scientific principles are involved in musical instruments? These are some of the questions to which attention will be given in this chapter.

PITCH AND FREQUENCY

What a musician calls the **pitch** of a simple musical tone, or its position in the musical scale, is judged mainly by the frequency of the sound waves that strike the ear. A musical **tone** is heard only if the vibrations of the source—and therefore of the sound waves coming from it—have a definite frequency. If the vibrations are irregularly timed, or if there is a jumble of unrelated vibrations, the sound is called a **noise.**

EXPERIMENT 31: Draw the tip of your fingernail across a ridged linen book cover and notice that the sound produced, while not particularly musical, has a definite pitch. The faster you move your finger, the higher the pitch becomes.

Not all sound waves can be heard. A normal human ear can respond to frequencies ranging from around 20 to just under 20,000 vibrations per second. Frequencies above the hearing range, especially those of several hundred thousand per second, are called **ultrasonic.** They can be produced by special methods (for example, by electrically-vibrated crystals) and are beginning to find many useful applications because of their ability literally to shake matter back and forth at a fast rate. Ultrasonic waves are used to destroy bacteria in water, to clean metals, dry paper, remove smoke from air, drill holes in hard or brittle materials, etc.

If a car approaches you with its horn blowing, the pitch of the tone seems to drop suddenly as the source sweeps past. The explanation is based on the fact that you judge the pitch of a sound only by the number of waves that strike the ear each second. When the listener and the source of sound are approaching each other, the waves strike more frequently than when both are, relatively, at rest and so a higher-than-normal tone is heard. When the two move apart, fewer waves hit the ear each second, giving the impression of a lower tone (Fig. 66). This is called the **Doppler effect,** after the scientist who first worked out its explanation. In astronomy, the effect on light waves is used to find the speeds of motion of the stars relative to the earth. The Doppler effect on radar waves can be used to measure the speed of an airplane or earth satellite.

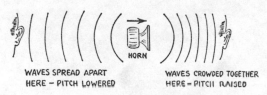

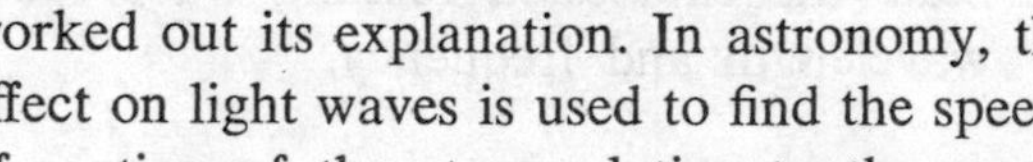

Fig. 66. The Doppler effect

INTENSITY AND LOUDNESS

There are ways of making sound waves visible, in a certain sense, so that they can be studied in the laboratory. The usual method is to allow the sound to strike a microphone, which converts the sound vibrations into corresponding electrical disturbances. These are then traced out in the form of a visible curve on the screen of what amounts to a television tube (oscilloscope). If, for instance, a gently vibrating reed or tuning fork is placed in front of the microphone, the pattern on the screen will look like Fig. 67a. The same reed or fork, when made to vibrate more strongly and give off a louder tone, will yield the pattern shown in Fig. 67b. The louder sound corresponds to a greater **amplitude** of vibration of the air particles, as shown by the higher crests and deeper hollows of the visible wave pattern. The physical quantity that corresponds to the observed loudness of the sound is called the **intensity;** the greater the amplitude in the waves, the greater is the intensity.

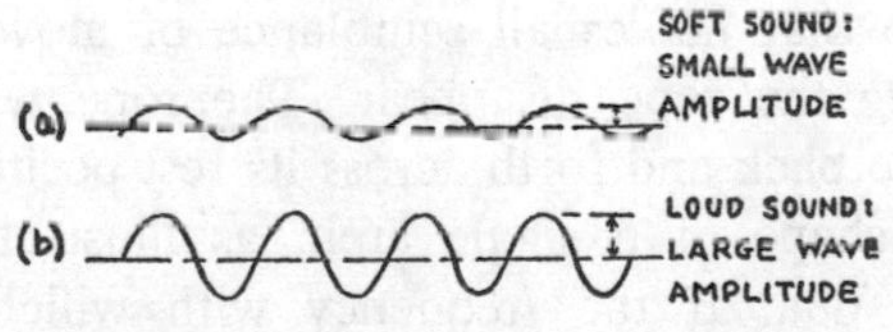

Fig. 67. Amplitude of waves

Besides depending on the amplitude of vibration of the source, another factor determines the intensity of the sound waves received by the ear, and that is the distance from the source. If the source is small and if there are no disturbances such as reflections of sound, the intensity will fall off inversely as the square of the distance. This means that at twice the distance, the intensity will be $(\frac{1}{2})^2 = \frac{1}{4}$ its former value, at 3 times the distance it will drop to $(\frac{1}{3})^2$, or $\frac{1}{9}$, etc.

The intensity of sound, as received at any place, is measured in a unit called a **decibel.** The table shows the rating, in decibels, of sounds having a great range of intensity.

TABLE 11

SOUND INTENSITY LEVELS

Source	*Rating, in decibels*
Faintest audible sound	0
Rustling of leaves	8
Whisper	10–20
Average home	20–30
Automobile	40–50
Ordinary conversation	50–60
Heavy street traffic	70–80
Riveting gun	90–100
Thunder	110

The intensity range over which the human ear is able to detect and respond to sounds is much greater than the decibel scale suggests. The extreme sounds listed above actually differ in *energy* by a factor of a hundred billion!

Indoor Sound

Listening to speech or music outdoors is not very satisfactory because the loudness falls off so rapidly with distance. In addition, the sounds seem somewhat flat and "dead." In an auditorium, reflection from the walls and other surfaces make the intensity more nearly uniform all over the audience, and by adding to the time that each sound impression lasts, give increased "life" to the tones heard. However, if the room is not properly designed, there may be annoying local concentrations of sound at some places and dead spots at others. Also, if the walls, ceiling or floor are made of hard, compact materials, the sound waves will be reflected back and forth many times before they are completely absorbed, giving the auditorium a long **reverberation time.** If this is too long, musical tones or spoken syllables will be confused with previously produced ones, leading to bad listening conditions. The remedy is to cover some of the reflecting surfaces with sound-absorbing materials such as drapes or special acoustic tiles made for that purpose.

Practice Exercise No. 24

1. In a fire siren, a jet of air is directed against a series of evenly-spaced holes in a rotating disk. As the disk speeds up, the tone

— (A) increases in frequency.
— (B) increases in wave length.
— (C) drops in pitch.
— (D) maintains constant pitch.

2. In order to emit sound, a body must

— (A) absorb sound waves.
— (B) vibrate.
— (C) reflect sound waves.
— (D) move toward the hearer.

3. As a man moves directly away from a steady source of sound at constant speed, the sound he hears will

— (A) increase in frequency and intensity.
— (B) stay constant in pitch but decrease in loudness.
— (C) decrease in frequency and intensity.
— (D) remain constant in both pitch and loudness.

4. To a man who moves from a position 20 ft from a bell ringing steadily in the open air to a position 60 ft from the bell, the intensity of the sound will appear to

— (A) decrease by a factor of 3.
— (B) decrease by a factor of 9.
— (C) increase by a factor of 10.
— (D) decrease by a factor of 1,200.

5. A concert hall has too long a reverberation time. Of the following, the best way to correct the condition would be to

— (A) limit the size of the audience.
— (B) install a curved ceiling.
— (C) lay heavy carpeting on the floor.
— (D) hang large mirrors on the walls.

STATIONARY WAVES

In experimenting with water waves (Experiment 30, p. 86), you probably noticed that two sets of ripples—say, a direct and a reflected set—can pass right through each other without any mutual effect. This is true of any kind of wave, including sound. For example, the sounds of a singer and his accompaniment are mingled in the air of a room, yet you can perfectly well make out each separately.

Let us go back next to Experiment 28 on p. 83, where a single wave, or pulse, was sent along a stretched rope. This time, instead of giving the end of the rope just one snap, suppose you shake it up and down in regular succession. Two continuous wave trains will now travel along it—the direct set going down the rope and the reflected set coming back. At any instant, the vibration of a given particle of the rope is determined by the resultant of the two wave motions as they pass. At the two ends of the rope, which are held fixed, the motion is of course always zero.

By trial, you can find a rate of shaking the rope that makes all semblance of movement *along* the rope disappear. The rope will vibrate back and forth across its rest position in the shape of a single arch, as illustrated in Fig. 68a. If the frequency with which you shake the rope is exactly doubled, you find that you again get a steady pattern. This time the rope breaks up into two equal loops and its middle point remains fixed even though it

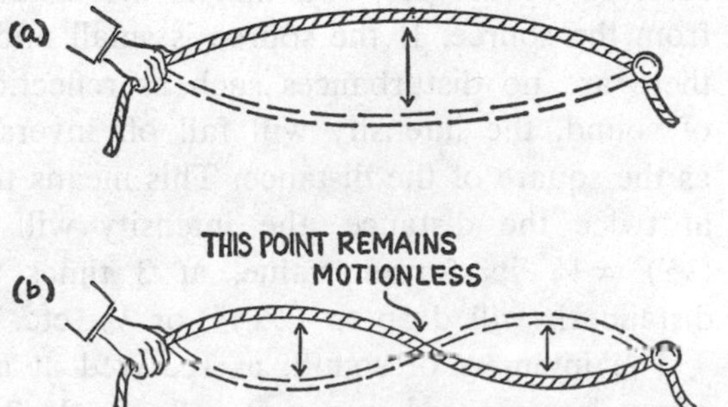

Fig. 68. Stationary wave patterns on a vibrating rope

is not held fast by anything from the outside (Fig. 68b). Similarly for vibration rates 3, 4, 5 . . . or any whole number of times the original rate (see figure). Points where the rope stays motionless at all times are called **nodes;** places half way between the nodes, where the movement is greatest, are called **loops.**

EXPERIMENT 32: Try to produce a few of the stationary wave patterns described in the last paragraph.

Vibration of Strings

There is a good reason for having talked at some length about the rope experiment: The motion of the rope is exactly the same as that of a wire or string in a **stringed musical instrument** such as the violin, harp or piano. If a string is bowed, plucked or struck at its center, it will vibrate with one loop, as in Fig. 69a, giving off the lowest-pitched tone that can be obtained from it. This tone is called the **fundamental.** By temporarily touching the string at its middle and plucking it at either of the quarter points it can be set into vibration in two loops, as in Fig. 69b. It then gives off its **first harmonic,** which has exactly *twice* the frequency of the fundamental. Musicians call this the **octave** above the fundamental. In similar ways the higher harmonics, having frequencies of 3, 4, 5, etc. times the fundamental, may be produced. Usually, when a string is set into vibration in any way, the fundamental and several of the harmonics are

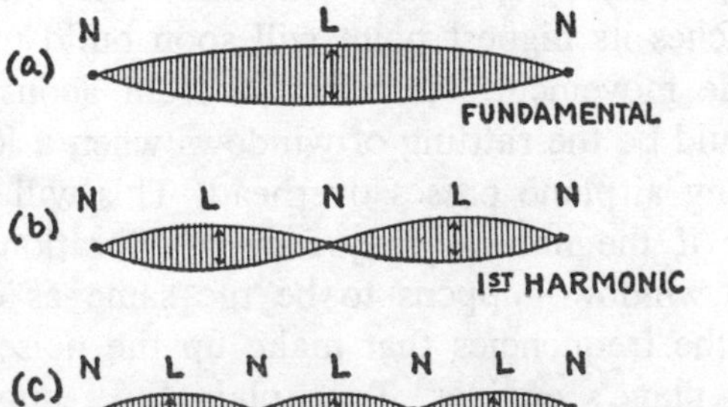

Fig. 69. There are nodes at the places marked *N* and loops at those marked *L*

all present to some extent. An important result of this will be described later (p. 92).

EXPERIMENT 33: Check some of the facts about vibrating strings by making a simple one-stringed guitar. Stretch a rubber band around a long pan, such as an ice-cube tray or baking tin (Fig. 70). Use a stick or pencil as a "bridge." With the bridge absent, pluck the string and note the pitch of its tone. Then insert the bridge at the middle of the string, pluck either half and notice that the tone produced is the octave of the first one. Placing the bridge at the quarter point will give the next octave. Try also to produce, one after another, the familiar *do-mi-sol-do* of the major chord by using the "open" string, then placing the bridge at distances 1/5, 1/3 and 1/2 from the left end, each time plucking the right-hand portion of the string. Another fact you can check is that tightening a string raises its pitch.

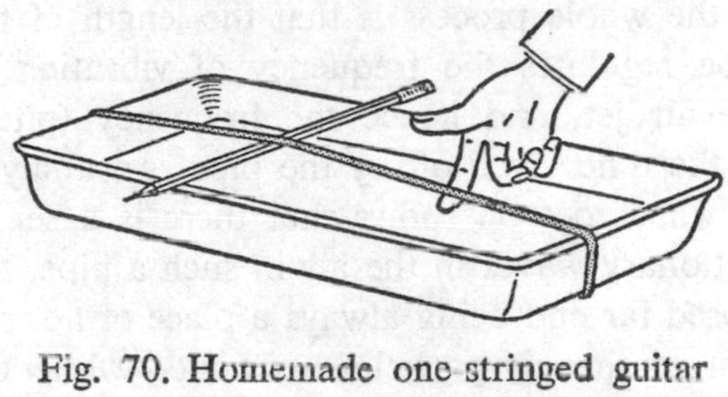

Fig. 70. Homemade one-stringed guitar

Altogether, experience shows that the frequency of a string can be raised by shortening it, by stretching it more tightly, or by making it lighter in weight. When playing stringed instruments like the guitar or violin, the pitch of a string is raised by "stopping" the string with the finger, and so effectively shortening it. In the piano, zither and harp, the various tones are produced by having individual strings, with different lengths, weights or stretching forces for each note.

Waves in a Pipe

Just as stringed musical instruments make use of stationary waves on a string, so **wind instruments** like the flute, trumpet and pipe organ depend on stationary compressional waves in the air inside a pipe. Here, compressions and expansions take the place of humps and hollows of the rope, and the waves are of course longitudinal instead of transverse. If a single compression is allowed to go down the air inside a long tube or pipe, it will be reflected from the far end and will return. Unlike the case of the string, however, there are two possibilities here.

Suppose, first, that there is a fixed wall at the far end of the tube, as in a "closed" organ pipe (Fig. 71a). The jet of air, blowing just inside the sharp lip of the tube, builds up a slight extra pressure there and this region of compression travels down the tube with the speed of sound. When it hits the closed end, it is reflected back. On reaching the open end once more, this compression pushes the air jet out of the tube. The pressure is at once relieved, the jet comes back into the tube again, and everything repeats. The net effect of the whole process is that the length of the tube regulates the frequency of vibration of the air jet, and hence the frequency (pitch) of the tone given off by the pipe. An analysis of what goes on shows that there is a set of stationary waves in the air in such a pipe, the closed far end being always a place of no motion of the air particles—a node—while the open end is a place of greatest motion—a loop.

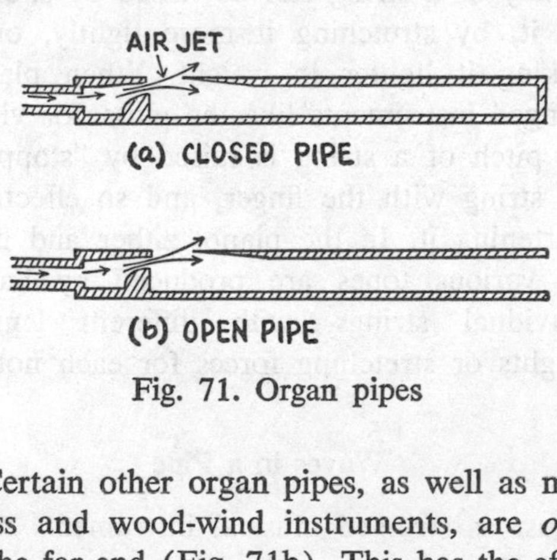

Fig. 71. Organ pipes

Certain other organ pipes, as well as most brass and wood-wind instruments, are *open* at the far end (Fig. 71b). This has the effect of changing the condition for reflection there; both ends of the pipe are now loops, but it is still the length of the pipe that controls the pitch of the tone.

EXPERIMENT 34: The simplest of all wind instruments is a tube or tall bottle which you blow by directing a stream of air across the open end, just inside the far edge. Try bottles of different length and observe that the longer ones give deeper notes.

In some organ pipes, and especially in instruments like the clarinet and saxophone, the air jet is replaced by a flexible reed. In the brass instruments, the lips of the player take the place of the reed. In instruments like the flute, clarinet, etc., the player changes the effective length of the pipe—and therefore the tone produced—by uncovering holes along the side of the tube. When the sound pulse gets to an opening, it is free to communicate with the outside air at that point, so the rest of the tube has no effect. Instruments like the cornet and tuba are made to produce their various notes by shunting in additional lengths of tubing by means of valves, as well as by tightening of the player's lips. In the slide trombone, continuous ("sliding") changes of pitch are possible.

RESONANCE; FORCED VIBRATIONS

A pipe regulates the frequency of vibration of the air jet that drives it, as described above. The process by which such vibrations build up is called **resonance.** A simple mechanical example would be a child's swing. In order to get it to swing high, it should not be pushed at random but in the exact tempo of its natural frequency of motion; in this case a very slight force applied each time the swing reaches its highest point will soon build up a wide movement. An example from acoustics would be the rattling of windows when a low-flying airplane passes overhead. This will occur if the natural frequency of vibration of the window happens to be the same as one of the frequencies that make up the noise of the plane's engines. To explain the response of an organ pipe to an air jet by such a process, we notice that the jet by itself produces only a noisy hissing sound—a mixture of many unrelated frequencies. The pipe, however, picks out one of these—the one it can reinforce by resonance—and rejects the others. The result is a strong set of standing waves in the air inside the pipe, part of the energy being sent out to the surrounding air in the form of sound waves of definite pitch.

A vibrating body may be made to transmit its movement to another body having a large surface, and thus produce a louder sound by setting a greater amount of air into motion.

EXPERIMENT 35: Pinch together the prongs of a dinner fork so that they are set into vibration. The sound is very faint, but if you now press the end of the handle firmly down against the top of a hard table the sound at once becomes remarkably loud.

This experiment illustrates the function of the sounding board of a piano, of the body of a violin or the diaphragm of a loud speaker. As contrasted with resonance, these are all examples of **forced vibrations.** A good sounding board must be able to respond equally well to *all* frequencies that it is intended to amplify. It must have no natural frequencies of its own in that range or the resulting sound will be "tinny."

Drums, bells, the xylophone, marimba, etc. are all examples of **percussion instruments.** The tones are produced by striking bars, plates or stretched skins, causing them to give their motion to the surrounding air. The vibrations of a bell are quite complex, and several higher forms of vibration are almost always present along with the fundamental. These other vibration frequencies, unlike those of strings or pipes, do not harmonize with each other, and produce a discordant, throbbing effect which is especially noticeable near a large church bell.

QUALITY OF SOUNDS

You have seen how a string or an air column can vibrate with its fundamental frequency or with any one of a set of harmonics whose frequencies are exactly 2, 3, 4, etc. times as great. These harmonics are present to some extent in any tone produced by an actual musical instrument. A **pure tone,** consisting of a single simple wave, like those pictured in Fig. 67, is seldom produced. The usual situation is represented more accurately by Fig. 72, curves *a, b* and *c,* showing that the source gives off a fundamental wave of a certain amplitude plus several harmonics, often of progressively smaller amplitude. Notice that the simple wave representing the first harmonic repeats itself twice as often as the fundamental, the next three times as often, etc., corresponding to the 1, 2, 3, etc. frequency ratio.

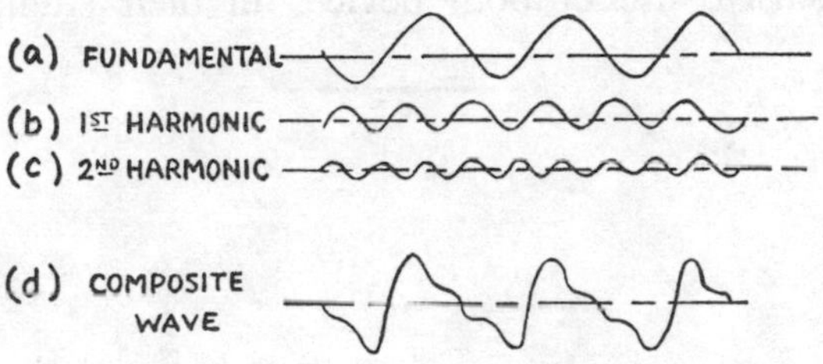

Fig. 72. How partial tones combine to form a composite tone

With harmonics present, the air will have to vibrate in all these various ways at one time. Actually, the separate vibrations will combine to give a single complex disturbance, as represented by curve *d* in the figure. This curve is obtained by adding the heights of the separate curves *a, b* and *c* at each point. It is just as truly a wave as any of the simpler ones, for it represents the regular repetition of a certain form of disturbance of the air. Its wavelength is that of the fundamental.

The resultant wave form of a tone, which depends on the relative strength of the harmonics, is what enables the ear to distinguish the same note played on various instruments. This characteristic of a tone is called **quality.** Typical wave forms of the tones of several instruments are shown by the curves in Fig. 73. There are electrical devices, called harmonic analyzers, which can "take apart" complex wave forms and show how much of each overtone is present. It is also possible to combine several simple wave forms and see the result-

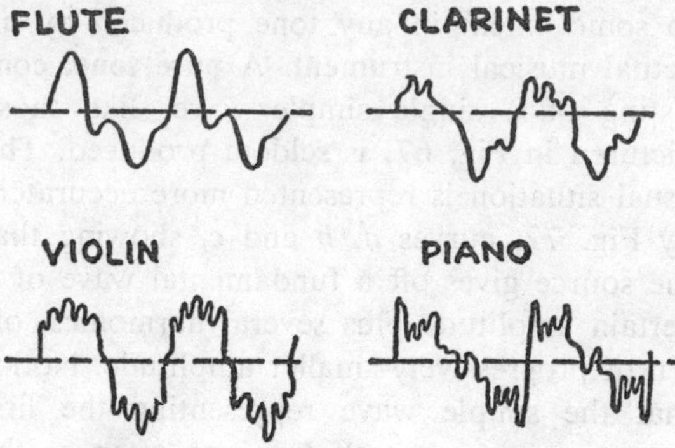

Fig. 73. Wave forms of various sources

ing complex wave on the screen of an oscilloscope tube. Acoustic researchers make extensive use of both devices in their studies.

Practice Exercise No. 25

1. Explain the difference between echo and reverberation.
2. Middle C on the piano has a frequency of 256 vib/sec. What is the frequency of the note one octave below this? One octave above?
3. Why do the bass strings of the piano have heavy, flexible wire wound around them along their entire length?
4. When water is poured into a tall jar, the pitch of the tone produced rises as the jar fills up. Explain.
5. Can you classify the human voice and the piano as wind, string or percussion instruments?

SUMMARY *Instructions:* (see page 17)

1. What is the main factor that determines the pitch of a tone?	
2. Describe the Doppler effect for sound.	The frequency of the sound waves as received by the ear or other detector.
3. How does the amplitude of a set of sound waves affect the intensity of the sound?	An apparent change in the frequency of received waves due to relative motion of source and receiver.
4. How does the intensity of sound from a small source depend on the distance from the observer?	Increased amplitude results in increased intensity.
5. Name the unit most commonly used to specify the intensity of a sound.	Intensity inversely proportional to the square of the distance.
6. What is meant by stationary waves?	The decibel.
7. Give the technical name for the state of vibration of a string or air column that has the lowest possible frequency.	A steady pattern formed by the combination of direct and reflected waves.
8. In strings or pipes, certain definite tones of higher frequency than the fundamental can be produced. What are they called collectively?	The fundamental.
9. Define resonance.	Harmonics.
10. What determines the quality of a tone?	The response of a system to a driving force that oscillates with the natural frequency of vibration of the system.
	The relative strengths (amplitudes) of the harmonics that are present.

SECTION FIVE

LIGHT

Chapter XIII

LIGHT AND LIGHTING

The greater part of what we know about our surroundings is brought to us by light. Light sent out by luminous objects such as lamps or the stars or reflected from a house or a planet is able to affect the eye and produce the sensation of vision. By direct sight and also by the use of optical instruments we get information from light in a great many ways. How this is done will be discussed in subsequent chapters, but in the present one we shall look into some facts about the physical character of light and light sources.

LIGHT TRAVELS IN STRAIGHT LINES

One of the most obvious facts about the behavior of light is that, in any uniform material or in empty space, it travels from one place to another in a *straight line*. You are familiar with the appearance of shafts of sunlight coming through a rift in the clouds, with the practice of sighting along the edge of a board to see if it is straight, with the impossibility of "seeing around corners." Further evidence for the straight-line travel of light is the sharpness of the shadow cast by an obstacle when placed in the light from a small, concentrated source. The boundary of the shadow is determined by straight lines that you can imagine drawn out from the source and passing through the extreme edge of the shadow-casting object. Such lines are called **light rays** (Fig. 74), and they may be drawn outward from the source in any number and in all directions. They are merely convenient guide lines, giving the direction in which the light is advancing at any point. In order for an object to be seen, rays coming from it must enter the eye.

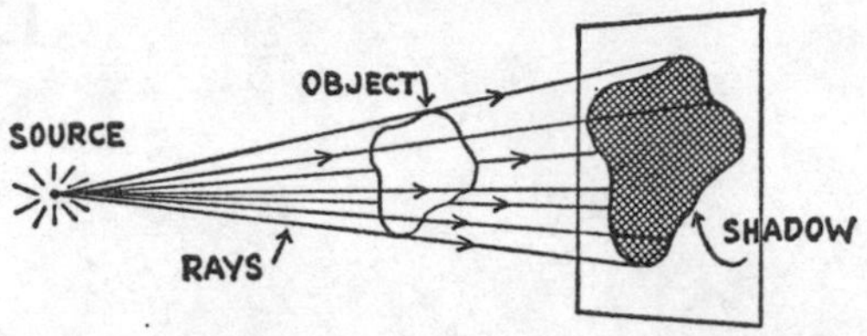

Fig. 74. The rays determine the shadow

If a source of light is large, every point of it must be thought of as a source of spreading rays. The result is that the shadow of an obstacle will now be made up of two parts, a central black one and an outer gray one. An **eclipse** of the sun occurs when the moon comes squarely between the earth and the sun (Fig. 75). Inside the central shadow cone no light is received from any part of the sun, while the cross-lined region gets light from part of the sun but not from all of it. As the earth turns, the shadow pattern sweeps across it. An observer who happens to be in the central region experiences a total eclipse while one in the outer region sees a partial eclipse.

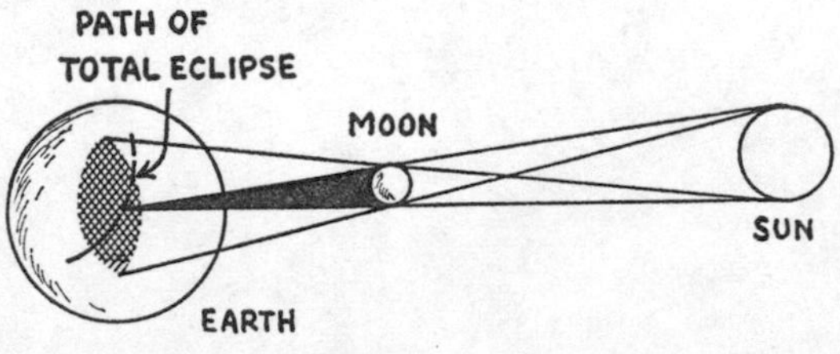

Fig. 75. Eclipse of the sun

EXPERIMENT 36: Make a **pinhole camera,** which utilizes the straight-line travel of light. Cut out one end of a cardboard box and cover this end with a piece of wax paper. Make a clean hole in the center of the opposite end of the box with a darning needle. In a darkened room, a candle flame or light bulb placed a few feet in front of the hole will be represented as a bright, inverted image on the wax paper screen (Fig. 76). Notice that the closer you bring the object to the camera, the larger its image will be. Surprisingly good pictures can be obtained with a pinhole camera by putting a photographic film in place of the screen, but because of the small amount of light that can come in through the pinhole, the exposures are inconveniently long. The remedy, of course, is to use a camera equipped with a lens. The action of lenses will be described later.

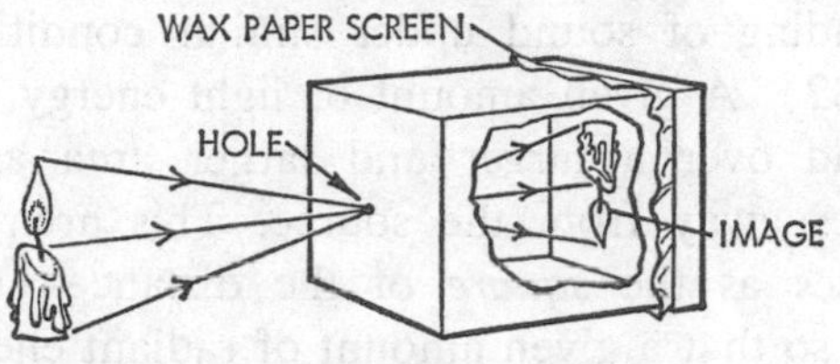

Fig. 76. Pinhole camera

SPEED OF LIGHT

On the basis of almost any reasonable idea as to what light is, we would expect it to take a certain time to go from one place to another, rather than to arrive instantly. However, in the early days of science there were many differences of opinion on this point. The first determination of the speed of light was made by the Danish astronomer Römer in the latter part of the seventeenth century. He observed that one of the moons of the planet Jupiter seemed to come out from behind the planet at later and later times when the earth was moving away from Jupiter, and at correspondingly earlier times when approaching. The total delay was nearly 1,000 sec, and Römer correctly interpreted this as the time taken by light to cross the earth's orbit, a distance now known to be about 186 million miles. Division of one figure by the other gives roughly 186,000 mi/sec as the speed of light. Römer's conclusion was not generally accepted until much later, when it was confirmed by other methods.

Most of the modern ways of measuring the speed of light in the laboratory are based on the accurate timing of a beam of light as it covers a known distance. When you realize that light travels nearly a thousand feet in a millionth of a second, the experimental difficulties involved become apparent, yet the speed is known to within a couple of miles per second. At the present time the best value is

$$c = 186{,}310 \text{ mi/sec} = 299{,}776 \text{ km/sec},$$

c being the standard symbol for the speed of light in a vacuum. The speed in any transparent material is found to be *less* than *c*. In air, the speed is only 0.03 per cent smaller, but in water it is about 25 per cent less and in glass about 35 per cent less than *c*.

LIGHT SOURCES

One of the more practical aspects of the study of light is concerned with illumination. In early times human activities were restricted largely to the hours when the sun was above the horizon. Beginning with crude torches and oil lamps, there has been steady improvement of light sources down to the various forms of electric lighting in general use today.

The most commonly used source of illumination is the **filament lamp,** in which the light is produced by passing a current of electricity through a very fine wolfram (tungsten) wire, or filament, placed inside a glass bulb in which there is either a vacuum or a filling of some inert gas such as nitrogen. This prevents the burning-through of the filament. The function of the current is to raise the temperature of the filament to around 2,500° C where it becomes "white hot."

The **carbon arc** is a very intense source of light and is used in motion-picture projectors, searchlights, etc. Two carbon rods are connected to an electric battery or generator. The tips of the rods are brought into contact and then drawn apart a short distance, producing a flame of burning carbon which continues to carry the current across the gap. Most of the light comes from the glowing tips of the carbons, which reach a temperature of 3,000 to 3,500° C.

Another kind of widely used light source uses the flow of a current of electricity through a gas or vapor at a pressure of a few thousandths of normal atmospheric. This kind of lamp is best known in the form of **tube-type lighting** used for advertising and display purposes. The tubes contain some permanent gas like neon or helium, or a mixture of such a gas and an easily vaporized metal such as sodium or mercury. The apparent color of the light depends on the materials used and on the color of the glass of the tube. Unlike the filament lamp or arc, the light of a gas-filled tube originates not in the intense heating of matter, but in a more direct conversion of electrical energy into light by the atoms of the gas. In fact, the study of the complex things that happen in such tubes has added much to our knowledge of the structure of the atom (Chapter XX).

Fluorescent lamps are now widely used. Here the passage of electricity through a mixture of argon gas and mercury vapor produces ultraviolet light (p. 119), which is invisible, but which causes a suitable chemical coating on the inside of the tube to glow with an intense visible light. The color of this light depends on the mixture of fluorescent materials used.

The efficiencies of most light sources are discouragingly low. Filament lamps, at best, convert into visible light only a few per cent of the electrical energy supplied to them. Some types of fluorescent lighting, however, are several times as efficient.

ILLUMINATION

The strength of a lamp or other source of light is specified by a quantity called its **luminous intensity.** This is measured in **standard candles**—a unit that goes back to the use of the ordinary wax candle as a source of light. In rating lamps at present, the actual comparison is made with standardized filament lamps kept in testing laboratories such as the Bureau of Standards. A filament lamp of moderate size has an intensity of about one candle for each watt rating. For example, the intensity of a 60-watt lamp is very nearly 60 candles.

The practical question facing the lighting engineer is how to determine the strengths and positions of lamps so that an adequate amount of light energy will fall on each unit area of the surfaces to be illuminated. The light from a small, unshaded source may be thought of as spreading out on the surface of a constantly expanding sphere, much like the spreading of sound under similar conditions (p. 82). A given amount of light energy will spread over a larger and larger area as it moves away from the source. This area increases as the *square* of the distance (Fig. 77), so that a given amount of radiant energy will be spread over 4 times the area at 2 times the distance, 9 times the area at 3 times the distance, etc. As a result, the illumination, or the energy falling on each unit area, will vary inversely as the square of the distance from the source. The illumination of any surface that is held perpendicular to the incoming rays will also depend directly on the strength of the source, so that the complete relation is given by

$$E = \frac{C}{d^2},$$

where E represents the illumination due to a small source of intensity C placed at a distance d from the surface in question. If C is measured in candles and d in feet, E is expressed in a unit called a **foot-candle.** The corresponding metric unit is called a meter-

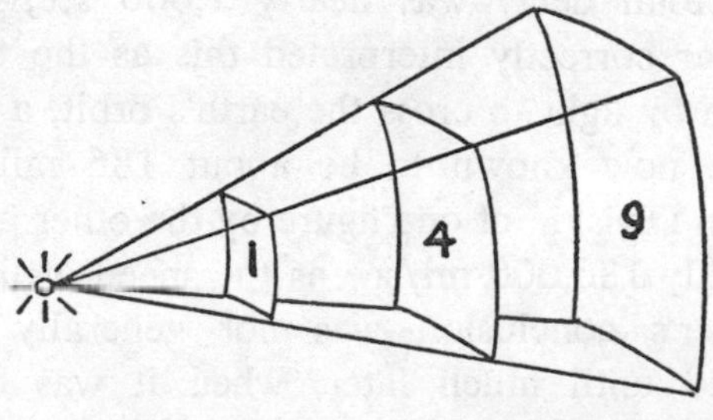

Fig. 77. Light spreads on the surface of a sphere

candle. Measurement shows that a surface receiving 1 ft-c of illumination is getting energy at the rate of about 0.00001 watt/cm². The eye is so sensitive that it can be stimulated by as little as a ten billionth of a foot-candle, equivalent to the illumination produced by a single candle nearly 20 miles away.

EXAMPLE 1: Light from a bare 60-c lamp falls directly on the page of a book 6×8 inches in size. If the illumination is to amount to 15 ft-c, how far from the page must the lamp be placed?

SOLUTIONS Using $E = C/d^2$ we have $d^2 = 60/15 = 4$, and $d = 2$ ft. The size of the page has nothing to do with the result as long as the lamp is small and sufficiently far away so that the rays strike the book practically perpendicular.

The intensity of a lamp is commonly measured by matching the illumination it produces with that from a standard lamp, and there are several devices, called **photometers,** that may be used for this comparison. Other instruments, called **illuminometers,** or foot-candle meters, are used by lighting engineers and architects to measure directly the total illumination of a surface, regardless of the strength, position or number of the contributing light sources. Modern foot-candle meters make use of photocells (p. 165) and are similar to the exposure meters used extensively by photographers.

EXPERIMENT 37: A simple photometer can be made by pressing together two paraffin blocks, such as the ones sold in grocery stores, with a sheet of tinfoil between. Hold the blocks together by using two rubber bands. In a darkened room, set up an unshaded lamp and a lighted candle about 5 ft apart and place the double block somewhere between the two sources, as shown in Fig. 78. Looking at the edges of the blocks, one will appear brighter than the other. Move the pair back and forth until both seem equally bright. When this is the case, the illumination will be the same from the two sides. Measure the distance from each light. You can now set C/d^2 for the lamp equal to C/d^2 for the candle and so compute the strength of the lamp. Note the rating of the lamp in watts and compare with your result, assuming 1 watt per candle.

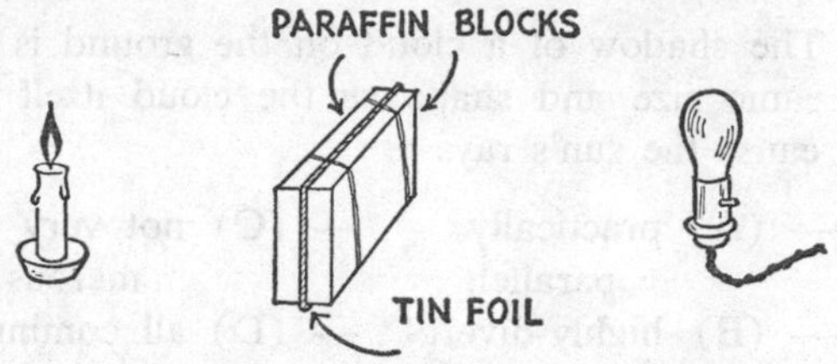

Fig. 78. Paraffin-block photometer

The following table gives standard illumination values which lighting experts recommend for specific uses:

TABLE 12

ILLUMINATION REQUIREMENTS FOR VARIOUS PURPOSES

Use	*Foot-candles*
Comparable with outdoor light. For photography, hospital operating rooms, etc.	1,000
Color matching in manufacturing	500
Extra-fine inspection work	200
Prolonged seeing tasks involving fine detail	100
Lengthy seeing tasks—drafting, sewing, etc.	50
Rough bench- and machine-work; reading or writing for short periods	20
Intermittent visual work; rough manufacturing, stockrooms, etc.	10
Auditoriums, corridors, etc.; general illumination in the home	5

Practice Exercise No. 26

1. Of the following, the only object that would be visible in a perfectly dark room would be

— (A) a mirror. — (C) a red hot wire.
— (B) any light-colored surface. — (D) a disconnected neon tube.

2. The shadow of a cloud on the ground is the same size and shape as the cloud itself because the sun's rays are

— (A) practically parallel. — (C) not very numerous.
— (B) highly diverging. — (D) all coming to a single point.

3. The length of time it takes light to go from the sun to the earth, 93,000,000 miles distant, is about

— (A) 2 min. — (C) 8⅓ min.
— (B) 50 sec. — (D) 173 hr.

4. A man 6 ft tall stands 12 ft from a pinhole camera. When he moves 4 ft closer to the camera, his image will become

— (A) 1.5 times as large as before. — (C) ⅓ as large.
— (B) ⅔ as large. — (D) 1.25 as large.

5. Mercury is about ⅓ as far from the sun as the earth is. Compared with the illumination received on earth, that received by Mercury will be

— (A) ⅓ as much. — (C) 9 times as much.
— (B) 3 times as much. — (D) ⅑ as much.

6. A standard candle and an electric lamp are found to produce equal illumination on a screen when the candle is 1 ft away and the lamp is 5 ft away. The rating of the lamp, in candles, is

— (A) 25. — (C) 0.04.
— (B) 5. — (D) 0.2.

THEORIES OF LIGHT

Ever since ancient times, people have speculated about the true nature of light. The philosopher Plato believed that light was something given off by the eye, and capable of making things visible when struck by it. Others thought light consisted of small particles shot out from luminous objects at high speed. Still others, among them Aristotle, preferred to think of light as something nonmaterial that goes on in the space between the eye and the object seen.

In the seventeenth century, the Dutch scientist Christian Huygens and the English scientist Robert Hooke suggested, independently of each other, that light may be a wave motion. Newton considered both the idea of light as a stream of particles darting out from luminous bodies and as a train of waves, but he definitely favored the particle idea, or **corpuscular theory,** as it was called. His reputation kept this theory active for nearly a century after his time, in spite of the fact that certain observations are almost impossible to explain on the particle basis, but are easily understood in terms of waves.

If we say that light is a wave motion, you immediately ask, "Waves in *what?*," knowing that all the kinds of waves with which we are familiar travel in some material—water, air, strings, etc. When this question first arose, physicists found themselves compelled to invent a carrier for the waves. This had to be something that filled all space, for light comes to us from the sun and stars through space that is virtually empty of all matter. They called this carrier the "ether," but no experimental evidence for its existence has ever been obtained, and the idea is considered unnecessary in modern science. As a result of the work of the British physicist Maxwell about a century ago, we now know that light waves consist of rapidly changing electric and magnetic forces that originate in the movement of electricity in the atoms or molecules from which the light comes. These **electromagnetic waves** will be discussed more fully later (p. 119).

When you look at a steady light, you get no impression of the fact that it may consist of waves, any more than hearing a steady tone gives any impression of wave-like nature of sound. For that matter, if sound or light were carried by streams of particles, the individual ones would fail to reveal themselves as long as they were very small and very numerous. The same thing, we saw, was true for the molecules of matter. So we must face the fact that we cannot hope to "see" individual light waves; our acceptance of the wave theory will have to depend on indirect evidence, as did our proof of the validity of the Kinetic Theory of matter.

As far as the facts about light described in this chapter are concerned, they can be equally well interpreted on either a particle or wave basis. Streams of particles would move off in straight lines, as light is observed to do, and so would waves under ordinary circumstances. The same thing may be said for the weakening of light as it spreads. We shall have to wait until we consider some of the observations about light described in the following chapters before we can find evidence for making a choice between the two rival theories.

Practice Exercise No. 27

1. How would you show that light comes from the luminous body rather than from the eye of the observer?
2. From what was said about Aristotle's idea of the nature of light, why would you say that this was closer to the wave theory than to the corpuscular theory?
3. Name one way in which light waves must differ from sound waves.
4. How would you account for the illumination relation $E = C/d^2$ (p. 100) on the basis of a corpuscular theory of light?

SUMMARY *Instructions:* (see page 17)

1. Under what conditions will light travel in straight lines?	
2. What is meant by a ray of light?	When it moves in a uniform material or in empty space.
3. For any given point on earth, what are the conditions under which a total eclipse of the sun takes place?	A line giving the direction in which light advances at any point.
4. State the approximate figure for the speed of light in empty space.	When the locality in question lies within the black, central shadow cone of the moon.
5. What is meant by the luminous intensity of a lamp?	186,000 mi/sec or 300,000 km/sec.
6. What relation holds between the luminous intensity of a small light source, the illumination it produces on a surface on which its light falls perpendicularly, and the distance from source to surface?	A number specifying the strength of the source. It may be measured in candles.
7. What name is given to any device used for measuring illumination?	$E = C/d^2$.
8. What is a photometer?	Illuminometer, or foot-candle meter.
9. Name the two theories that have been advanced concerning the nature of light.	A device for measuring the luminous intensity of a light source.
10. According to modern ideas, what is the physical nature of light waves?	Wave theory and Corpuscular (particle) theory.
	They are electromagnetic—a combination of electric and magnetic forces.

Chapter XIV

REFLECTION AND REFRACTION OF LIGHT

In the preceding chapter it was pointed out that light travels in straight lines in a uniform material. But when light or any other type of wave motion comes to a non-uniform region or hits a reflecting surface it changes its direction. These changes produce important effects. For one thing, any object that is not self-luminous must be able to reflect light to the eye from its surroundings in order to be seen. Further, the operation of any optical instrument that uses lenses, mirrors or prisms, whether it is a pair of eyeglasses or an astronomical telescope, depends essentially on the production of certain changes in the direction of rays of light. The present chapter will take up questions of this kind.

REFLECTION OF LIGHT

Law of Reflection

The reflection of waves was discussed to some extent in Chapter XI in connection with sound, and in Experiment 30 (p. 86) you actually observed the reflection of water waves. Circular ripples spreading out from the source were reflected from the flat board in the form of circles turned the opposite way.

It is much simpler to discuss the travel of waves of any kind by drawing certain rays rather than by tracing the progress of the waves themselves. Fig. 79 shows how a single ray of light is reflected from a **plane** (flat) **mirror.** It is customary to measure the directions of both the **incident** (incoming) **ray** and the **reflected ray** with respect to the **normal** (perpendicular) to the surface. Experience shows that **the angle of incidence always equals the angle of reflection,** and that **the normal and the two rays all lie in one plane.*** This **Law of Reflection** is a general description of what happens to any ray. By applying it to particular sets of rays, the reflection of light from any kind of surface can be worked out. Notice that a perfectly smooth and elastic ball will rebound from a surface in accordance with the law just stated. This means that the reflection of light is just as readily explained on a corpuscular theory of light as on the wave theory.

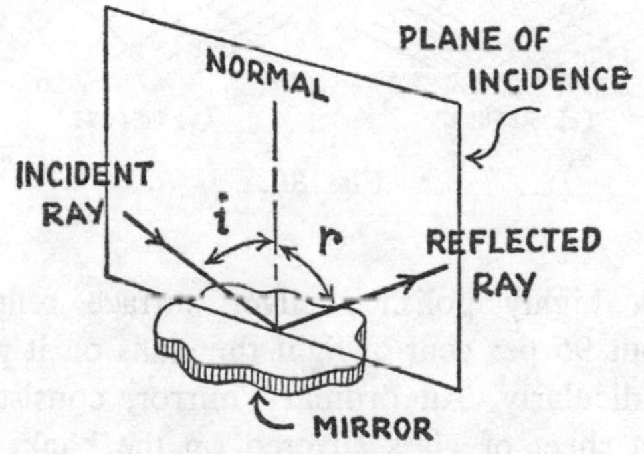

Fig. 79. The angle of incidence equals the angle of reflection

At a considerable distance from a small source of light, a limited portion of the spherical waves will be practically plane. The rays, which are always perpendicular to the waves, will in this case be very nearly parallel (Fig. 80a). Sunlight is an example. If a parallel beam of light hits a plane mirror, the Law of Reflection tells us that the rays will also be parallel after reflection (Fig. 80b). This is called **regular reflection.** By contrast, when such a beam of light strikes a rough or irreg-

* The two rays, of course, lie on *opposite* sides of the normal—that is, the light goes "straight on."

ular surface, **diffuse reflection** takes place (Fig. 80c). At *each point* on the surface the angles of incidence and reflection are equal, but the various portions of the surface have different directions, and so do the reflected rays. As a result, a rough surface will be visible from almost any position, while in order to receive light from a mirror your eye must be in the particular direction in which the incident beam is reflected. We recognize materials from the effect of their surface texture on the light they diffusely reflect. A perfectly smooth, clean mirror would not be visible; what you would see would be the source of light rather than the mirror.

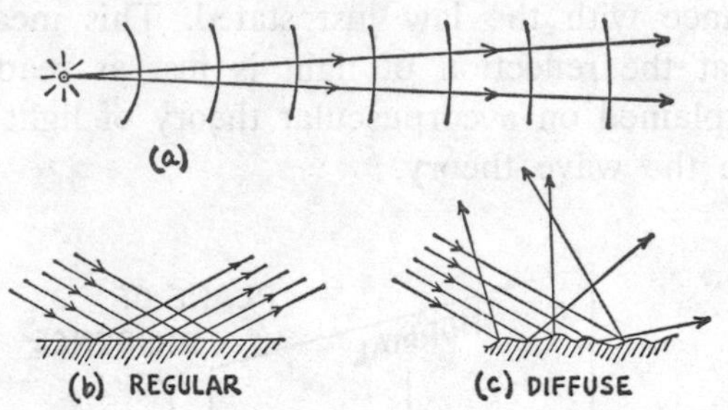

Fig. 80.

A highly polished silver surface reflects about 95 per cent of light that falls on it perpendicularly. An ordinary mirror, consisting of a sheet of glass silvered on the back, reflects about 90 per cent. The surfaces of a transparent substance, such as a sheet of glass, reflects some light even though they may not be silvered. You notice, for instance, that at night the interior of a lighted room in which you are sitting can be seen reflected in the windows. Only about 8 per cent of light falling perpendicularly on a sheet of glass is reflected, half of this from the *rear* surface; but at large angles of incidence ("grazing" incidence) almost all of the incoming light is reflected at the front surface. This explains why the reflection of the sun in a lake is not extremely bright when the sun is overhead but is too dazzling to look at when the sun is low in the sky.

Plane Mirror

We usually say that we look *into* a mirror to see our reflection. Of course, nothing actually goes on behind the reflecting surface, but it can be shown that light originating at any point in front of the mirror will *appear* to come from a point an equal distance directly behind the mirror. This point is called the **image** of the source (Fig. 81a). Because light rays do not actually originate there but only seem to do so, the image is said to be **virtual.** The image of a real object of any size is found by taking one point after another and locating its image. The familiar result is that the complete image is the same size as the object and the positions of object and image are symmetrical with respect to the mirror (Fig. 81b).

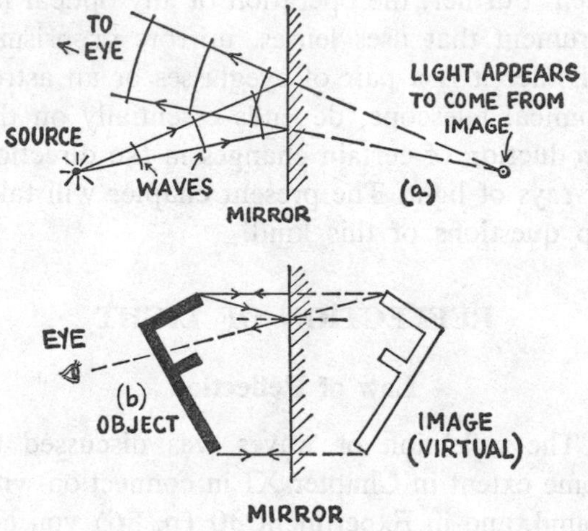

Fig. 81. Images in a mirror

When you look at yourself in a plane mirror you do not see yourself exactly as you appear to others, but with right and left reversed. If you wink your right eye, your image winks its left eye. The object and image are identical in all details, but the parts are arranged in reverse order, like the two gloves of a pair.

How big must a mirror be in order to see all of a given object in it? No matter how small a mirror may be, you will be able to see the entire image, although you may have to move about in order to see all parts of it (Fig. 82).

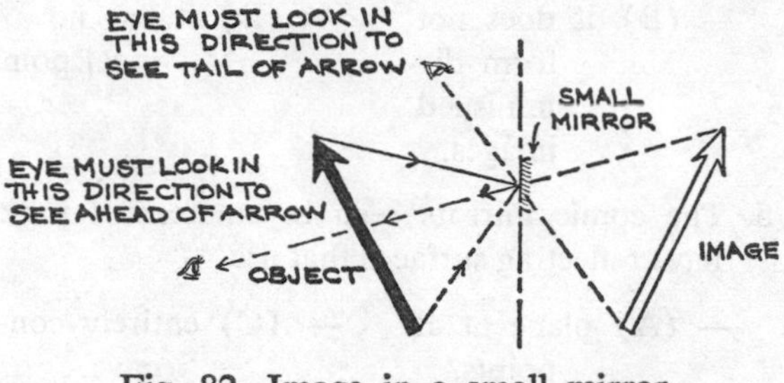

Fig. 82. Image in a small mirror

EXPERIMENT 38: Stand two mirrors up a few inches apart so that they face each other and are parallel. Stand a small object, such as a fountain-pen cap, between them and when you sight over the top edge of one of the mirrors you will see an endless row of images in the other. Any image formed in one mirror acts as the object for another image formed in the other mirror, and this goes on indefinitely. There should be a similar row of images in each of the two mirrors, as you can check by looking in from the opposite side.

Curved Mirrors

A bright steel ball, a round Christmas tree ornament or one type of rear-view mirror are all **convex mirrors.** You can see a virtual image by looking into such a reflector. The image will always be erect (right side up) and smaller in size than the object, and the closer the object is to the mirror, the larger the image will be. These are all results of the fact that parallel rays striking such a mirror *diverge* after being reflected (Fig. 83a). Notice

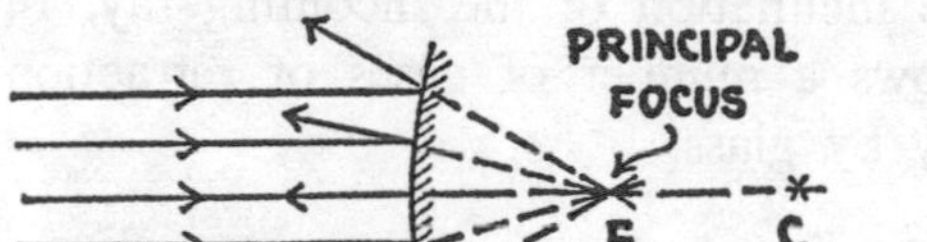

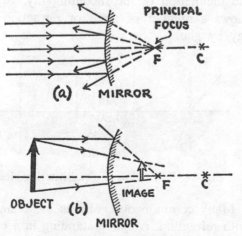

Fig. 83. Convex mirror

that each ray obeys the Law of Reflection, the normal at each point being the radius of the sphere of which the mirror is a part. If the mirror surface is not too large a part of the sphere, all the reflected rays will appear to come from a single point behind the surface, called the **principal focus.** By tracing rays, the image of any object in a convex mirror may be found (Fig. 83b).

A more useful form of curved reflector is the **concave mirror.** An example is the kind of inexpensive hollow-surfaced shaving mirror that can be bought in any drug store. You know from experience that you can see an erect, enlarged virtual image of your face in such a mirror; but under other conditions, this mirror is able to form a real image—one that can be thrown onto a screen, as in the projection of lantern slides or motion pictures.

EXPERIMENT 39: Face a shaving mirror toward the sun. The rays will be collected and brought to a focus at a point two or three feet in *front* of the mirror. Find this focal point by moving a small card back and forth until a tiny bright point, an image of the sun, is seen on it. A match-head held at this point for a few seconds will ignite. The distance from this point to the mirror surface is called the **focal length** of the mirror, and is one-half the radius of the sphere of which the mirror is a part. Now, in a darkened room, form a real image of a candle or lamp by placing it a little farther from the mirror than the focal length. A large, inverted real image will be seen on the opposite wall. Move the light source back and forth until the image is sharp. Note that the image is also reversed left to right.

Like a convex spherical mirror, a concave one will not form a perfect image if the mirror surface is too large a part of its sphere. It is found that this trouble can be avoided by changing the curve of the cross-section of the mirror from a circle to a *parabola,* a curve slightly more "pointed" than a portion of a circle. If a small, concentrated light source is placed at the focus of a concave parabolic mirror, the reflected rays will go forward perfectly parallel, as in a **searchlight.** Reverse the light path and you have a **reflecting telescope** (p. 114) of the type represented by the huge astronomical instrument at the Mt. Palomar Observatory in California. The surface of such a mirror must be ground accurately to within a millionth of an inch.

Practice Exercise No. 28

1. In order to avoid objectionable glare when reading, one should

— (A) use very low illumination.
— (B) avoid anything printed on rough paper.
— (C) have the light coming from over one shoulder.
— (D) use a bare, unshaded lamp.

2. When a man walks directly toward a vertical mirror at a speed of 4 ft/sec he

— (A) approaches his image at the rate of 4 ft/sec.
— (B) recedes from his image at the rate of 4 ft/sec.
— (C) approaches his image at the rate of 8 ft/sec.
— (D) stays a constant distance from his image.

3. In order just to see himself from head to foot when standing before a vertical plane mirror, a man 6 ft tall must have a mirror

— (A) 3 ft high.
— (B) 3×3 ft in size.
— (C) at least 3 ft wide but of any arbitrary height.
— (D) 6 ft high.

4. A convex mirror makes a good rear-view mirror for a car because

— (A) it forms erect, reduced images.
— (B) it does not form diminished images.
— (C) its images can be thrown on a screen.
— (D) it has no focal point.

5. The comic mirrors seen in amusement parks have reflecting surfaces that are

— (A) plane at all points.
— (B) convex and spherical.
— (C) entirely concave.
— (D) irregularly curved.

REFRACTION OF LIGHT

The action of mirrors depends on the fact that light hitting a surface is turned back into the space from which it comes. This always happens to some extent, but if the surface is that of a transparent material, some of the light passes through into the second substance. If the light comes in at an angle with the normal, it will change its direction sharply on going through the boundary. This change of direction of the rays is called **refraction.**

Law of Refraction

If a ray of light goes from a thinner substance, such as air, into a denser substance, such as glass, it will be bent *toward* the normal to the surface of separation; if from a denser to a rarer material, it will bend *away* from the normal. The amount of the deflection will not be constant, but will change with the inclination of the incoming ray. Fig. 84 shows a number of cases of refraction of a ray by glass.

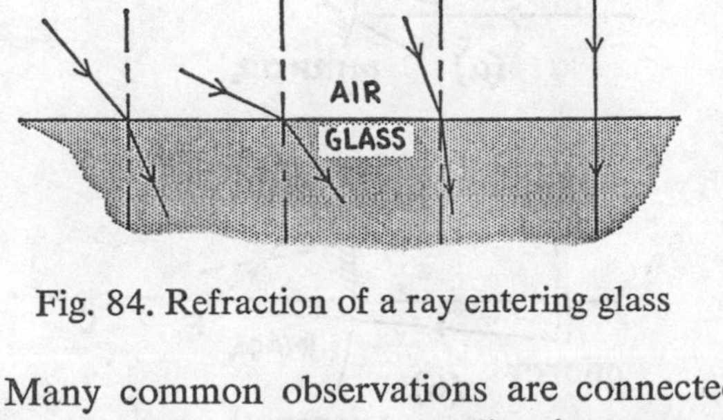

Fig. 84. Refraction of a ray entering glass

Many common observations are connected with refraction. A spoon standing in a cup of water seems to be broken where it passes through the surface (Fig. 85a). This is because any underwater object is seen by light reflected by it and coming up through the surface. Rays coming from any point are refracted as in Fig. 85b, and so appear to come from another point which lies closer to the surface. The result is that the immersed part of the object seems to be swung upward as noted.

Light that passes completely through a parallel-sided piece of glass is refracted, the rays being bent equal but opposite amounts at each surface—toward the normal in one case and away in the other. As a result, the beam that comes through is parallel to the original one, but is displaced to one side (Fig. 85c).

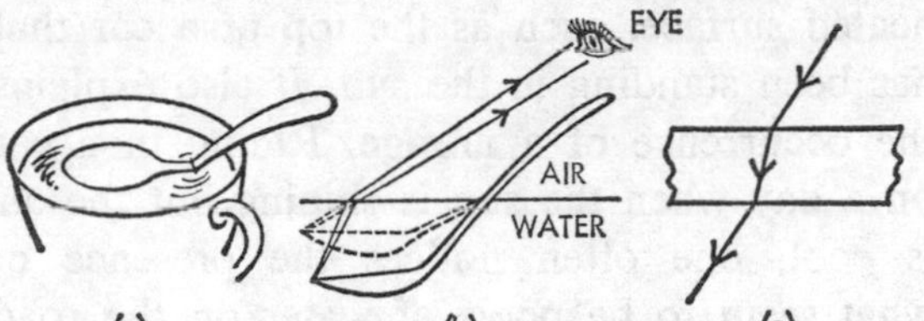

Fig. 85. Refraction effects

EXPERIMENT 40: Look at a pencil through a thick piece of glass held at an angle to your line of sight. The part of the pencil seen behind the glass appears to be moved to one side.

Wave Theory of Refraction

The observed direction of a refracted ray can be accounted for by the wave theory of light. Think of a parallel beam of light coming through air and striking a flat glass surface, as in Fig. 86. *AB* is a plane wave front that is just about to enter the glass at the point *A*, while *CD* is a wave front that has just gotten completely in. During the time that the light waves travel a distance d_a in the air, they evidently travel a distance d_g in the glass, so we can say that

$$\frac{V_a}{V_g} = \frac{d_a}{d_g}$$

where V_g is the speed of light in glass; V_a is the speed in air, which we can take to be practically the same as *c*, the vacuum speed, the difference being unimportant for most purposes.

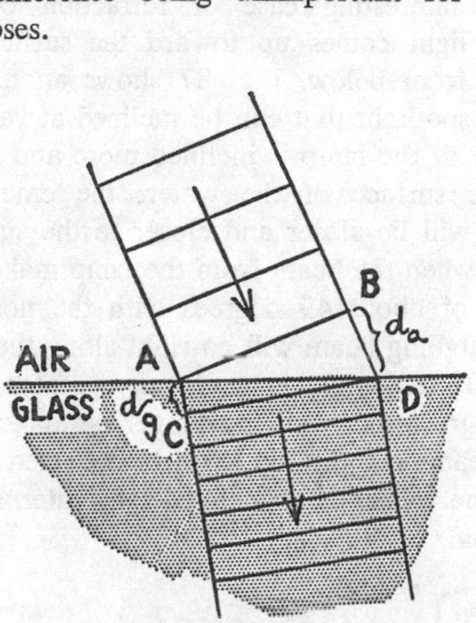

Fig. 86. Refraction of plane waves

The ratio of the speed of light in a vacuum to the speed in a given material is called the **index of refraction** of the material. This quantity, represented by the symbol *n*, determines the extent of the bending of the rays. Thus the Law of Refraction may be considered to give the change in direction of a ray in terms of the value of *n* and the construction of Fig. 86. It states also that the incident ray, the normal to the surface, and the refracted ray all lie in one plane.

TABLE 13

INDEX OF REFRACTION OF VARIOUS SUBSTANCES

Substance	*Index n* $(=c/V)$
Air	1.0003
Ice	1.31
Water	1.33
Gasoline	1.38
Olive oil	1.47
Glass, ordinary	1.5
Glass, dense optical	1.6–1.9
Diamond	2.42

TOTAL REFLECTION; MIRAGES

An interesting case of refraction occurs when light comes up toward the surface of water from below. Fig. 87 shows an underwater spotlight that can be inclined at various angles. If the lamp is inclined more and more to the surface of the water, the emerging beam will lie closer and closer to the surface until, when the beam from the lamp makes an angle of about 49 degrees with the normal, the outgoing beam will go right along the surface. If the angle is made any greater than 49 degrees there will no longer be an emerging beam—all the light will be reflected back into the water. This is called **total internal reflection.**

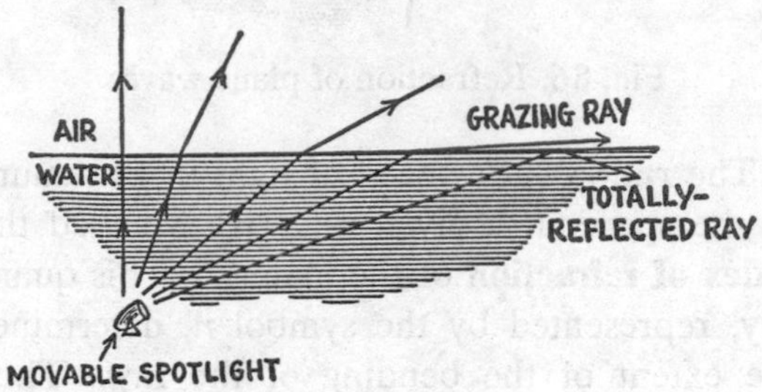

Fig. 87.

Light can be "piped" along a rod of transparent plastic material by total reflection, and dentists and doctors use this method to get concentrated light without objectionable heat.

Fig. 88. "Piped" light

Total-reflection prisms are used in high grade binoculars. The slant surface acts as a perfect mirror because the angle of incidence is 45 degrees here and this is greater than the critical angle for glass—about 42 degrees; it is physically impossible for any light to get out (Fig. 89).

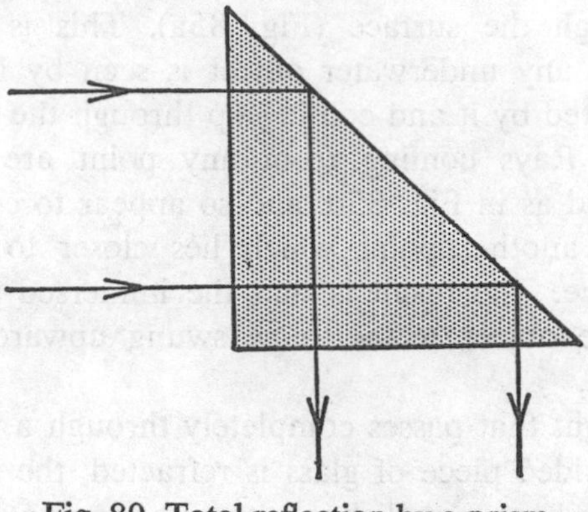

Fig. 89. Total reflection by a prism

Light passing through air that is not all at the same temperature is refracted. This accounts for the twinkling of the stars and the wavering appearance of objects seen over a heated surface, such as the top of a car that has been standing in the sun. It also explains the occurrence of a **mirage.** Riding in a car on a day when the sun is shining but the air is cool, one often notices the presence of what seem to be pools of water on the road some distance ahead. The "water" always disappears before you get to it; what you see is merely light from the sky that is refracted to your eye by warm air near the ground. The effect is exactly what was represented for sound waves by Fig. 60, p. 83.

LENSES

Refraction finds its most useful application in **lenses,** which are an essential part of many optical devices such as microscopes, projectors, eyeglasses, telescopes, cameras, range finders, etc. The purpose of a lens is to change the curvature of light waves—that is, to bend the rays—usually in order to form an image. Lenses are ordinarily made of optical glass, sometimes of plastic. In practice, the two surfaces are ground to spherical form. The commonest lens shapes are shown in Fig. 90. Those which are thicker at the center than at the edges are called **converging lenses,** those thicker at the edges are **diverging lenses.** The reason for these designations will be explained.

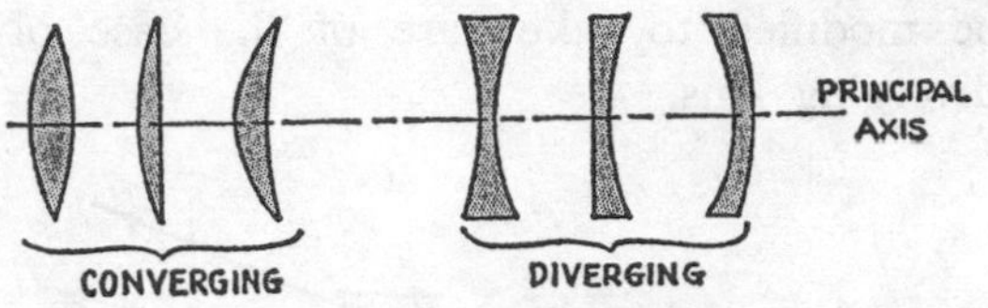

Fig. 90. Lens shapes

The ability of a lens to bring light to a focus is measured by what is called its **focal length.** Consider a beam of parallel light (plane waves) coming in along the axis of a converging lens, as shown in Fig. 91. Because the speed of light in glass is less than in air, the part of a wave that passes through the thick middle portion of the lens will be held back more than the outer parts. After getting clear through the lens, the waves (which were originally plane) will now be parts of spheres that close down to a point F, the **principal focus** of the lens. If there is nothing to stop them, the waves again expand as they go on to the right. The distance of the principal focus from the lens is called the **focal length** of the lens. Its magnitude depends on the curvature of the two surfaces and on the index of refraction of the material of which the lens is made. The whole situation is reversible: If a point source of light is placed at the principal focus of a converging lens, the waves will be "straightened out" and made plane by passing through it.

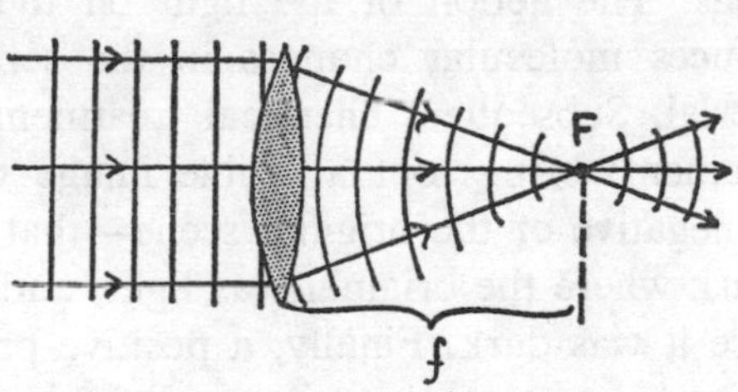

Fig. 91. Converging lens

Image Formation

Now that we know what a converging lens does to light coming from a great distance (plane waves), let us see what happens when a source of light is placed nearer to the lens, but at some point P beyond the principal focus (Fig. 92a). The lens is still able to reverse the curvature of the waves, and they close down to a point Q that lies beyond the focal distance on the right side of the lens. However, if the object is placed anywhere *within* the principal focus, the lens can no longer change the direction of curvature of the waves and there is only a virtual focus at some point on the *near* side of the lens. This is the case when a lens is used as a **simple magnifier.**

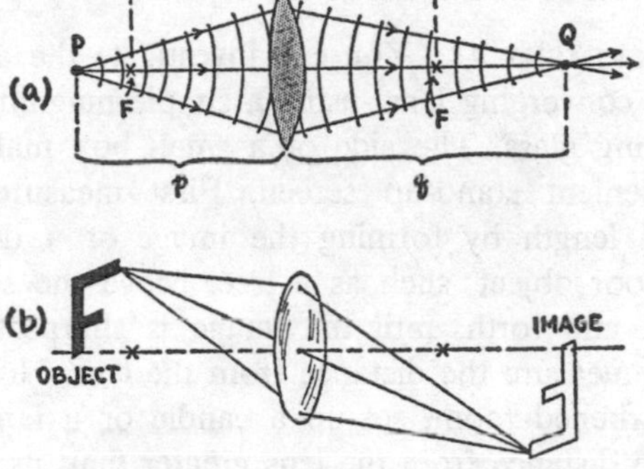

Fig. 92. Real image formed by a converging lens

If the point source at P in Fig. 92a is replaced by an extended light-giving object, a complete image of this object will be formed at Q. Rays from each point of the object are brought to a corresponding focal point of the image. The image is real; rays actually cross to form it, and it can be caught on a screen. It is also inverted, and if the object extends in a direction perpendicular to the page, it will be reversed from side to side as well (Fig. 92b).

How can we find the location and size of a real image? The relation giving the distance is found to be

$$\frac{1}{p}+\frac{1}{q}=\frac{1}{f}$$

where p is the object distance, q the image distance and f the focal length of the lens. The size of the image is given by

$$\frac{h_i}{h_o}=\frac{q}{p}$$

where h_i is the height of the image and h_o is the height of the object.

EXAMPLE 1: A lamp is 30 in. from a converging lens whose focal length is 10 in. Where will the image be found? If the lamp is 2 in. tall, what will be the height of the image?

SOLUTION: Using the lens formula,

$$\frac{1}{30}+\frac{1}{q}=\frac{1}{10}, \text{ or } \frac{1}{q}=\frac{1}{10}-\frac{1}{30}=\frac{1}{15}.$$

Inverting both sides, $q=15$ in. The second formula above gives $h_i=2\times 15/30=1$ in. Thus the image will be located 15 in. beyond the lens and will be half as tall as the object.

EXPERIMENT 41: You can investigate the action of a converging lens, using a simple magnifier or reading glass. The side of a small box makes a convenient stand-up screen. First measure the focal length by forming the image of a distant outdoor object, such as a tree. Move the screen back and forth until the image is sharpest and then measure the distance from the lens. Now, in a darkened room, set up a candle or a lamp at some distance from the lens greater than its focal length and locate the image by trial. Measure p and q and check the lens equation. Note also the relative sizes of object and image and compare with the ratio of their distances from the lens.

Diverging Lenses

Diverging lenses do not form real images under any circumstances, and are used mainly in combination with converging lenses. If you replace the lens used in the above experiment by a diverging lens (obtained, for example, by unscrewing the eye lens of an opera glass), you will get no image on the screen at any distance, but only a circle of uniform light. When parallel light strikes a diverging lens, the refracted rays spread apart from each other, all of them *seeming* to come from a point on the near side of the lens (Fig. 93). This is a **virtual focus.** The distance of this point from the lens is called the focal length, just as for a converging lens. Diverging lenses always form virtual, erect images that are smaller than the object. The lens formula can be modified to take care of the case of a diverging lens.

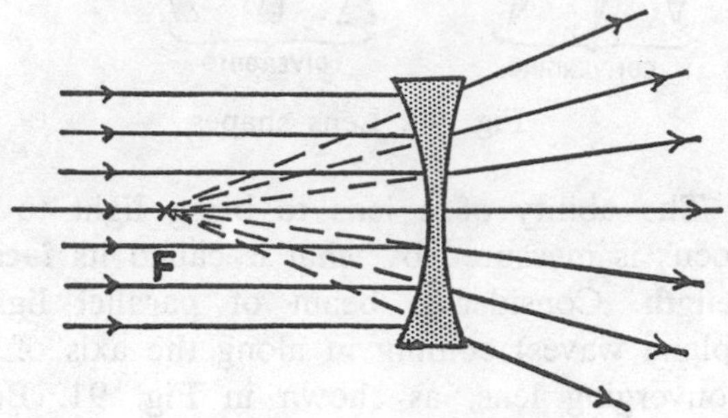

Fig. 93. Diverging lens

SOME OPTICAL INSTRUMENTS

Camera and Eye

In principle, the set-up of Experiment 41 constituted a **camera.** Essentially, it lacked only an enclosure for keeping out unwanted light and a film for making a permanent record of the image. In any but the simplest photographic cameras, the single lens is replaced by a combination of lenses for improving the sharpness and other characteristics of the image. Also, a diaphragm is provided for varying the size of the lens opening and so regulating the brightness of the image when pictures are taken under various lighting conditions. The action of the light on the film produces molecular changes in the sensitive material. Subsequent chemical treatment (development) brings out a visible image which is a negative of the original scene—that is, it is dark where the original was light, and light where it was dark. Finally, a positive print is obtained by passing uniform light through the negative onto sensitized paper, which is chemically developed to give the finished picture.

The **human eye** is optically very similar to a camera—a motion picture or TV camera, as a matter of fact, because the image is continually changing. An enclosure, the eyeball itself, contains a lens-shaped organ whose focal length can be shortened by muscles capable of squeezing it into a thicker shape. A watery fluid in front of the lens and a jelly behind it contribute to the refraction, producing an image on the **retina,** or sensitive rear surface (Fig. 94a). Although the image on the retina is inverted, we have learned to interpret it right side up. The retina contains millions of delicate nerve endings whose sensation is carried to the brain. The **iris** is a variable-sized diaphragm controlling the amount of light entering the eye.

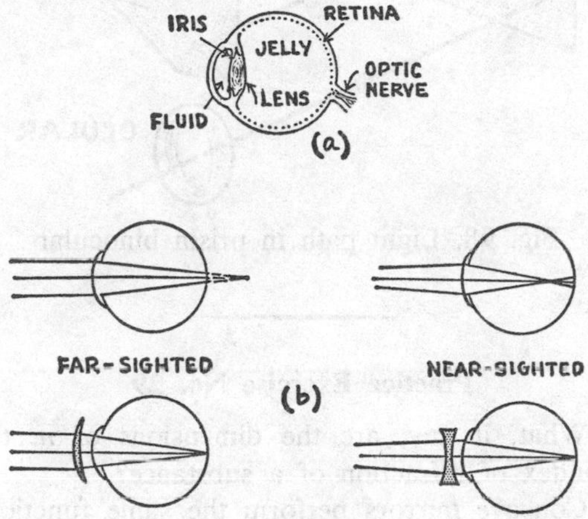

Fig. 94. The eye

Eyeglasses are probably used in greater numbers than any other optical instrument. In a normal eye, the muscles are able to compress the lens enough to make possible the distinct seeing of objects as close as about 10 inches away. A **near-sighted** eye is one that is too long, front to back, for the formation of sharp images of such nearby objects. The rays cross in front of the retina instead of on it. The remedy is to place in front of the eye a diverging lens of the proper focal length, as shown in Fig. 94b. In a **far-sighted** eye, the rays strike the retina before they have had the chance to cross, and a suitable converging eyeglass lens is used to correct this difficulty. In an eye having the defect of **astigmatism,** the front surface of the eyeball is not curved equally in all directions like a sphere, and this produces indistinct images. Prescribing a **cylindrical lens**—one that is curved in one direction only—remedies this condition. If there is both astigmatism and near- or far-sightedness, the two kinds of lens needed for correction are combined in a single piece of glass.

We have two eyes in order to locate and better perceive objects in space. Each eye sees things a little differently, for the separation of the eyes permits you to look around the sides of an object, in a certain sense, and so recognize that the object has depth. A **stereoscope** is an instrument that allows each eye to see separately two pictures of an object taken from slightly different positions, making the scene stand out in space.

Microscopes and Telescopes

A **compound microscope** is a combination of two converging lens systems—an **objective** of very short focal length and an **ocular** of moderately short focal length. Fig. 95 shows the arrangement, each system being represented for simplicity as a single lens. The thing to be examined is brought up close to the objective, which forms a real image of it inside the tube. This image is not caught on a screen but merely exists in space. The ocular, used a simple magnifier, then produces an enlarged, reversed virtual image out in front of the instrument, the eye converts this into a real image out in front of the instrument, and finally the eye converts this into a real image on the retina. By special methods used by metallurgists and medical researchers, magnifications of as much as 2,500 are attained. The **electron microscope** (p. 165), operating on a different principle, can attain magnifications ten or more times as great.

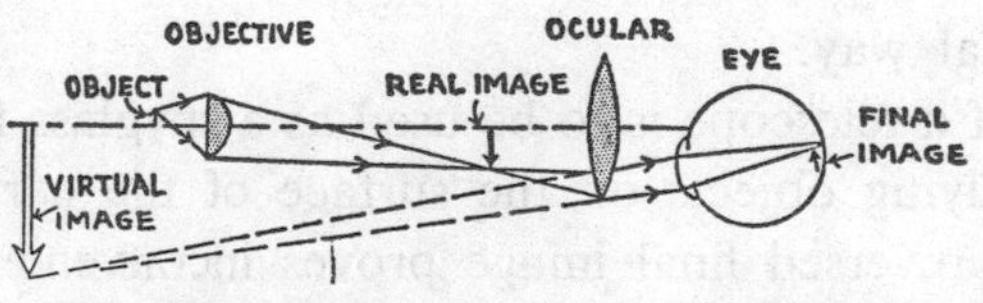

Fig. 95. The compound microscope

A **refracting telescope,** like a microscope, consists of an objective which forms a real image and an ocular for magnifying it, but here the objective has a very long focal length

(Fig. 96). Because of the optical unsteadiness of the atmosphere, magnifications of more than about 1,500 to 2,000 are seldom used in astronomy. Even more important to astronomers than magnification is the **light-gathering power** of a telescope, which determines how faint a star can be and yet be seen. This depends on the area of the objective, and is one reason for making telescopes of large diameter.

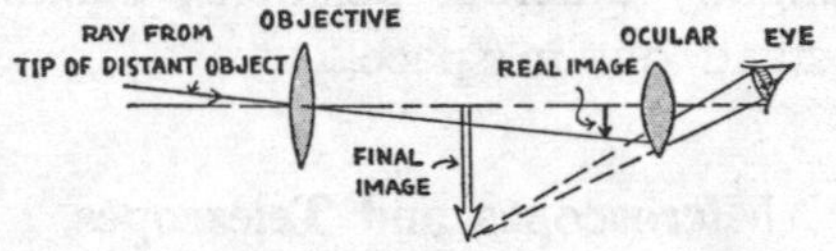

Fig. 96. The refracting telescope

The largest refracting telescope in existence has an objective 40 inches in diameter. The making of larger lens systems than this is impractical, and all the very large astronomical instruments now constructed, including the 200-inch Mt. Palomar telescope, are **reflecting telescopes,** in which a parabolic mirror replaces the objective system. One arrangement is diagrammed in Fig. 97. As in Experiment

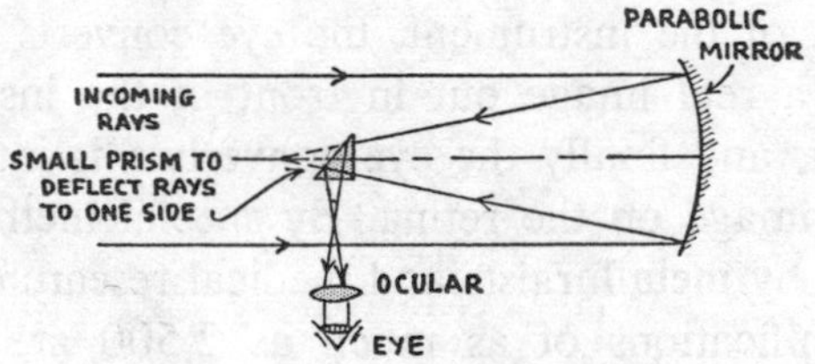

Fig. 97. The reflecting telescope

39 (p. 107), the mirror forms the first image. This is then examined by an ocular in the usual way.

If a telescope is to be used as a spyglass for studying objects on the surface of the earth, the reversed final image proves inconvenient. In this case, an additional lens can be placed in the tube to put the image the right way around again. In the **prism binocular,** this reversal is accomplished more effectively by reflecting the rays back and forth between two right-angled prisms. Another advantage of this arrangement is that it shortens the total length of the instrument. It also gives better depth perception by effectively increasing the distance apart of the observer's eyes.

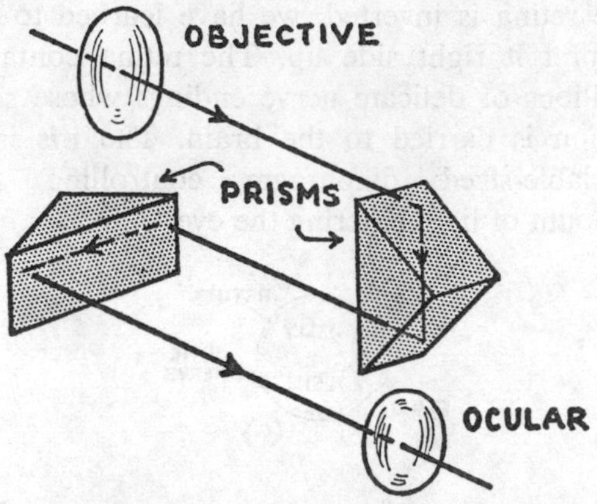

Fig. 98. Light path in prism binocular

Practice Exercise No. 29

1. What, if any, are the dimensions of *n,* the index of refraction of a substance?
2. Concave mirrors perform the same functions as converging lenses, convex mirrors the same ones as diverging lenses. Explain.
3. What are bifocal eyeglasses?
4. A camera has an objective of focal length 10.0 in. Use the lens formula to find how far from this camera must a person stand in order to be in sharp focus when the objective is racked out to a distance of 10.5 in. from the film.
5. The head of a common pin is 1/14 in. across. If all of it could be seen at one time in a microscope under a magnification of 2,500, how big across would it appear to be?
6. The objective mirror of the Mt. Palomar telescope has a diameter of 200 in., while the pupil of the eye has a diameter of 0.2 in. Since the amount of light that each receives is proportional to the area of its circle, prove that this telescope has about a million times the light-gathering power of the eye.
7. What is meant by an f/4.5 camera objective? How does the brightness of the images it forms compare with those produced under the same conditions by an f/9 objective? Consult a book on photography.

SUMMARY *Instructions:* (see page 17)

1. State the Law of Reflection of light.	
2. What causes diffuse reflection of light from a surface?	The angle of incidence is equal to the angle of reflection; and the incident and reflected rays, together with the normal to the mirror, lie in one plane.
3. Why is the image of an object in a plane mirror said to be virtual?	Roughness or irregularity of the surface, causing parallel incident rays to be reflected in many different directions.
4. In comparison with the object, how would you describe its image as formed in a plane mirror? Discuss comparative size, position, orientation, etc.	Because rays of light, after striking the mirror, merely *seem* to come from such an image.
5. Which kind of curved mirror forms only virtual images?	Image same size as object and same distance from mirror, but reversed in one direction.
6. What name is given to the change in direction of a ray of light as it goes through a non-uniform material, or as it passes from one material into another?	Convex.
7. Define the index of refraction of a substance.	Refraction.
8. What is meant by the focal length of a converging lens?	The ratio of the speed of light in a vacuum to its speed in the material in question.
9. State the lens formula.	Plane waves, entering a converging lens, will close down to the principal focus on the far side of the lens. The distance of this point from the lens is the focal length.
10. What is the principal difference in construction between reflecting and refracting astronomical telescopes?	$1/p + 1/q = 1/f$, where p is the object distance, q the image distance and f the focal length of the lens.
	In the reflecting instrument, a concave mirror replaces the objective lens (converging) of the refracting telescope.

Chapter XV

WAVE OPTICS AND COLOR

Color adds tremendously to the interest and attractiveness of the world about us. Its influence ranges from the fine arts to the advertising and packaging of goods, and psychologists find that the colors in our surroundings have significant emotional effects. In this chapter the physical basis for producing and combining colors will be described. Certain other important aspects of the wave character of light will also be explained.

THE SPECTRUM

The ancients were aware of the brilliant hues produced when sunlight passes through transparent gems and crystals. Newton, while still a university student, became concerned with the undesirable fringes of color that surrounded the images in refracting telescopes, and he performed a simple experiment that revealed the true character of color. Holding a triangular glass prism in the path of a narrow beam of sunlight, he found that the rays were fanned out into a band of color after passing through (Fig. 99). The sequence was the same as the one seen in the rainbow, with red at one end merging gradually into orange, then yellow, green, blue and violet.* Newton suspected that these shades are all present to begin with in the colorless beam of sunlight —what we call **white light;** but in passing through the prism, the various colors are refracted by very slightly different amounts. Once spread out this way, the eye is able to recognize each color for what it is. The spreading process is called **dispersion,** and the

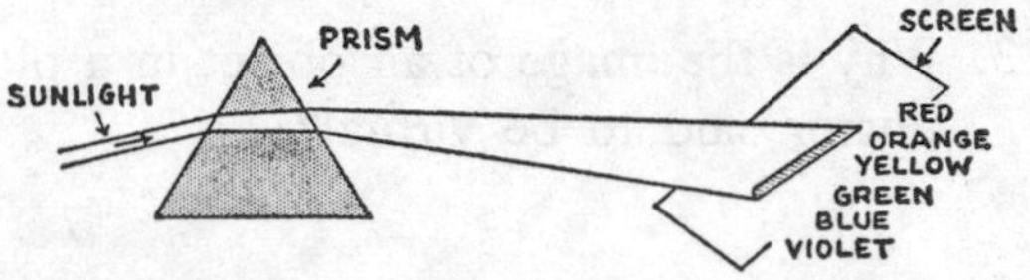

Fig. 99. Breaking down white light

color sequence that results is called a **spectrum.**

Careful experimenter that he was, Newton tested his supposition about the nature of white light by placing a second prism behind the first, but in a reversed position, and found that the rays were re-united into a colorless path of white light (Fig. 100a). As a further experiment, he cast a spectrum on a card, cut a small hole in the card at one point, and placed another prism behind the opening (Fig. 100b). His purpose was to see if the color coming through the hole could be further broken up by the second prism. This did not happen: Green light, for instance, coming through the opening was bent aside by the second prism, but the transmitted light had the same green hue as before.

What Newton established, then, is that **white light consists of a mixture of colors.** The

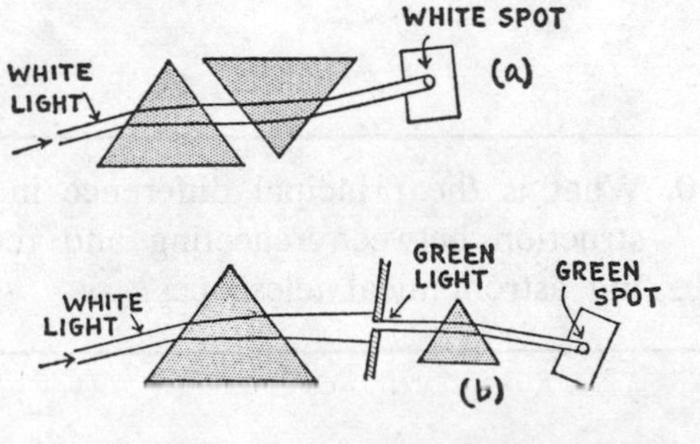

Fig. 100. Newton's further experiments on dispersion

* Sometimes an additional range of color, **indigo,** is designated between blue and violet.

various colors are refracted by slightly different amounts in glass, which means that the index of refraction (p. 109) is really slightly different for each color. It follows, on the wave theory, that what we perceive as **color is really wavelength,** and that the waves representing various colors travel with different speeds in matter. The difference is not very big—in ordinary glass red light travels only about 1 per cent faster than violet. In a vacuum, all colors travel with the same speed. At the extreme red end of the spectrum the wavelength is about 1/30,000 of an inch (0.00007 cm), decreasing gradually through the sequence of colors to about 1/60,000 of an inch (0.00004 cm) at the extreme violet.

EXPERIMENT 42: Repeat some of Newton's tests. In the absence of a regular optical prism (a small one can be bought very cheaply from dealers in salvage materials), use a crystal glass pendant, or make a water prism by holding a rectangular glass dish, partly filled with water, in an inclined position. Let sunlight hit the prism and catch the spectrum on a white card. See that the card is shielded from the direct sunlight. The experiment can also be done indoors by placing a bare lamp behind a narrow slit in a card, putting a rather long-focus converging lens at a distance away just greater than its focal length, and placing a white card at the proper distance to catch a sharp image of the slit. Now put the prism, edge up, just beyond the lens, and the white slit image will give way to a colored spectrum which lies below it on the screen. Recombine the colors into a white spot of light by using another lens or a concave mirror to bring them together.

Since different wavelengths are refracted by slightly different amounts, there is some separation of colors whenever light passes through any transparent material. A lens acts to some extent like a prism, causing the color effects that Newton noticed in refracting telescopes. He avoided this difficulty by inventing the reflecting telescope. Later, it was found possible to accomplish the same result by using combinations of lenses made of different kinds of glass.

The **rainbow,** one of the most commonly observed examples of dispersion, is formed when sunlight passes through myriad droplets of water suspended in the air after a shower. The rays are refracted on entering a drop, reflected from the back surface and refracted again on coming out (Fig. 101). But while going through, the light is also dispersed, so that the several colors come through at slightly different angles. The total effect produced by all the drops is the observed rainbow.

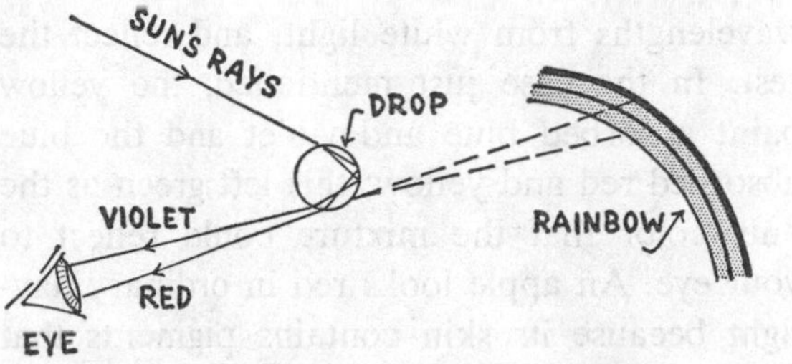

Fig. 101. Optics of the rainbow

Color Mixing

When we say that the spectrum is made up of the colors red, orange, yellow, green, blue, and violet, we must remember that these divisions are made merely for convenience. The whole spectrum really consists of an endless number of colors (wavelengths). Experts can distinguish thousands of shades. The eye also recognizes colors that are not found in the spectrum, but which are effects produced by mixing various spectrum colors. Purple, for instance, is a mixture of blue and red; pink is a mixture of red and white; browns are produced by mixing red and yellow. It has been found by experience that virtually any recognizable color can be produced by mixing different proportions of the three colors red, green and blue-violet. These may be called the **primary colors.** For example, if three such spots of light are thrown on a screen as shown in the figure, the place where all three overlap will appear white. Other regions, where only two overlap, give the colors shown.

Mixing Pigments

In the previous paragraph you found out what happens when various *colors*, or wavelengths, of light are mixed in the eye. This is not to be confused with what occurs when different *paints* or *pigments* are mixed. For example, Fig. 102 shows that when yellow and blue-violet *light* are mixed the result is white. However, when yellow and blue-violet *paints* are mixed, the outcome is green paint. Paints or pigments **absorb** or subtract out certain wavelengths from white light, and reflect the rest. In the case just mentioned, the yellow paint absorbed blue and violet and the blue absorbed red and yellow; this left green as the only color that the mixture could reflect to your eye. An apple looks red in ordinary daylight because its skin contains pigments that can absorb the other colors. The same apple seen in red light appears pale and whitish because it reflects nearly all the light falling on it. In green light, however, it looks black, because it is not able to reflect much of the incoming light (black is merely the absence of light). We see from all this that the apparent color of an object depends very much on the quality of the light by which it is seen. This fact must be kept in mind in any practical operation that involves the matching of colors, for example in the textile industry.

The chemical processes that go on in plants require red light. As long as the plant is alive, the red part of sunlight is absorbed by a substance called chlorophyl, and so the remaining wavelengths—largely green—are reflected, giving the plant its characteristic color.

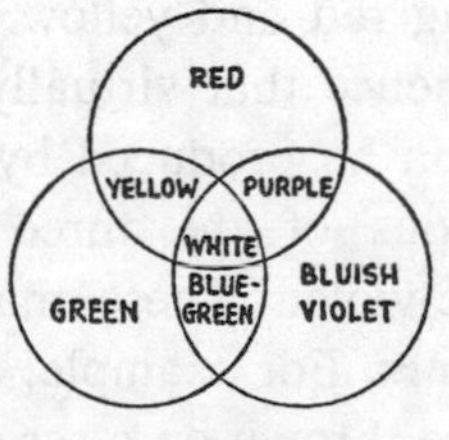

Fig. 102. Mixing colors

EXPERIMENT 43: Make some markings with red and with green ink or water colors on a white sheet of paper and examine them, first under red and then under green light. (A sheet of colored cellophane held in front of either the lamp or the eye can be used.) Explain what you observe.

In **color printing processes,** pictures of the object are taken through three colored filters, each corresponding to one of the primary colors. A printing block is made from each, and they are linked with the proper colors and printed one over the other on white paper. In **color photography,** the film has three different layers of sensitive material, one capable of registering blue light, another green, the third red. In development, the film goes through a complex process in which each layer is dyed the proper color, so that when light is passed through the film in the projector the pictures are thrown on the screen in natural color.

Practice Exercise No. 30

1. From Fig. 101 it is evident that the color of the outer edge of the rainbow will be

— (A) purple. — (C) violet.
— (B) red. — (D) yellow.

2. The effect produced in the eye by a mixture of purple and yellow light will be

— (A) white. — (C) blue-violet.
— (B) blue-green. — (D) green.

3. A tailor, wishing to match thread for a blue overcoat, should do so

— (A) under a yellow light. — (C) near a window.
— (B) under a blue light. — (D) in semi-darkness.

4. A certain piece of paper looks red under red light but appears black under blue light. When seen in daylight, it may appear

— (A) colorless. — (C) white.
— (B) blue. — (D) red.

5. When seen through a piece of red glass, the leaves of a plant

— (A) appear almost black. — (C) are seen in their natural color.

— (B) become nearly invisible. — (D) take on a bluish hue.

THE SPECTROSCOPE

The simple arrangement used by Newton for producing spectra can be improved in several ways: In place of a round hole for admitting the light, a narrow slit perhaps less than a hundredth of an inch wide is used. This greatly reduces overlapping of colors in the final spectrum. Lenses are placed before and after the prism to improve the definition, and the spectrum is magnified by an ocular (Fig. 103). The complete instrument is called a **spectroscope.** If a permanent record is wanted, the ocular is omitted and a photographic film is put in the focal plane of the second lens. In this case the instrument is called a **spectrograph.**

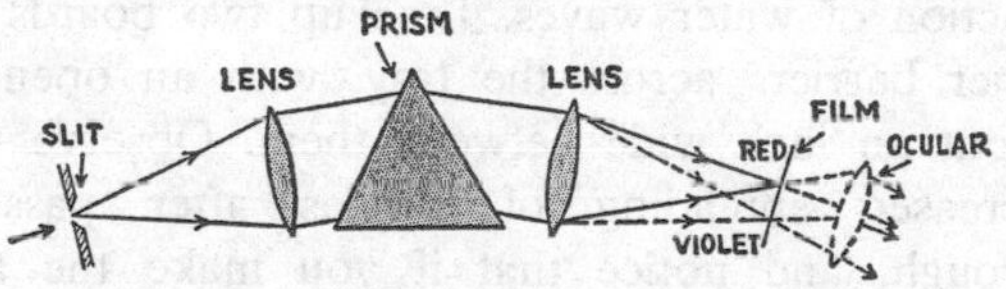

Fig. 103. Principle of the spectroscope or spectrograph

What is seen when the radiations from various substances are examined and analyzed by a spectroscope? Sunlight, the light from a filament lamp, a pot of molten iron or a candle flame all give the rainbow-like band of color already described. This is called a **continuous spectrum;** all wavelengths are present and there are no gaps from extreme red to extreme violet.

The situation is different when gases or vapors are made to give off light. Then what is seen in the spectroscope is a number of sharp, **bright lines** against a dark background. Each line is an image of the slit in a given wavelength of light, and so we conclude that a gas can give out only a definite set of wavelengths. The pattern of lines is different for each chemical element present in the light source, and so once the patterns are known, the elements present in any source can be identified (Fig. 104). This process enables us to find out what elements even the sun and stars contain. In recent years it has also been found possible to find the approximate amount of each substance by measuring the brightness of the lines. These techniques of **spectrochemical analysis** are taking the place of regular chemical methods in many industries, in medicine, in crime detection, etc.

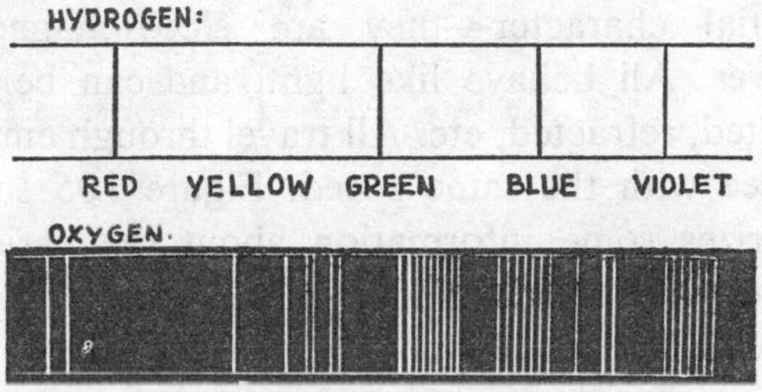

Fig. 104. Examples of line spectra

ELECTROMAGNETIC WAVES

It happens that the human eye is limited in the ability to see only light whose wavelength lies between about 1/30,000 and 1/60,000 of an inch, but there are other waves of a similar nature—some shorter, some longer—that differ from visible light only in the ways by which they can be produced and detected. The waves that fall beyond the violet end of the visible spectrum make up the **ultraviolet** region; the ones beyond the red end are called the **infra-red.** Each is present to some extent in sunlight, but the shorter ultraviolet waves are much stronger in the light of a mercury vapor lamp (sunlamp), for instance, and infra-red is given off generously by a hot stove or heating coil.

X rays are still shorter than the ultraviolet, about one thousandth the wavelength of visible light. A special high-voltage vacuum tube is needed to produce them in quantity, and their outstanding characteristic is the ability to penetrate considerable thicknesses of most materials. Besides their use in medicine, they serve to reveal flaws in metal parts, alterations of paintings and documents, etc. Even shorter and more penetrating than X rays are the **gamma rays** given off in atomic processes. Their uses are similar to those of X rays.

On the long-wave side of the infra-red are radiations that are produced by electric circuits in which alternating currents flow (p. 153). These **electric waves** include the ones used in radio and television. All these types, from the shortest gamma rays to the longest electric waves, are of the same essential character—they are **electromagnetic waves.** All behave like light, and can be reflected, refracted, etc. All travel through empty space with the same speed. Figure 105 summarizes some information about the various kinds of electromagnetic waves, and is worth careful inspection.

DIFFRACTION

In Chapter XIII it was pointed out that light travels in straight lines while passing through any uniform region. Of course, if light strikes a mirror or if the density of the material through which it passes is not the same at all points, it will change its direction; these possibilities were considered in Chapter XIV in connection with reflection and refraction. But even in uniform space, light and other forms of wave motion are found to bend somewhat if they graze the edge of a barrier or go through very small openings. In fact, Huygens (p. 102) first got the idea that light consists of waves when he noticed that sea waves spread out sidewise when coming through the opening in a breakwater. Certainly we are all familiar with the fact that sound waves bend around corners very considerably—you do not have to be in line with an open window to hear sounds from outdoors. This bending of waves when they pass near the edge of an obstacle or through small openings is called **diffraction.** The fact that it can be observed for light, under proper conditions, is strong evidence in favor of the wave theory.

EXPERIMENT 44: Use a tray of water, as in the set-up for Experiment 30, p. 86, to produce diffraction of water waves. Line up two boards or other barriers across the tray, with an opening about an inch wide between them. Observe the increased spreading of ripples after passing through, and notice that if you make the apperture smaller, the bending becomes more pronounced.

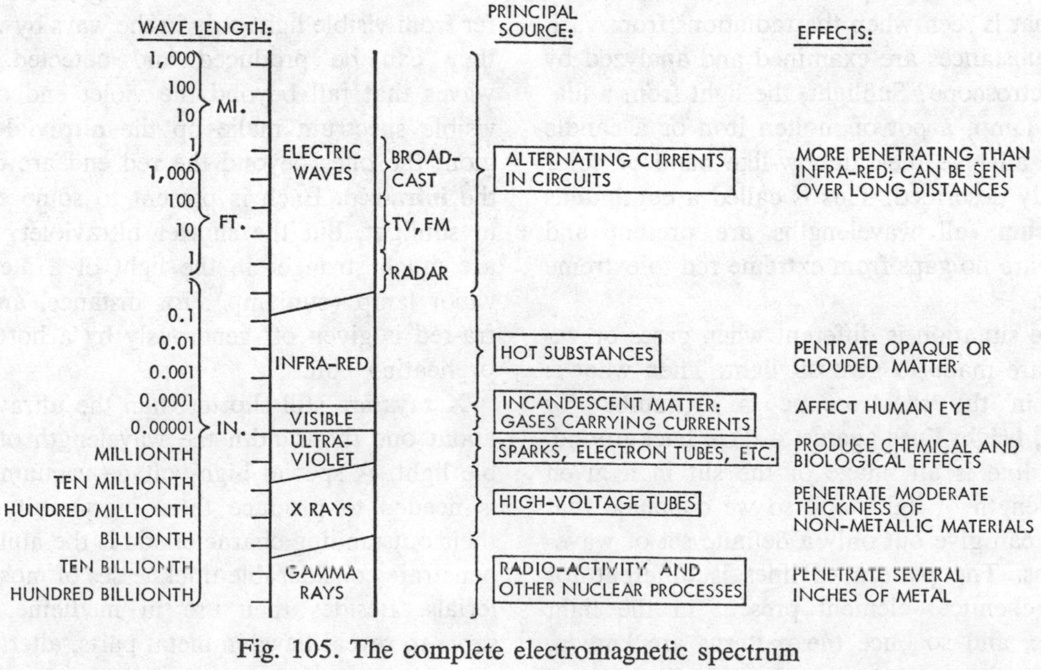

Fig. 105. The complete electromagnetic spectrum

The iridescent rainbow play of color that you see when white light is reflected almost edgewise from a phonograph record is due to the fact that the various wavelengths of light are diffracted by different amounts when reflected by the regularly spaced ridges with which the surface is covered. In fact, a surface covered by fine, evenly spaced channels or ridges can be used as a substitute for the prism in a spectroscope. Such **diffraction gratings** are made by special machines that rule extremely fine scratches on metal or glass plates by means of a diamond point. A good grating of this kind may have 15,000 or more rulings to the inch, and is capable of giving much greater dispersion than any prism. As fine as such optical gratings are, they are too coarse for producing diffraction of the very much shorter X rays. But crystals of certain minerals can serve as natural gratings for this purpose. The regular spacing of the atoms in a crystal is just of the right order of size for diffracting X rays and thus can serve to measure their wavelengths. Then, using X rays of known wavelength, the exact arrangement of the atoms in other crystals can often be worked out.

EXPERIMENT 45: Look at a distant lamp through a handkerchief or through the fabric of an umbrella. In place of a single spot of light you will see a square arrangement of fainter, smeared-out colored images due to diffraction of light by the two sets of threads of the cloth—really two diffraction gratings at right angles to each other.

INTERFERENCE

The beautiful display of colors seen on a soap bubble or on a spot of oil on a wet pavement is not due to pigments or to diffraction but to the **interference of light.** It depends on the fact that two sets of waves arriving at the same place will add up their effects if they get there *in step,* but will cancel each other if they get there *out of step.* The English scientist Thomas Young discovered the interference principle around 1800 and saw that it furnishes us with further confirmation of the idea that light is a wave motion.

In all examples of interference, light from a single source is, in effect, reflected from two surfaces that are very close together, as in the examples mentioned in the preceding paragraph. When you look at a soap film, part of the light that comes to you has been reflected from the front surface, part from the back. If the two reflected rays of a given wavelength come back exactly out of step with each other, they cancel and no light of this color reaches your eye from this point of the film (Fig. 106). Of course, whether this happens depends on both the wavelength of the light and on the thickness of the film at that place. Since white light consists of many different wavelengths and since a soap film is not of uniform thickness, the result is that you see a variety of colors, each one being white light *minus* the particular wavelength that is cut out by interference. For example, where green is destroyed, the film will have a reddish hue.

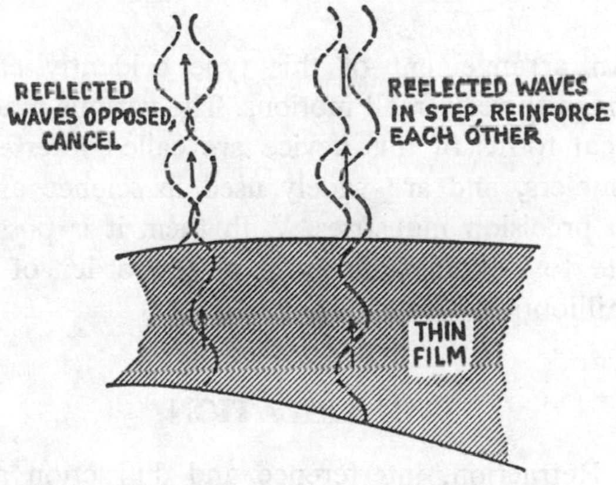

Fig. 106. Coloration of a soap film

A useful application of interference is to **non-reflecting coatings** for glass. The surface is covered with a chemical film of just the right thickness to kill off most of the light that would ordinarily be reflected and cause glare. When applied to a camera objective this improves the quality and brightness of the image by cutting out reflections from the various lens surfaces.

EXPERIMENT 46: Get two rectangular strips of clear glass several inches long and place one on top of the other. Fasten their ends together with rubber bands and separate the plates slightly at one end by inserting a strip of paper. Now take a piece of blotting paper that was previously soaked in strong salt water and dried, and hold it in a gas flame in a darkened room. This produces a yellow light of a single color, which gives better contrast than white light. Look at the reflection of the flame in the pair of plates and you will see that they are crossed by evenly-spaced dark stripes as a result of interference of light reflected from the front and back of the "wedge of air" between the plates. Squeeze the pair more tightly together at one end and the stripes will move some distance along the plates.

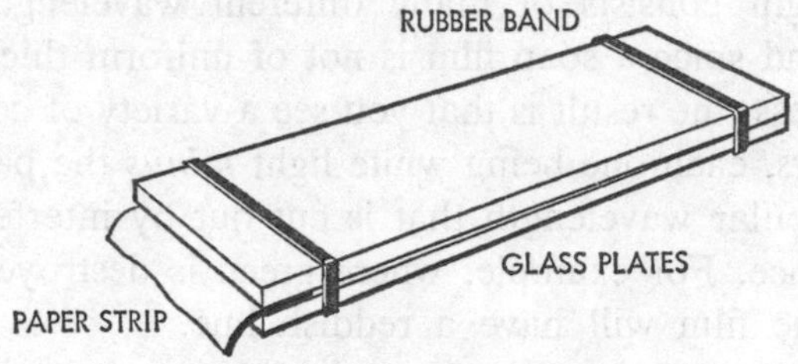

Fig. 107. Homemade interferometer

An arrangement of this type evidently can magnify very small motions. The various practical forms of this device are called **interferometers,** and are widely used in science and in precision industries. With them it is possible to measure distances of the order of a millionth of an inch.

POLARIZATION

Refraction, interference and diffraction all serve to establish the wave theory of light. But what *kind* of waves are light waves—longitudinal, like sound, transverse, like waves in a rope, or a mixture of the two, like sea waves? The answer is that **light waves are transverse.** The proof comes from a study of what is called the **polarization** of light.

Consider what happens when a beam of ordinary light passes through certain crystals. The arrangement of the atoms in such a crystal is known to give it a sort of ribbed structure, equivalent to a large number of parallel slots. If two such crystals are placed one behind the other, light will get through both when their "slots" are parallel, but will be completely cut off if the slots are crossed (Fig. 108). The only assumption that will explain this observation is that the vibrations of ordinary light are in all possible directions in a plane perpendicular to the ray. A single crystal will then hold back all the vibrations except the one that is lined up with its own grain. A beam of light whose vibrations are thus confined to one direction is said to be **plane-polarized.** This polarized beam gets through the second crystal when the two sets of slots are parallel, but will be gradually cut off as the second crystal is rotated to the perpendicular position. A manufactured polarizing sheet material, called Polaroid, has now replaced natural crystals for most of these uses.

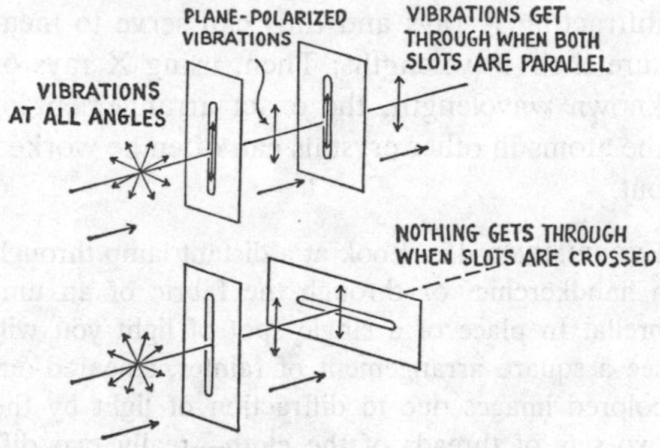

Fig. 108. Polarization of light

Polarized light can be used to find just how the stresses are distributed in machine parts. A model of the part is made out of plastic and subjected to the kind of stress the original would get in actual use. When viewed by polarized light, colored bands appear which reveal the exact stress pattern in the piece.

Practice Exercise No. 31

1. For light traveling in a vacuum, the wave equation (p. 85) can be written $c =$ frequency $\times$ wavelength. What is the frequency of vibra-

tion of orange light of wavelength 0.00006 cm?

2. Describe the kind of spectrum you would expect to get from (a) moonlight; (b) a luminous tube containing neon gas; (c) a candle flame whose light is due mainly to glowing solid particles of carbon.
3. The Doppler effect (p. 88) is observed for light. Light waves from a star approaching the earth are shortened. Would the lines of its spectrum be displaced toward the red end of the spectrum or toward the violet?
4. When you look at the moon through a window screen you see a cross of light through the moon's image. Explain.
5. An inventor once suggested distilling soap solution in order to get out the colored dyes seen on soap bubbles. Is this a sound scientific idea?
6. Explain why sound waves cannot be polarized.

SUMMARY *Instructions:* (see page 17)

1. What main conclusion is drawn from Newton's principal experiment with sunlight and a prism?	
2. What is meant by dispersion?	That white light (sunlight) consists of all the colors of the spectrum (rainbow).
3. The sensation of color is associated with what physical characteristic of light?	The spreading-out of the colors to form a spectrum.
4. Distinguish between the mixing of colored lights and the mixing of pigments (paints).	Wave length.
5. What is a spectroscope?	Superimposed light beams add up to give a new color; e.g., red added to green gives yellow. Mixed paints give colors by subtracting (absorbing) certain wavelengths of the light that strikes them.
6. Describe the appearance of the spectrum of a glowing gas.	An instrument for examining spectra.
7. Name the regions of electromagnetic waves that are shorter than visible light.	A pattern of bright, crosswise lines seen against a dark background. Each line is the image of the slit of the spectroscope in a particular wavelength of light.
8. Name the regions that are longer than the visible.	Ultraviolet, X rays, gamma rays.
9. What is meant by diffraction?	Infra-red and electric waves.
10. Define interference of light and describe the conditions under which it occurs.	The bending-aside of waves when they pass the edge of an obstacle or go through small openings.
11. What fact about light waves is demonstrated by the phenomenon of polarization?	The net effect of superimposing two sets of light waves. Depending on how they arrive at a given place, they may cancel or reinforce each other. In practice, both sets of waves must come originally from a single source.
	That light waves are transverse.

SECTION SIX

MAGNETISM AND ELECTRICITY

Chapter XVI

MAGNETS AND ELECTRIC CHARGES

MAGNETISM

More than twenty-five centuries ago, the ancient Greeks found that pieces of a certain kind of rock called magnetite were able to attract iron. The Chinese discovered that a splinter of this rock, if hung by a thread, would always set itself in the north-south direction, and they used such an arrangement as a compass for guiding their ships. The reason for the interesting behavior of these natural **magnets** remained a mystery for many centuries, and it is only within the last few decades that magnetism has become so widely applied to many electrical devices that we find indispensable in modern life. The relationship between magnets and electricity will be brought out in a later chapter.

Magnet Poles

An ordinary steel bar can be made magnetic by stroking it always in one direction with either end of a piece of magnetite. Thereafter it will behave exactly like the piece of magnetite. Besides iron and steel, only a very few other materials can be noticeably magnetized —the chemical elements nickel and cobalt, and certain special alloys.

If a magnetized bar is dipped into a heap of iron filings or chips, heavy tufts cling to the bar near each end (Fig. 109). The effects of the attraction seem to be located at two places, one near each end, called the **poles** of the magnet. When the bar is suspended as a compass needle, the pole that turns toward the north is called a **north** (or simply N) **pole,** and the other is called a **south** (or S) **pole.**

While experience shows that an ordinary piece of iron is always attracted by either pole of a magnet, two magnet poles will be found either to attract or repel each other, depending on their kind. By bringing one end of a magnet near the ends of a suspended magnet or compass needle, as in Fig. 110, we find the simple rule that **like poles repel each other and unlike poles attract.** By using different magnets at various distances apart, it is further found that the **force** of attraction or repulsion **between poles** is directly **proportional to the strengths of the poles and inversely proportional to the square of the distance** between them. Any action of one magnet on another can then be described as the net effect of the forces between the pairs of poles.

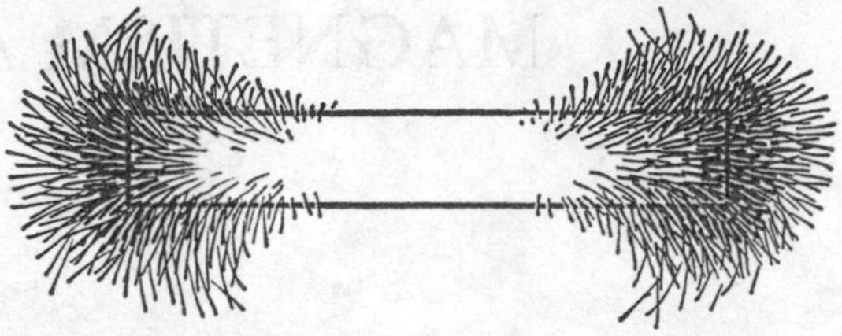

Fig. 109. Bits of iron cling to the magnet near its poles

If a bar magnet is cut in two, it is found that a new pole now exists near each cut end, opposite in kind to the pole at the other end of the piece. No matter how many times the cutting process is carried out, this is found to happen; it is impossible to have a piece of steel with only one pole on it. This suggests that when the limit is reached in such a cutting-up process, each piece would still be equivalent to a bar magnet having two poles. In fact, if we make the assumption that magnetic ma-

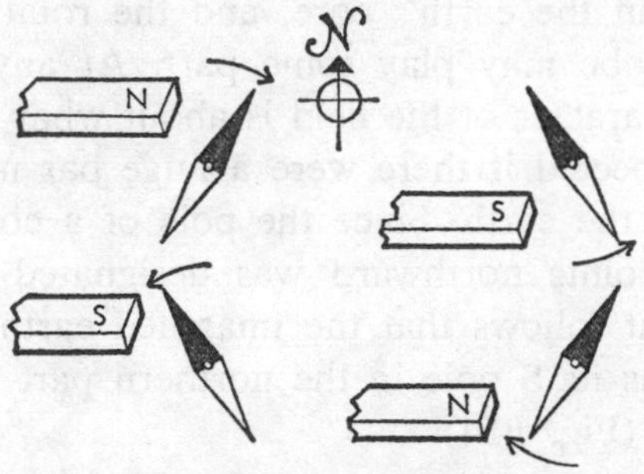

Fig. 110. Like poles repel; unlike poles attract

terials are composed of tiny individual magnetic units, many observations can be explained. In an unmagnetized piece of iron, for example, these units can be thought of as arranged in random directions. When the bar is magnetized—say, by stroking with a magnet—these small units become lined up, all in the same general direction. The poles of the whole bar represent merely the outside effect of all the individual magnetic units acting together. These tiny units may consist of individual atoms or molecules, or of groups of atoms lined up to form small crystals called magnetic **domains.**

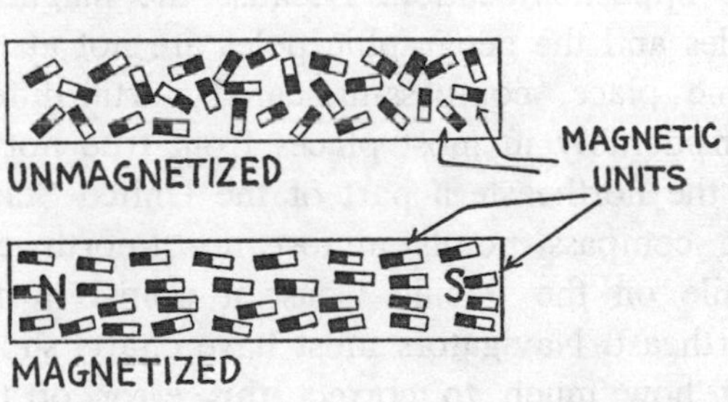

Fig. 111. The bar becomes a magnet when the individual magnetic units are lined up

If a magnet is heated red hot and allowed to cool again it will no longer be magnetic —the jostling of the molecules will have knocked the magnetic units out of their former alignment.

The theory also explains what is called **induced magnetism.** A steel magnet will pick up several tacks or small nails, chain fashion. If the uppermost nail is carefully held in a clamp and the magnet then removed, the whole chain goes to pieces (Fig. 112). Each nail attracted the ones next to it only as long as the magnet was near, and we say that magnetism was **induced** in the nails by the permanent magnet. It kept the units of the iron lined up. Soft iron becomes only temporarily magnetic under the influence of the nearby permanent steel magnet, but a piece of hard steel retains much of its magnetism afterward.

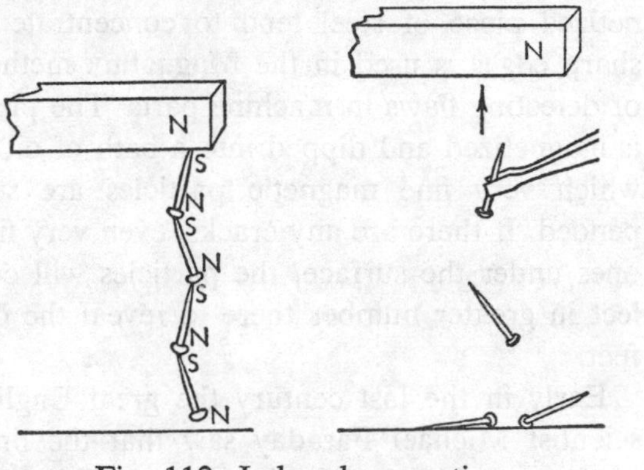

Fig. 112. Induced magnetism

Magnetic Fields

A permanent magnet will exert a force on a piece of iron or on another magnet some distance away. The space around magnets, where their effects are felt, is called a **magnetic field.** It is strongest near the magnet or magnets that cause it, but extends out indefinitely into the surrounding space.

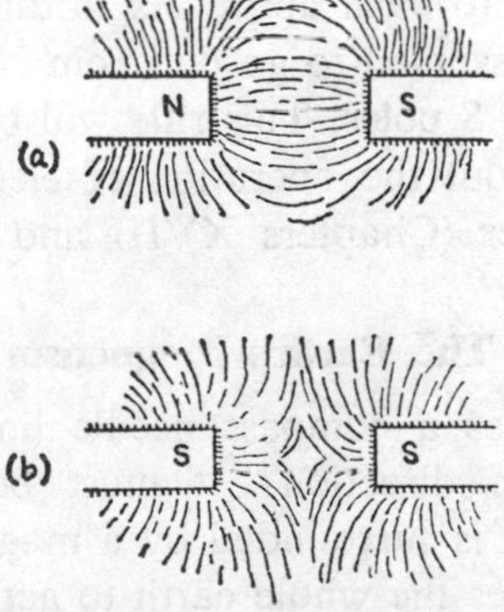

Fig. 113. Iron filings reveal the magnetic lines of force

EXPERIMENT 47: Toy horse-shoe magnets or small but powerful bar magnets can be bought very inexpensively in a toy store or hobby shop. Try the experiment just described. Also, lay a card on top of one or more of these magnets, scatter some iron filings uniformly over the whole card, then tap it with a pencil. The filings become magnets by induction and arrange themselves in curved lines somewhat as shown in Fig. 113. These curves are called **magnetic lines of force.**

The fact that the lines of force of a magnetized piece of steel tend to concentrate at sharp edges is used in the **Magnaflux** method of detecting flaws in machine parts. The piece is magnetized and dipped into a bath of oil in which very fine magnetic particles are suspended. If there are any cracks, even very fine ones under the surface, the particles will collect in greater number there to reveal the defect.

Early in the last century the great English scientist Michael Faraday saw that the lines of force, while purely imaginary (like light rays, or the earth's equator), could help his thinking about the behavior of magnets if he assumed that they acted like stiffened rubber bands. For instance, the filings show that the lines of force between two poles of opposite kind go across from one pole to the other. If they were really stretched rubber bands, this would tend to pull the poles together, which is what actually happens. For two poles of the same kind, the lines bend away from each other, and if they are assumed to act like stiff fibers, this would account for the fact that the poles tend to push apart. As to direction, the lines are assumed to go out from N poles and come in to S poles. This rule will be useful in talking about the operation of electrical machines later (Chapters XVIII and XIX).

The Earth's Magnetism

Why does a compass needle line up in a north-south direction? It must be that the earth itself is surrounded by a magnetic field. What causes the whole earth to act as a magnet is not completely understood. Part of the effect seems to be due to strong electric currents in the earth's core, and the rotation of the globe may play some part. At any rate, the character of the field is about what would be expected if there were a huge bar magnet inside the earth. Since the pole of a compass that points northward was designated an N pole, it follows that the imagined earth magnet has its S pole in the northern part of the globe (Fig. 114).

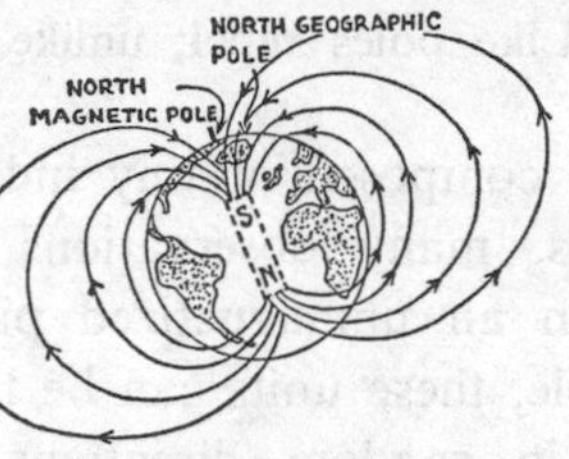

Fig. 114. Earth's magnetism

At any place on the surface of the earth in, say, the northern hemisphere, the lines of the field dip down into the ground at an angle. The place where the lines go straight down is called the **North Magnetic Pole,** and is located in northern Canada nearly 1,500 miles from the geographic north pole. There is a corresponding **South Magnetic Pole** in nearly the opposite location. Because the magnetic poles and the geographic poles are not at the same place, compass-indicated north differs considerably in most places from true north. In the northeastern part of the United States the compass points almost north-northwest, while on the Pacific Coast it points north-northeast. Navigators must have charts showing how much to correct this error of the compass, but the field is found to change slowly over a period of years, so that the government must issue new maps from time to time. At irregular intervals there also occur sudden, violent changes in the field, which may seriously affect telegraph, radio and TV communication. These "magnetic storms" are believed to be connected with increased activity of the sun.

Practice Exercise No. 32

1. Of the following, the one that will be attracted by *either* pole of a bar magnet is

— (A) the N pole of another bar magnet.

— (B) the S pole of another bar magnet.

— (C) an unmagnetized piece of nickel.

— (D) bits of broken glass.

2. Two identical bar magnets are placed side by side, with like poles together. This combination will

— (A) pick up bits of steel, but not iron.

— (B) pick up more iron filings than one such magnet.

— (C) fail to attract a cobalt rod.

— (D) repel iron nails.

3. If one end of a soft iron rod is held close to the S pole of a strong magnet

— (A) the rod will be a strong magnet after the bar magnet is removed.

— (B) there will be, temporarily, an S pole near the other end of the rod.

— (C) the rod will spring away as soon as it is let go.

— (D) the far end of the rod will not attract iron filings.

4. In flying from Chicago to Calcutta via the North Pole, the plane's magnetic compass would point

— (A) northward at all times.

— (B) southward at all times.

— (C) northward part of the time.

— (D) directly toward the geographic pole at all times.

5. A magnetized needle free to pivot in any direction will come to rest in a horizontal position when at

— (A) the North Magnetic Pole.

— (B) the South Magnetic Pole.

— (C) a place about midway between the North and South Magnetic Poles.

— (D) a place about 1,500 miles from the North Magnetic Pole.

STATIC ELECTRICITY

The fact that we use dozens of electrical appliances, from toasters to TV sets, in our daily lives emphasizes the practical importance of the science of electricity. These relatively recent developments seem to have little to do with the fundamental observation, made more than 25 centuries ago, that a piece of amber, previously rubbed with cloth, is able to attract and pick up bits of straw or paper. Much later it was discovered that other materials besides amber have this characteristic, which was called **electrification,** a name that comes from the Greek word for amber. In the following sections the behavior of electrified bodies will be described.

ELECTRIC CHARGES

Any two substances, when rubbed together under suitable conditions, become electrified, or acquire a **charge of electricity,** as we say. In dry weather, a plastic or hard rubber comb becomes charged and often makes crackling noises when run through your hair; or if you shuffle your feet on a wool rug, then bring your finger near a pipe or radiator, a spark will be produced, accompanied by a slight electric shock. The charges that rest on a comb, on your body or on any object are referred to as **static electricity,** while a charge in motion constitutes an **electric current**—the useful agency in most electrical appliances.

You can electrify a stick of hard rubber or sealing wax by rubbing it with a piece of fur or flannel. You can also electrify a glass rod or tube by rubbing it with a silk handkerchief. In either case, the attraction of bits of paper shows a charge to be present, but in a very definite way the charge on the hard rubber and the charge on the glass are of an opposite nature: Two electrified pieces of hard rubber will be found to repel each other; but an electrified piece of hard rubber rod and an electrified piece of glass will attract each other. This is represented by Fig. 115. Such experiments show that charges are of two kinds, and that **unlike kinds attract each other, while like kinds repel.** It was Benjamin Franklin who gave the names "positive" and "negative" to the two sorts of charge. The kind found on the glass rod he called positive (+) that on the hard rubber, negative (−).

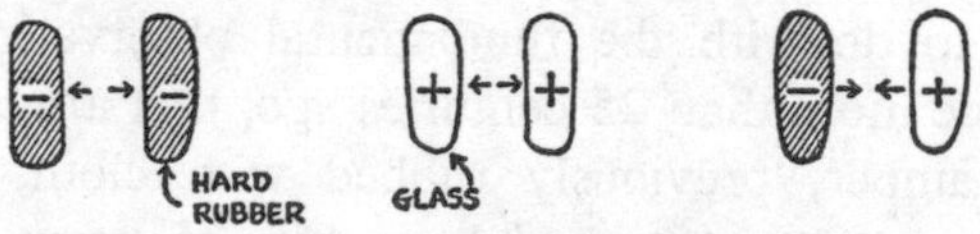

Fig. 115. Like charges repel; unlike charges attract

ATOMS AND ELECTRICITY

The charging of bodies is now understood in terms of the structure of the atoms composing the body. Some of the facts will be given now, but the reasons for believing them will not appear until later.

Every atom consists of a compact central **nucleus** carrying a positive charge, around which are distributed a number of **electrons,** each negatively charged. The nucleus owes its positive charge to the fact that it contains particles called **protons.** All protons are alike, and all carry the same amount of + charge. All electrons are alike, and each carries a −

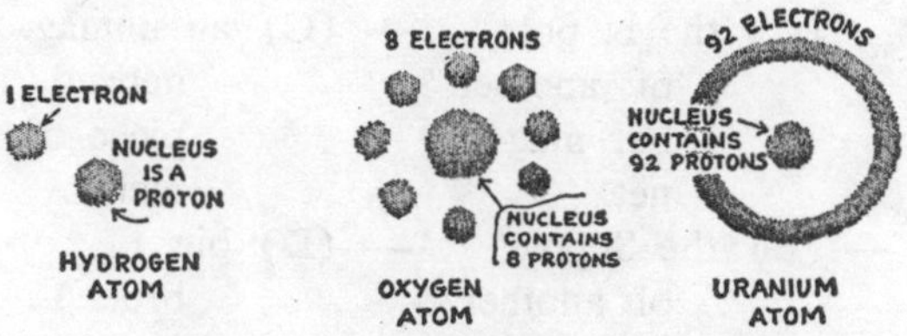

Fig. 116. Distribution of protons and electrons in certain atoms

charge, equal in amount to the + charge of a proton.

In its normal condition, the atom is electrically neutral—there are just as many electrons outside the nucleus as there are protons in it. However, certain atoms are able to hold temporarily more than their normal number of electrons, so when two different materials such as glass and silk are put into good contact by rubbing, the glass gives up some electrons to the silk. Thus the silk now has a negative charge, while the glass has a *deficiency* of negative charge, which means it has a positive charge. Charges are not "produced" by rubbing, they are merely separated out. It is usually the electrons that move from one place to another, the nuclei of the atoms remaining fixed in place.

CONDUCTORS AND INSULATORS

A charged body, if it is to keep its charge, must be supported by something that does not allow electrons to pass freely along it. Suitable materials, such as glass, hard rubber, sulfur, porcelain, are called **insulators** or **non-conductors.** On the other hand, many substances, especially metals, allow charge carriers to pass easily, and are called **conductors** of electricity.

If a charged rod is touched to an insulated metal object, some of the charge will pass from one to the other, and the metal body is said to receive a charge by **conduction.** This charge will spread over the entire surface of the conductor. If the charged object is now connected to a very large body (such as the earth) by means of a wire, it is said to be **grounded,** and loses its charge. If negative to begin with, its excess electrons flow off

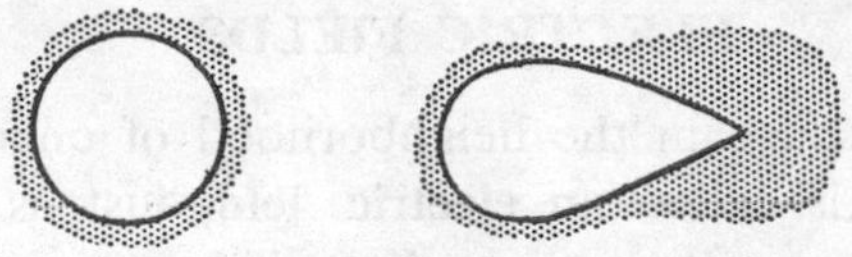

Fig. 117. (a) Distribution of charge on a round conductor (left) and on a pointed conductor (right)

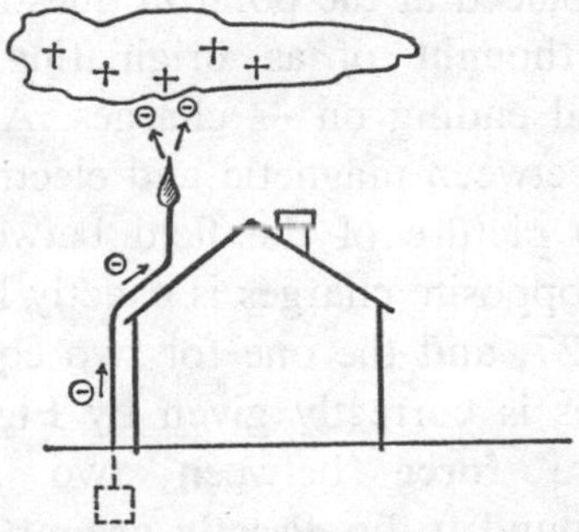

Fig. 117. (b) The action of a lightning rod

through the ground wire; if originally positive, the required number of electrons come up to it from the ground. The earth acts merely as a very large storehouse of charge of either kind.

Because a charge always goes entirely to the outside of a conductor, a sheet-metal box or even a wire cage that is grounded will act as an electrical shield, cutting off the effects of charges that may exist on the outside. Radio sets and other electrical apparatus can thus be shielded against external disturbances.

Franklin's famous kite experiment identified lightning as a discharge of electricity—an electric spark. Following this up, he devised the **lightning rod.** If a charge is put on a pointed conductor, most of the charge piles up at the point. If the point is quite sharp, the charge may actually leak off to the surroundings. A lightning rod is merely a pointed conductor placed at the top of a structure and connected by a heavy wire to a metal plate buried in moist earth. Suppose a positively-charged cloud passes over a house. Its attraction makes electrons flow up to the rod from the earth. On reaching the pointed rod, the electrons leak off and quietly neutralize the charge of the cloud before it can cause damage by suddenly finding a path to earth through the structure itself.

The discharging effect of points is used in the electrical smoke and dust **precipitator.** The particles become charged by the electricity streaming from the points (Fig. 118), are thus driven away and collect on the grounded plate. Not only is pollution of the air avoided, but the reclaiming of valuable materials from the dust may make the whole operation quite profitable.

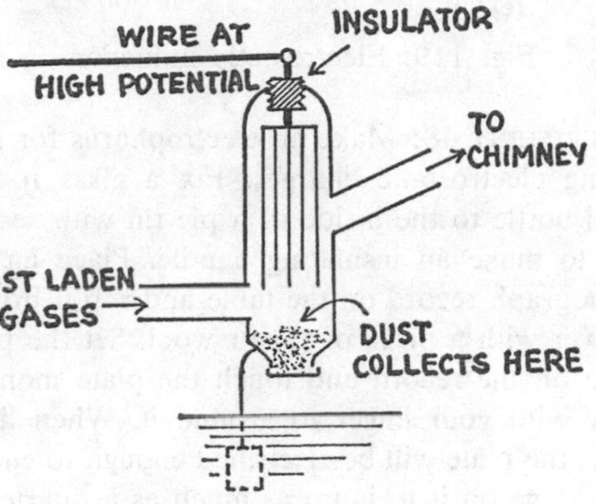

Fig. 118. Smoke and dust precipitator

ELECTROSTATIC INDUCTION

In studying magnetism, it was found that a piece of iron could become a magnet by induction merely by being brought near a permanent magnet. In a similar way, charges can be **induced** in a neutral body by bringing it near a charged one. In Fig. 119 the insulated, uncharged object is represented as having a uniform mixture of + and − charges all through it. When the + rod is brought near one end, some of the electrons are attracted toward that end. Now, touching the body with a finger provides a ground connection through which additional electrons may come onto the body in response to the attraction of the + charge on the rod. If the ground connection is now broken, the body will be left with an excess of electrons, and when the rod is finally removed they will redistribute themselves more uniformly. Although it is never actually touched by a charged object, the body acquires a charge by induction. In a similar way, a negatively charged rod can be used to give an object a + charge.

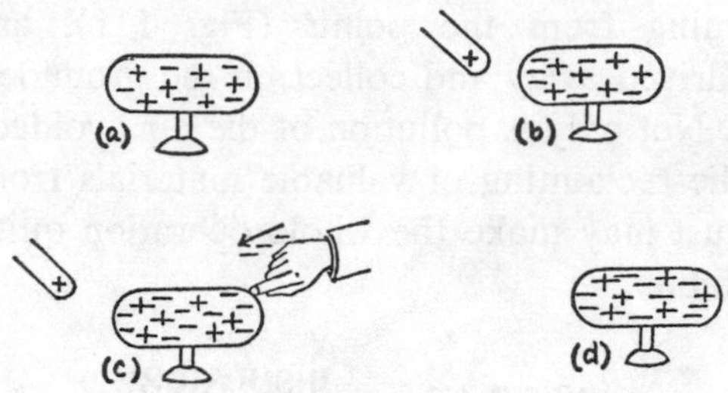

Fig. 119. Electrostatic induction

EXPERIMENT 48: Make an **electrophorus** for generating electrostatic charges. Fix a glass rod or small bottle to the inside of a pie tin with sealing wax to make an insulating handle. Place an old phonograph record on the table and rub it briskly all over with a piece of fur or wool. Set the plate down on the record and touch the plate momentarily with your finger to ground it. When lifted away, the plate will be electrified enough to enable the charge on it to jump as much as a quarter of an inch through the air to your knuckle. Without rubbing the record again, you can get a fresh charge on the disk over and over before the original charge on the record has leaked away.

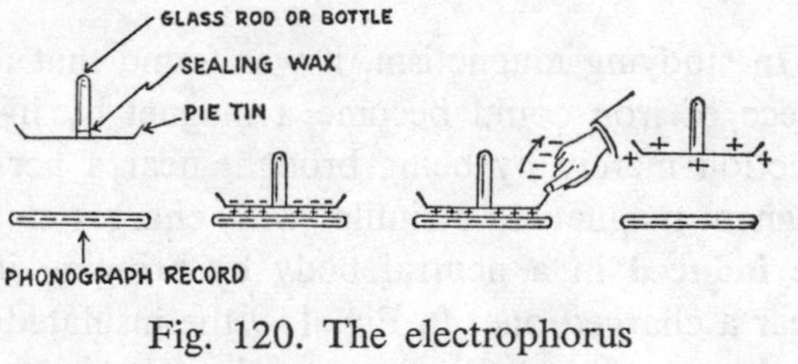

Fig. 120. The electrophorus

The diagram shows the stages in the charging process. The work you do each time the disk is lifted away from the record in opposition to the attraction between the charges on the two pays for the seemingly unlimited amount of electrical energy that is produced. Continuous-operating **electrostatic generators** based on a similar principle produce large amounts of charge at millions of volts. They are used in studying the effect of lightning on power lines and for "atom smashing" experiments.

ELECTRIC FIELDS

The space in the neighborhood of charged objects is called an **electric field,** just as the region around magnets is called a magnetic field (p. 127), and again lines of force are used to map out electric fields. Each line gives the direction of the resultant force on a small + charge placed at the point in question. The lines are thought of as originating on + charges and ending on − charges. A further similarity between magnetic and electric fields is that the picture of the field between two equal and opposite charges is exactly like Fig. 113a, p. 127, and the one for two equal and like charges is correctly given by Fig. 113b. Again, the **force** between two charged bodies is found to be **directly proportional to the amounts of charge and inversely proportional to the square of their distance apart.** The amount of charge on an object can be measured by bringing a standard charge up to a certain distance and measuring the force that one exerts on the other. The practical unit of quantity of charge is called one **coulomb,** after the French experimenter of that name. One coulomb is about the amount of charge that flows through a 100-watt filament lamp every second, yet it is equivalent to 6,300,000,000,000,000,000 electrons.

POTENTIAL AND CAPACITANCE

If a steel ball is placed on a hill it will roll down, and we can say that it does so because there is a resultant downhill force acting on the ball (Fig. 121a). But we can also describe what happens in another way by saying that the ball will move from a position of higher gravitational potential energy to one of lower (p. 53). Or, in discussing two connected water tanks like those in Fig. 121b, it can be said that water will have a tendency to flow from the left hand tank to the right because at the connecting pipe the pressure is greater from the left than from the right. When the valve is opened, the flow will take place and will continue as long as any pressure difference exists. In a corresponding elec-

TABLE 14

COMPARISON OF MAGNETIC, ELECTROSTATIC AND GRAVITATIONAL FORCES

Characteristic	*Magnetism*	*Electrostatics*	*Gravitation*
Materials	Only a few substances are magnetic.	Any substance can be electrified.	All matter exerts gravitational attraction.
Individuality of force centers	Single pole never found on one object.	A single kind of charge may be put on a body.	Every particle is a center of force.
Direction of force	Two opposite kinds of pole. Like repel, unlike attract.	Two opposite kinds of charge. Like repel, unlike attract.	Only one kind of mass. Force is always attraction.
Law of force	Force varies inversely as square of distance between centers.		
Shielding	Force can be shielded to some extent with soft iron, etc.	A metal enclosure acts as a good shield.	No known material screens off gravitational force.

trical case we say that a charge will have a tendency to move from one place to another if an electrical **potential difference** (abbreviated as "PD") exists between the two places. For instance, if two insulated metal balls (Fig. 121c) are at different electrical potential, charge will flow from the higher to the lower when they are joined by a conducting wire. If the potential difference is high enough to begin with, the insulating ability of the air between them may be insufficient, and a spark will pass from one to the other.

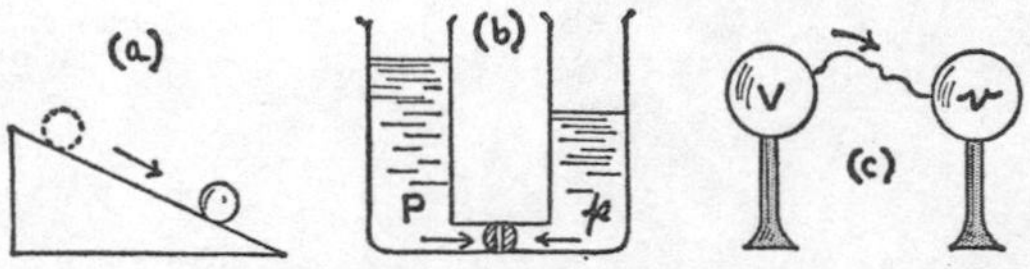

Fig. 121. Potential difference

The more charge you put on an insulated conductor, the higher its potential (that is, its PD with respect to the earth) becomes. This is similar to the increase of air pressure inside a balloon as you force more air in. The ability of a conductor to take on more charge as its potential is raised is measured by its electrical **capacitance.** The capacitance of a conductor may be increased greatly by putting a grounded conductor close to it. A "sandwich" consisting of two flat metal plates separated by a thin sheet of insulating material such as air, glass, mica or waxed paper constitutes an electrical **capacitor.** The charge-

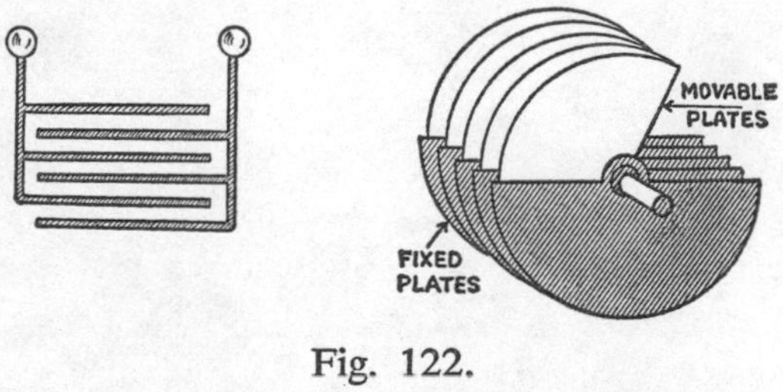

Fig. 122.

Multi-plate capacitor (schematic)

A radio capacitor; turning the shaft changes the capacitance

storing ability may be increased by using many layers, with the alternate plates connected together (Fig. 122). Capacitors are indispensable parts of radio, telephone and TV circuits, and many other electronic devices.

Practice Exercise No. 33

1. Using the idea of electrostatic induction, make sketches to explain why any neutral object will be attracted by a charged rod carrying either + or — electricity.
2. A small cork ball hanging by a silk thread is attracted when a charged glass rod is brought near, but if the ball moves over and touches the rod, it will bound away immediately afterward. Explain.
3. During a thunderstorm violent rising currents of air carry drops of water upward within the clouds. Can you explain how these drops become charged?
4. Friction between tires and road sometimes causes a considerable charge to accumulate on a car, and the potential of the car body may reach several thousand volts. What is the function of the flexible strap that some motorists hang from the axle of their car?
5. An insulated metal ball has an excess of 3 billion electrons on it, and an identical metal ball has a deficiency of 4 billion. a) Do they attract or repel each other? b) If the two are touched together and then separated, what will be the kind and amount of charge on each one and the nature of the force between them?

SUMMARY *Instructions:* (see page 17)

1. What are the *poles* of a magnet?	
2. Describe qualitatively the force acting between two magnetic poles.	The places, one near each end of a magnetized bar, where the force of attraction for bits of iron seems to be concentrated.
3. In principle, what is the nature of the process of magnetizing a steel bar?	Like poles repel, unlike poles attract.
4. What is a magnetic field?	It consists in lining up the elementary magnetic units of which the material is composed.
5. Describe the general nature of the earth's magnetic field.	The region near a magnet or magnets where their (magnetic) effects are appreciable.
6. What is meant by saying that a body has an electric charge?	The field is roughly that of a bar magnet whose axis (line of poles) makes somewhat of an angle with the rotational axis. The field changes slowly in time.
7. In terms of the electron concept, how are positively and negatively charged objects distinguished?	That, as a result of rubbing with a different substance, it has acquired the ability to attract light objects of any kind.
8. How does the force that one charged body exerts on another depend on the circumstances of a particular set-up?	A positively-charged object has a deficiency of electrons; a negatively-charged one has an excess.
9. What idea is suggested by the term "the difference in electrical potential" between two places in an electrostatic field?	The force varies directly as the two amounts of charge and inversely as the square of the distance apart of the two objects.
10. What property of a conductor is measured by its capacitance?	The tendency of a charged object to move from one of these places to the other.
	Its ability to take on more charge as its potential is raised.

Chapter XVII

ELECTRIC CURRENTS

An electric current has already been described as electric charge in motion. In a solid conductor, such as a wire, the current consists of a swarm of moving electrons, while in certain liquids and in gases the carriers may include positively and negatively charged atoms, as will be explained later. In addition, a beam of electrons or charged atoms may be made to go through a vacuum, no conductor being involved at all. Such a beam amounts to a current just as much as one in a wire. In this chapter you will find a description of the basic facts concerning the flow of electricity in circuits consisting of solid and liquid conductors.

CURRENT STRENGTH

There is a close correspondence between an electric current in a wire circuit and the flow of a liquid through pipes. The rate at which the liquid flows past any point in a system of piping may be measured by the amount passing in each unit of time—for instance, in gallons per second, cubic feet per hour, etc. In the electrical case, the **strength of the current** (usually called simply the "current") is similarly measured by the **amount of charge passing per unit of time.** The practical unit is the **ampere,** named for the French scientist and mathematician A. M. Ampère. One ampere is a rate of flow of one coulomb of charge per second, which means (p. 132) 6.3 billion billion electrons per second. In spite of this large number, the electrons in a metal are so crowded together that their movement in a current of moderate strength amounts only to a slow drift, corresponding to a speed of only around a hundredth of an inch per second. The reason that a light goes on the moment the switch is closed is not that electrons race around to it at high speed, but that the conductors are always "filled" with electrons, just as a pipe system is full of water (Fig. 123).

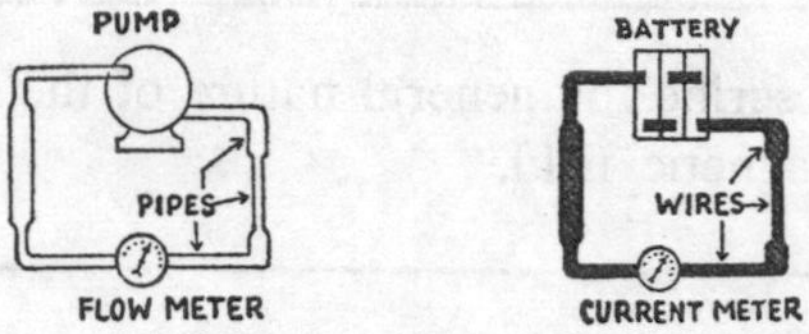

Fig. 123. Analogy between a hydraulic circuit and an electric circuit

The water system consisting of a series of pipes joined to a circulating pump corresponds to a simple electric circuit made up of a series of wires connected to a battery. The purpose of the pump is to maintain a pressure difference between its inlet and outlet in order to keep the water circulating. Similarly, the function of the battery is to maintain an electrical PD between its two terminals, and it is this PD which keeps the current going in the circuit.

ACTION OF A CELL; IONS

How does a battery accomplish this effect? Near the end of the eighteenth century the Italian biologist Galvani found that the muscle of a frog's leg would twitch when it was touched at the same time by two metals, such as brass and iron. Galvani believed the movement was due to some kind of "animal electricity," but Volta showed that similar effects could be produced without using animal tissue at all. He built the first battery by stacking alternate zinc and copper disks separated by pieces of leather soaked in salt solution, and was able to obtain from it the same kinds of action as from a charged capacitor, except that the operation could be repeated many times over.

A single unit of such a battery is called a **voltaic cell.** The mechanism of operation of a cell was not explained by chemists until long after the time of Galvani and Volta. The typical chemical cell represented in Fig. 124 is made by placing a rod of zinc (chemical symbol Zn) and a rod of copper (Cu) in a solution of hydrochloric acid (HCl).

It is found that when HCl molecules dissolve in water they break apart, or **dissociate,** into two pieces. One part is the chlorine atom; but instead of being a normal Cl atom, it has an extra electron attached to it and is called a chlorine **ion.** The attached electron is indicated by writing a minus sign on its symbol: Cl^-. This electron was obtained from the hydrogen atom which, having had this negative charge taken away from it, has now become the positive hydrogen ion H^+. In a similar way, many other chemical substances dissociate in solution to form ions.

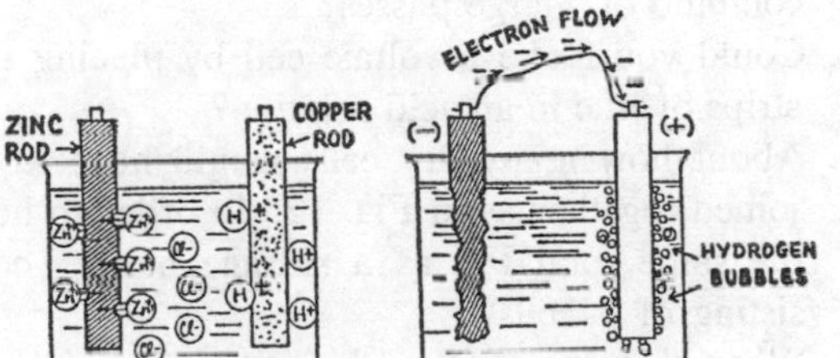

Fig. 124. Chemical cell

When the Zn rod is put into the liquid, the Zn atoms have a strong tendency to detach themselves from it. Each such atom comes off as a doubly-charged ion, Zn^{++}. Every time this happens, a pair of electrons is left behind on the rod. Soon no further Zn ions come off because of the back attraction of the negative charge on the rod. The accumulating Zn ions repel the H ions, making the latter collect near the copper rod. The copper does not dissolve to any extent, and nothing further happens until the outside circuit is completed by connecting a wire between the two rods. Then the electrons that have piled up on the Zn rod flow over this wire to the Cu rod, where they neutralize the positive charges carried there by the H ions. Having given up their charge, the H ions are again ordinary atoms of hydrogen, and hydrogen gas begins to bubble out of the liquid at the surface of the copper rod. The action goes on until the Zn rod is completely used up.

EXPERIMENT 49: Scrub a penny and a dime with scouring powder until they are bright and clean. Hold the two coins in contact at one edge and insert the tip of your tongue between their flat surfaces. The bitter-sour taste is due to the ions formed in the saliva by this simple voltaic cell.

BATTERIES

A voltaic cell can maintain a PD of about 1.5 **volt** between its terminals when only very small currents are drawn from it. If a battery is made up by connecting a number of such cells as shown in Fig. 125, the PD across the

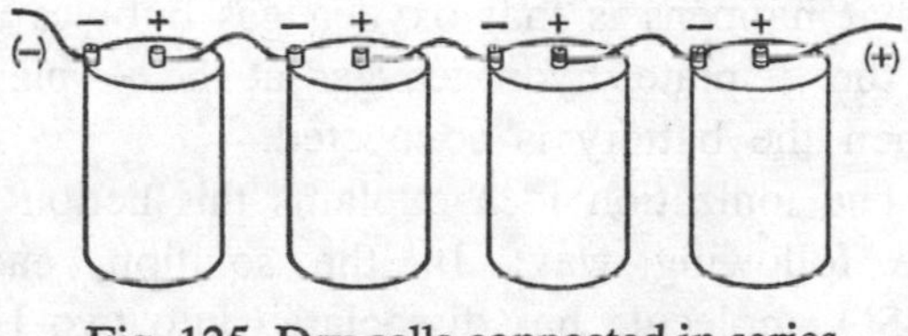

Fig. 125. Dry cells connected in series

whole battery will be this number times 1.5 volts. The most widely used form of voltaic cell is the **dry cell,** used in flashlights, portable radio sets, etc. The construction is shown in Fig. 126.

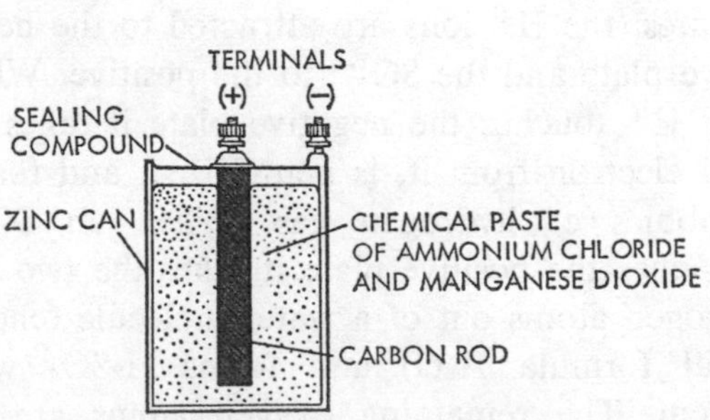

Fig. 126. Cross-section of a dry cell

A **lead storage cell** consists of a lead plate and one containing lead peroxide placed in a sulfuric acid solution. The action is similar to that of a voltaic cell, except that the plates do not dissolve but can be restored to their original state by passing a "charging" current through the cell in the opposite direction. The cell may be used repeatedly. The usual automobile storage battery is made up of six such cells and its total "voltage" when fully charged is just over 12. The electrical condition of such a battery may be tested by using a hydrometer (p. 28) to measure the specific gravity of the solution.

ELECTROLYSIS

Pure water is a very poor conductor of electricity, but can be made conducting by dissolving any substance that breaks up into ions. Suppose a little sulfuric acid (chemical formula H_2SO_4) is dissolved in water and that two metal plates, one connected to each terminal of a battery, are placed in this solution. The plates may be made of platinum, which is not acted upon chemically by the acid. What happens is that oxygen gas bubbles up at the + plate, hydrogen gas at the − plate, when the battery is connected.

The ionization idea explains this action in the following way: In the solution, each H_2SO_4 molecule has dissociated into two H^+ ions and one $SO_4^=$ ion. As already explained, each H^+ ion is a hydrogen atom lacking its usual electron, and since there are two of these for each SO_4 group, the latter ion must have two added electrons, and so is written $SO_4^=$. When the battery is connected to the plates, the H^+ ions are attracted to the negative plate and the $SO_4^=$ to the positive. When an H^+ touches the negative plate it takes on an electron from it, is neutralized, and forms bubbles of hydrogen gas. When an $SO_4^=$ reaches the positive plate it takes the two hydrogen atoms out of a water molecule (chemical formula H_2O) and forms H_2SO_4 with them. The remaining oxygen atoms are set free and form bubbles of oxygen gas. In this way, water is broken up into its two constituents, oxygen and hydrogen. Such a process is called **electrolysis,** and a study of it has added much to chemical knowledge.

On the practical side, aluminum and several other metals became commercially available only after it was found possible to extract them from natural minerals by electrolysis. If the liquid in an electrolytic cell contains ions of a given metal, they may often be made to deposit on the negative plate in the form of a thin, firmly adhering coating of the metal. The process is then called **electroplating,** and gold, silver, copper, chromium and other metals are commercially plated on various articles in this way. In making **electrotypes,** such as used in printing this book, a wax impression of the original type is coated with graphite to make it a conductor and is then plated with copper. The wax is later removed and the thin copper shell is backed up with some cheaper metal to make it strong enough for use in the process.

Practice Exercise No. 34

1. How strong is the average current, in amperes, in a lightning flash lasting 0.0002 sec if 1 coulomb of charge passes?
2. Could you make a voltaic cell by placing two strips of zinc in an acid solution?
3. About how many dry cells would have to be joined together as in Fig. 125 in order to have the same total PD as a storage battery consisting of 9 cells?
4. When a storage battery is in use, sulfuric acid is being removed from solution. Sulfuric acid has a greater specific gravity than pure water. Where would you expect a hydrometer to float higher—in the liquid from a discharged cell or from a fully-charged one?
5. What is actually "stored" in a storage battery —electricity, kinetic energy, chemical energy or heat? Explain.

A SIMPLE CIRCUIT

A simple electrical circuit consisting of a source of PD and a series of conductors was diagrammed in Fig. 123. A useful addition is a switch for opening and closing the circuit. If we want to know the magnitude of the current and the PD between any two points, suitable measuring instruments called, respectively, **ammeters** and **voltmeters** may be used. The operation of such devices will be explained in the next chapter.

Fig. 127 shows an electrician's diagram of such a circuit, using the standard symbol for each part. *B* is a battery made up of three cells. The long stroke represents the + terminal, the short thick line the — terminal of each cell. The zigzag line *R* is any conductor through which we wish the current to go, while the heavy straight lines represent heavy connecting wires. The ammeter *A* is connected directly *into the circuit* at any point, while the voltmeter *V* is *in a side circuit*, its terminals being connected to the two points whose PD we wish to know—in this case, the ends of the unit *R*. The current that passes through *V* is negligible compared to the current in the main circuit. When *K* is closed, a steady current flows in the circuit and the meters take on steady readings.

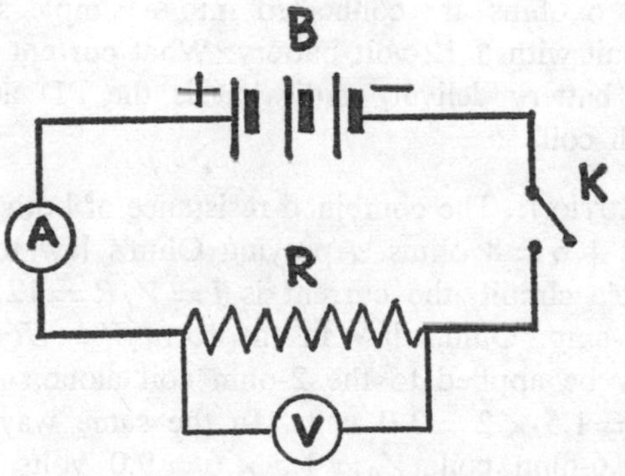

Fig. 127. Electrician's diagram of a simple circuit

What determines the strength of the current that flows in the circuit? The answer to this important question was first given early in the last century by the careful experiments of a German scientist, G. S. Ohm. By connecting pieces of wire of various lengths, cross-sections and materials in place of *R* in a circuit like the one in the diagram, he found that the current is directly proportional to the cross-section area of the wire and inversely proportional to its length, and also depends on the kind of metal of which the wire is made. The best conductors are found to be silver, copper and gold.

OHM'S LAW

The dependence on length and cross-section is just what we would expect if a wire offers resistance to the flow of current, just as a pipe in a water system offers resistance to the flow of water. Ohm further found that, with a given wire in the circuit, **the current is proportional to the PD between the ends of the wire.** This relation can be written

$$I=\frac{V}{R},$$

where *I* is the strength of the current, *V* is the applied PD and *R* is the **resistance** of the conductor. This is the famous **Ohm's law** of current electricity. You already know that the practical unit of *I* is the ampere, and that of *V* is the volt. Then the corresponding unit for *R* is called one **ohm.** Thus, by Ohm's law, a one-ohm resistor is one that allows a current of 1 amp to flow when a PD of 1 volt is applied to its ends. For example, the resistance of the hot filament in a 60-watt lamp is over 200 ohms, while that of the heating element of an electric iron may be only about 20 ohms. The total resistance of the connecting wires in a simple circuit like the one in Fig. 127 may be only a few hundredths of an ohm. The most direct way to find the resistance of a conductor is to put it in a simple circuit, measure the PD across it and the current through it by suitable meters, and then compute the resistance using Ohm's law.

EXAMPLE 1: Find the strength of the current through a filament lamp if the resistance of the filament is 220 ohms and it is used on a 110-volt line.

SOLUTION: The applied PD can be taken to be 110 volts, so Ohm's law gives $I=110/220=0.5$ amp.

EXAMPLE 2: What is the resistance of the heating element of an electric toaster that carries a current of 5.0 amp on a 110-volt line?

SOLUTION: Ohm's law gives $R=V/I$, or $R=110/5=22$ ohms.

The resistance of a given conductor usually increases slightly as its temperature is raised, as observed originally by Ohm. Once the rate of increase has been measured for a given kind of wire, the process may be turned around and temperatures determined by noting the change in resistance of a coil of such wire inserted in the material whose temperature is to be found. Such an instrument is called a **resistance thermometer.**

PD in a Circuit

Ohm's law can be applied to a whole circuit or to any part of a circuit, and this often makes it possible to reduce effectively certain groups of resistors to a single unit whose resistance can be computed from those of the individual parts. As an illustration, suppose that a number of resistors (they may be coils, lamps, heating elements or any conducting units) are connected **in series**—that is, in such way that the entire current flows through one after the other, as represented in Fig. 128. There will be a drop of potential along each of the resistors, and the total fall of potential in the whole wire circuit will be the sum of these separate PD's. The positive terminal of the battery can be thought of as the highest potential peak in the whole circuit; from here the potential drops as the moving charge goes through one resistor after another, and finally it gets down to the negative battery terminal —which has the lowest potential in the circuit. Inside the battery, chemical action "boosts"

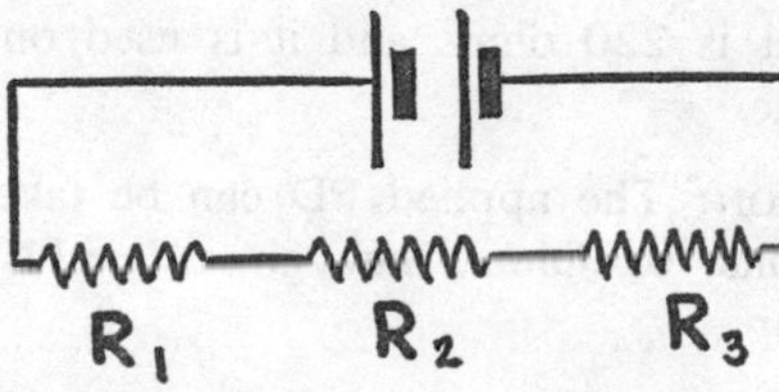

Fig. 128. Resistors in series

the moving charge back up to the high level, and it goes around the circuit again and again. The close similarity with balls rolling down a slope is suggested by Fig. 129.

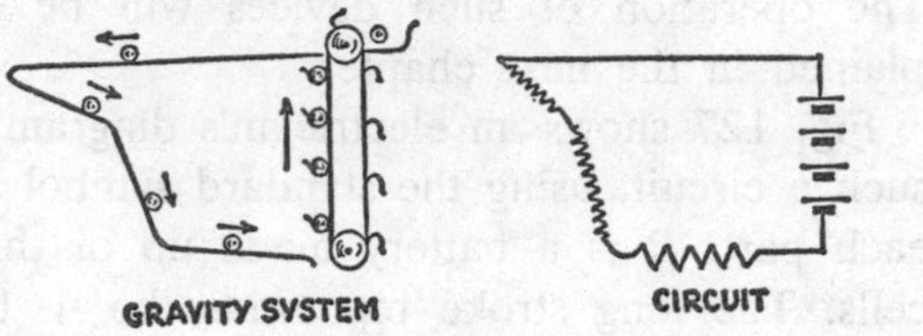

Fig. 129. The battery "boosts" the charges up again

Resistors in Series

Suppose we have a series circuit like the above, except that it may contain any number of resistors so connected. If the resistance of the first one is called R_1, that of the second one R_2, and so on, then the combined resistance of the whole set (call it simply R) will be merely the sum of the separate ones, or

$$R=R_1+R_2+R_3 \ldots \text{etc.}$$

EXAMPLE 3: Two coils of resistance 2 ohms and 6 ohms are connected into a simple series circuit with a 12-volt battery. What current does the battery deliver, and what is the PD across each coil?

SOLUTION: The combined resistance of both coils is $2+6=8$ ohms. Applying Ohm's law to the whole circuit, the current is $I=V/R=12/8=1.5$ amp. Ohm's law in the form $V=IR$ may now be applied to the 2-ohm coil alone, giving $V_2=1.5\times 2=3.0$ volts. In the same way, for the 6-ohm coil, $V_6=1.5\times 6=9.0$ volts. The sum of these two PD's is 12 volts, the voltage of the battery, as it must be.

Ordinary 110-volt lamps are used on electric railways, where the PD supplied from the line is generally 550 volts, so five such lamps are joined in series and the whole line voltage is applied to the set. This makes the PD across each lamp 110 volts—the normal operating voltage. A disadvantage of the arrangement is that if one lamp burns out the whole set goes out.

Resistors in Parallel

In order to get around difficulties like the one just mentioned, the appliances in a household circuit are connected in a different way, which makes them independent of each other. In Fig. 130 the resistors are said to be joined **in parallel.** The main current, instead of going through one after the other, divides and a part of it goes through each. The separate currents then rejoin and complete the circuit. In this type of circuit, each resistor has the same voltage applied to it—that of the battery. If any unit is disconnected, the remaining ones continue to function as before.

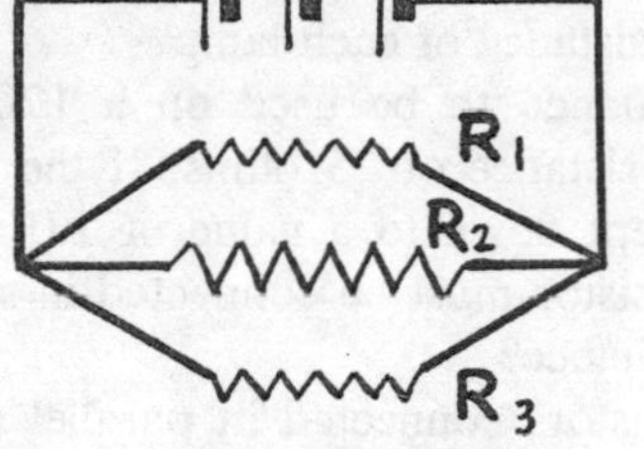

Fig. 130. Resistors in parallel

It is found that the combined resistance of a number of resistors connected in parallel is given by

$$\frac{1}{R}=\frac{1}{R_1}+\frac{1}{R_2}+\frac{1}{R_3}\ldots \text{etc.}$$

Here R_1, R_2, etc. stand for the values of the separate resistances, and R is the equivalent total resistance of the set. In using this relation, avoid the mistake of assuming that both sides of the equation can be inverted *term by term*. All the fractions on the right side must first be brought over a common denominator.

EXAMPLE 4: Three resistors of 4, 6 and 12 ohms, respectively, are connected in parallel, and a 6-volt battery is applied to the combination. What current is delivered by the battery, and what current flows in each branch?

SOLUTION: The first thing to do is compute the equivalent resistance of the set. Using the above relation,

$$\frac{1}{R}=\frac{1}{4}+\frac{1}{6}+\frac{1}{12}=\frac{6}{12}=\frac{1}{2};$$

inverting,

$$R=2 \text{ ohms.}$$

Notice that the value of R is less than any of the individual resistance values. This is reasonable, since every conductor added in parallel provides an additional path for the current. The current in the entire circuit is given by Ohm's law as $I=V/R=6/2=3.0$ amp. The current in the 4-ohm coil is $I_1=V/R_1=6/4=1.5$ amp. In the same way, the current in the 6-ohm branch is $6/6=1$ amp, and that in the 12-ohm branch is $6/12=0.5$ amp. The sum is 3.0 amp, as it must be.

While series and parallel connections are two very important arrangements of resistors, there are other more complicated hookups that are also used in practice. These often can be handled by using an extension of Ohm's law, but the details may get somewhat complex.

EXPERIMENT 50: The two cells and lamp of a 3-volt flashlight, together with an extra lamp, can be used to check the principles explained above. First connect the cells and lamps in series, using short lengths of bell wire or any pieces of wire whose ends are scraped clean. To make contact at the center terminals of the lamps or cells, tape the wires on, as shown in Fig. 131. Notice that the lamps glow only dimly, since the PD across each is just half what it should be. Now **short-circuit** one lamp by shunting a piece of wire across it. Most of the current will then go through the

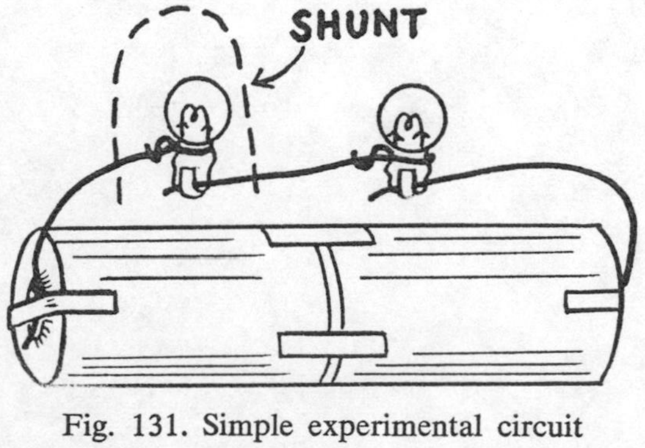

Fig. 131. Simple experimental circuit

"short," which has less resistance than the lamp filament, and so the other lamp brightens up. Put aside the shunt, then connect both lamps in parallel and observe that they light normally. Finally, put both lamps in series with a single cell and notice that they are very dim, since each has only half the normal PD applied to it.

ELECTRIC POWER AND ENERGY

The *power* expended in any appliance—the rate at which it uses electrical energy—is given directly in watts by multiplying the current in amperes by the PD in volts.*

In symbols,

$$P_{\text{watts}} = I_{\text{amp}} \times V_{\text{volts}}.$$

For example, an electric iron that draws 3.5 amp when connected to a 120-volt line would have a power rating of $3.5 \times 120 = 420$ watts.

Since power is defined as energy divided by time, energy may be expressed as power multiplied by time, and this is the way electrical energy is sold, the unit being the **kilowatt-hour.** Thus, when you write a check for your monthly electric bill you are paying for the total amount of electrical *energy* that the company delivered to you during that period. The total energy consumed by a number of appliances is found by adding up the products of power rating and time of use for all of them.

EXAMPLE 5: In a home laundry a 550-watt iron is used for a total of 20 hours each month, a washing machine (185 watts) for 12 hours and two 60-watt lamps for 25 hours. If electrical energy costs 4 cents per kilowatt-hour in this locality, what is the monthly cost of the appliances used?

SOLUTION: Remembering that 1 kw = 1,000 watts, the total energy used will be $0.55 \times 20 + 0.185 \times 12 + 2 \times 0.06 \times 25 = 16.22$ kw-hr. At the 4-cent rate, this will cost about 65 cents in all.

* To refresh your memory on the definition of the watt, look back at p. 54.

Practice Exercise No. 35

1. If both the diameter and the length of a copper wire are doubled, what effect does this have on its resistance?
2. Christmas tree lights are usually connected in a series of 8 lamps when used on a 120-volt line. If the current in each is 0.2 amp, what is the resistance of each lamp?
3. An appliance to be used on a 120-volt line has a resistance of 25 ohms. If the current is to be kept down to a value of 2.0 amp, how big a resistor must be connected in series with the appliance?
4. Two resistors connected in parallel are joined to a battery. If one of the resistors has 3 times the resistance of the other, compare the currents in the two. What fraction of the *total* current goes through each?
5. A 3-ohm coil and a 6-ohm coil are connected in parallel and the combination is joined in series with a 2-ohm coil and a 12-volt battery. Find the current in the 2-ohm coil.
6. In the last problem, find the current in each of the other coils.
7. A 30-watt automobile lamp is supplied by the 12-volt storage battery. What is the resistance of the hot filament of the lamp?

SUMMARY *Instructions:* (see page 17)

1. Define electric current.	
2. What is meant by the strength (or intensity) of an electric current?	Charge in motion.
3. Of what does the current in a metallic wire consist?	The amount of charge passing any point in unit time: $I=Q/t$.
4. What are the carriers of charge when a current flows through certain solutions?	The drift of a large number of electrons.
5. What is meant by electrolysis?	Plus and minus ions formed by the dissociation of molecules of a suitable dissolved substance.
6. State Ohm's law.	The transport and separation of substances by passing a current through a solution containing ions.
7. If a number of resistors are connected in series, what is the amount of their total resistance?	The strength of the current in a metallic conductor held at constant temperature is given by $I=V/R$, where I is the current, V the PD across the conductor and R its resistance.
8. The same question for a number of resistors connected in parallel.	Total resistance is the sum of the separate resistance values: $R=R_1+R_2+\ldots$
9. State the formula for computing the amount of power expended in any circuit element in which the current is I amp and the PD is V volts.	Total resistance given by $1/R=1/R_1+1/R_2+\ldots$
	$P_{\text{watts}}=I_{\text{amp}}\times V_{\text{volts}}$.

Chapter XVIII

HEATING AND MAGNETIC EFFECTS OF ELECTRIC CURRENTS

The usefulness of an electric current is determined by the physical effects it is able to produce. The chemical changes involved in electrolysis were discussed in the preceding chapter. Two other effects of great importance, the production of heat and the production of magnetic fields, will be described in this chapter.

HEAT DEVELOPED IN A CONDUCTOR

The work done by a battery or other source of PD in moving charges around a circuit may be converted into various forms. Part of the energy may be changed to mechanical work if there are motors in the circuit, part may be changed into radiation if there are lamps, etc.; but always, some will appear in the form of heat. In a wire, for example, the electrons that are made to move through it continually bump into the atoms of the material, delivering some of their energy to them in the form of random heat motion.

The heat produced in a conductor is sometimes merely an unavoidable loss, as in motors or storage batteries, but in certain applications such as industrial furnaces, heating coils, ranges, etc., the production of heat is the main purpose of the unit, and it becomes important to know how to calculate how much heat will be obtained. To do this, recall (p. 142) that the power W (in watts) expended in maintaining a current I (in amp) in a conductor where the PD is V (in volts) is given by $P = I \times V$. If the current flows for a time t (in sec), then the total work done, or energy delivered, W (in joules) is given by $W = I \times V \times t$. But according to p. 54, 1 joule is equivalent to 1/4.18, or 0.24 calorie, and so if all the work done by the source of PD is changed to heat in a conductor, the amount of heat produced will be, in calories,

$$Q = 0.24\ I \times V \times t.$$

EXAMPLE 1: How much heat is produced in one minute by an electric iron that draws 4.0 amp when connected to a 115-volt line?

SOLUTION: Substitution in the above relation gives $Q = 0.24 \times 4.0 \times 115 \times 60 = 6{,}624$ cal.

For some purposes it is more convenient to have the quantity of heat given in terms of current and resistance, rather than current and voltage. Using Ohm's Law, we can substitute $I \times R$ for V in the formula, getting

$$Q = 0.24\ I^2 \times R \times t.$$

This expression shows, for instance, that if there are a number of resistors connected in series (same current in each), the greatest amount of heat will be produced in the one having the highest resistance. Since the resistance of a conductor changes with temperature, the heat produced by the current will change the value of R, and care must be taken to use the value that corresponds to the temperature reached in any particular case.

EXPERIMENT 51: Almost all of the electrical energy put into a filament lamp is converted into heat. The heating effect can be measured by immersing a lighted lamp almost to its socket (careful not to let the water touch the socket itself!) in a can of water placed on folded newspapers.

Use a thermometer and a watch to record the length of time it takes a 25-watt lamp to warm the water by 10°. Repeat with a 60-watt lamp, and you will find that in the same length of time the temperature will rise about 60/25=2.4 times as much, or 24°.

Applications of the Heating Effect

The electric arc (p. 99), which may be used for lighting, for heating certain types of industrial furnaces or for welding metals together, utilizes the heat evolved by the current. So do a variety of household appliances such as waffle irons, heating pads, coffee-makers, electric blankets, and many more.

If the wires of an electric circuit carry too heavy a current they may become hot enough to burn away their insulation and may start a fire. To prevent overloading of a circuit, **fuses** are often placed in series with the circuit to be protected. A fuse is a strip of wire having a high resistance and made of some metal that melts at a relatively low temperature. If, for some reason, the current should become dangerously high, the fuse will melt and so break the circuit before any other damage can result. The plug fuses used in many house circuits (Fig. 132) are rated to blow out when the current reaches 15 or 20 amp.

Fig. 132. Cutaway view of a fuse plug

OERSTED'S DISCOVERY

Some of the most important technical applications of electricity depend on the fact that **a current produces a magnetic field** in its neighborhood. This connection between magnetism and electricity was discovered by the Danish physicist H. C. Oersted a century and a half ago. He noticed that a compass needle placed just below a wire carrying a current would take up a position nearly perpendicular to the wire while the current was flowing. When the direction of the current was reversed, the needle again set itself at right angles to the wire, but with its ends reversed (Fig. 133). The effect lasts only while the current flows. It is not due to the wire as such (copper is non-magnetic), but in some way to the existence of the current itself. In fact, currents in solutions or in gases and charges streaming across a vacuum are found to give the same effect.

Field Due to a Current

The lines of magnetic force that mark out the field due to a current in a straight piece of wire are found to be circles that go around the wire in one direction (Fig. 134). This can be checked by carrying a small compass needle around the wire or by scattering iron filings on a card through which the wire passes. The field is strongest near the wire and gets weaker as you go farther out in any direction. If the current is reversed, the lines are again circles, but go around in the opposite sense.

There is a simple way of relating the direction of the field to that of the current caus-

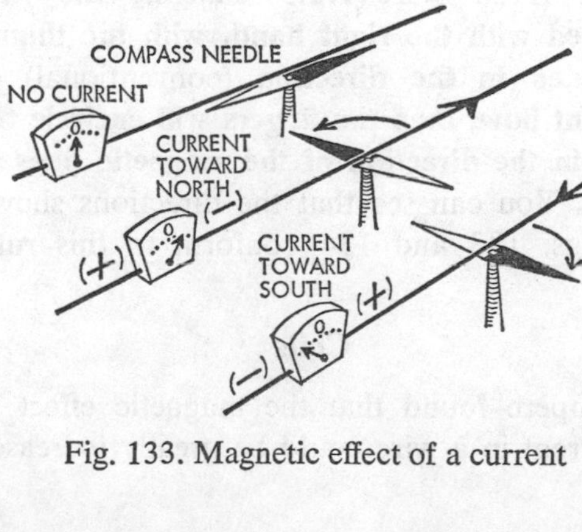

Fig. 133. Magnetic effect of a current

ing it. In the first place, we must make definite what is meant by the direction of the current is a wire. In terms of what we now know about the nature of the current in a wire, the obvious way to specify this would be to say that the current is the direction in which the electrons move. However, long before the discovery of electrons, the current in a circuit had always been taken to flow from the + terminal of the battery around to the − terminal. This is plainly opposite to the direction of actual electron flow (electrons are negative), but it is too late to change the conventional designation, which is always used by practical electricians, and we must be content to remember that this **conventional direction** of current is really **opposite to the electron flow.** From here on, any reference to direction of current will be assumed to refer to the conventional direction unless otherwise mentioned.

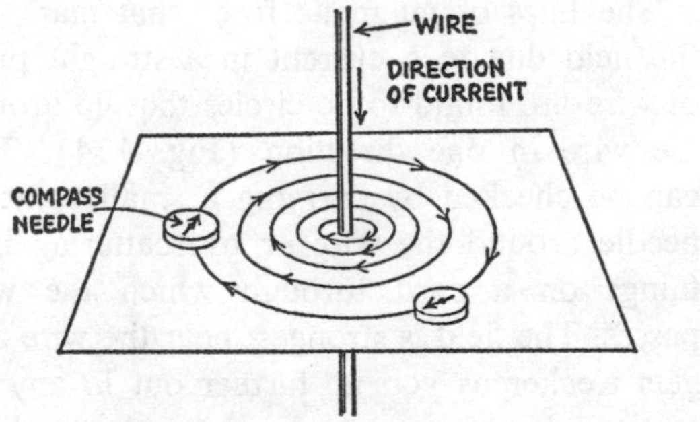

Fig. 134. Lines of magnetic force around a straight current

The simple rule for the relation between the directions of current and field is known as the Right Hand Wire Rule: **Imagine the wire grasped with the right hand, with the thumb extended in the direction** (conventional) **of current flow; then the fingers will encircle the wire in the direction of the magnetic lines of force.** You can see that the directions shown in Figs. 133 and 134 conform to this rule.

Coils

Ampère found that the magnetic effect of a current in a wire could be greatly increased by winding the wire in the form of a spinal coil, or **solenoid.** The effects of the many turns add up to give a field exactly like that of a bar magnet, and the lines can be followed even inside the coil (Fig. 135). The magnetic strength of such a coil may be increased hundreds and even thousands of times by placing a soft-iron core inside it. The device is then called an **electromagnet** (Fig. 135). It has the advantage over a permanent magnet that it can be made much stronger, and that its strength can be controlled and its polarity reversed by suitably changing the current in the coil.

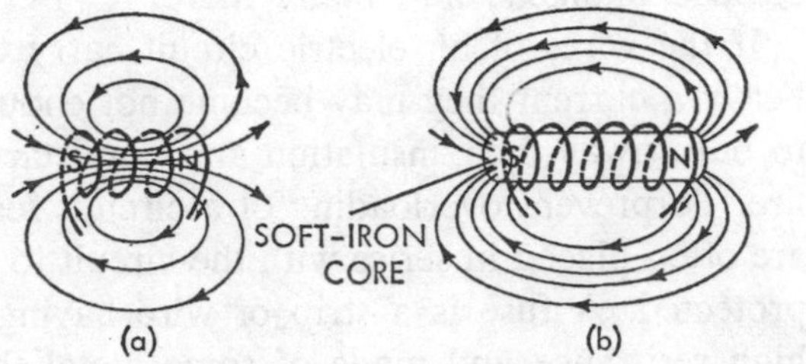

Fig. 135. The solenoid becomes an electromagnet by the insertion of an iron core

There is a definite relation between the direction of the current in the coil and the direction of the magnetic field produced. This is contained in the **Right Hand Coil Rule,** which can be figured out from the simple right hand rule for a straight wire as given above: **Grasp the coil with the right hand so that your fingers go around it in the direction of the current in the wires; then the extended thumb will point in the direction of the N pole of the coil** (Fig. 136). Notice the reversal of what the fingers and thumb stand for, as compared with the right hand rule for a straight wire.

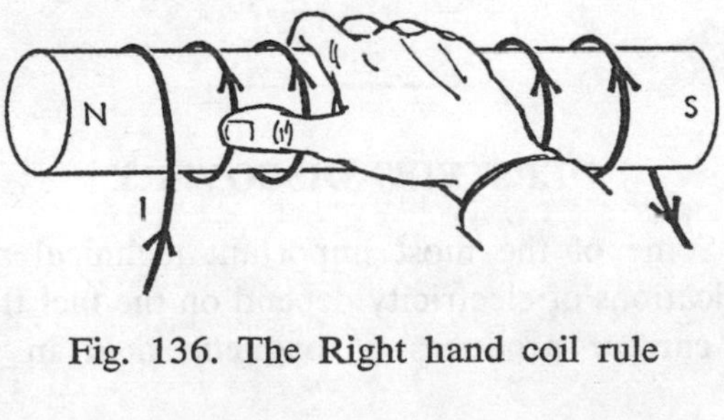

Fig. 136. The Right hand coil rule

Uses of Electromagnets

Electromagnets in various forms have a great variety of uses. "Lifting magnets" strong enough to hold loads of many tons are used to load and transport scrap iron, steel bars and machine parts. The load is engaged or released simply by closing or opening the switch that controls the current in the coils. Some magnets of this type can lift as much as 200 lb for each square inch of pole face.

Examine an electric doorbell or buzzer and observe that there is a horse-shoe electromagnet, each arm wound with many turns of fine wire.

A **relay** is a device that allows a weak current to open and close a circuit in which a heavier current flows. It is, in principle, a switch that may be operated from a distance. A sensitive relay may operate on as little current as a millionth of an ampere.

Electromagnets are essential elements in the construction of the telephone receiver (p. 156) and radio loudspeaker, and in atomic research devices such as the mass spectrograph, cyclotron, betatron, etc.

Practice Exercise No. 36

1. The wires leading to a filament lamp do not become as hot as the filament itself because the filament has a greater

— (A) length. — (C) resistance.
— (B) diameter. — (D) current flowing in it.

2. When a 100-watt water heater is allowed to run for 5.0 min, it raises the temperature of ½ pint (225 gm) of water by

— (A) 0.53 C°. — (C) 72 C°.
— (B) 32 C°. — (D) 0.22 C°.

3. The century in which Oersted discovered that a magnetic effect can be produced by an electric current was the

— (A) eighteenth. — (C) twentieth.
— (B) nineteenth. — (D) sixteenth.

4. A vertical wire carries a heavy current flowing from bottom to top. A compass needle placed on a table just east of the wire will point

— (A) north. — (C) east.
— (B) west. — (D) south.

5. A spiral coil is wound on an upright post, with the current going around it in a clockwise direction as seen from above. Then it is true that the lines of force will

— (A) begin and end on various turns of a wire. — (C) decrease in number if the current is increased.
— (B) concentrate most just beyond the ends of the coil. — (D) enter the coil at the top.

Force on a Current

Experience shows that a current-carrying wire placed in a magnetic field is acted on by a sidewise force. As an example, suppose that in Fig. 137a, a wire extends in a direction perpendicular to the lines of the field of the magnet. Then, with the field and current as shown, the wire is found to be pushed to the right. The three directions—current, field and force—are mutually perpendicular, like the three edges of a brick that go out from a corner. This mechanical effect can be thought of as the action of the field of the magnet on the field produced by the current in the wire, and the idea of lines of force will give its direction. In Fig. 137b both the lines of the mag-

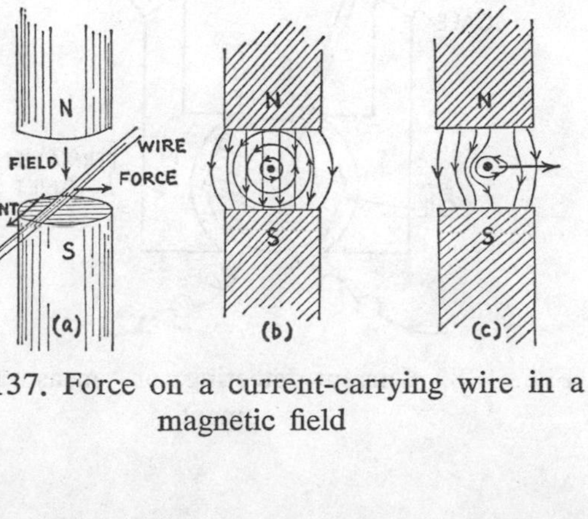

Fig. 137. Force on a current-carrying wire in a magnetic field

net's field and those of the current in the wire have been drawn. But two sets of lines can always be combined into a single set, for at any point the two forces themselves can be combined into a single resultant. At any point to the right of the wire the two fields are in opposite directions, and so partially cancel; to the left of the wire the two are in the same direction and reinforce each other. The combined field is shown in (c). Remembering that the lines tend to act like stretched bands, the effect of a field of this shape would be to force the wire over to the right, as shown.

Moving-Coil Meters

The commonest forms of ammeters and voltmeters operate on the basis of the forces acting on current-carrying wires in a magnetic field. The field is usually that of a strong permanent magnet, and the current to be measured is passed through a rectangular coil mounted on good bearings (Fig. 138). A stationary soft-iron core inside the coil acts to concentrate the field. When current flows in the coil, the action of each wire that extends in the direction perpendicular to the page is like that described above, and the net effect is to turn the coil in one direction on its axis. This turning is opposed by a pair of hair springs, and since the magnetic forces are proportional to the current, the amount that the coil turns will be a measure of this current.

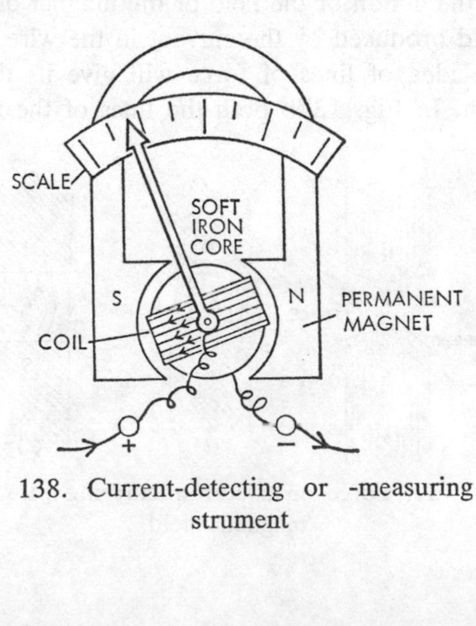

Fig. 138. Current-detecting or -measuring instrument

If such an instrument is to be an ammeter, the coil is connected as in Fig. 139a and most of the main current in the circuit bypasses the coil and goes through the low-resistance shunt. But a definite fraction will go through the coil, and the scale can be marked to read directly the total current passing through the meter. On the other hand, if the instrument is to be a voltmeter, it must have a high resistance, so that the current it draws is not appreciable. In this case a stationary coil of high resistance is connected in series with the moving coil (Fig. 139b). The movement of the coil is determined, as above, by the current flowing in it. By Ohm's law, this is proportional to the applied PD, and so the scale can be marked directly in volts. Moving-coil instruments can be made sensitive enough to respond to currents as small as a hundred-billionth of an ampere.

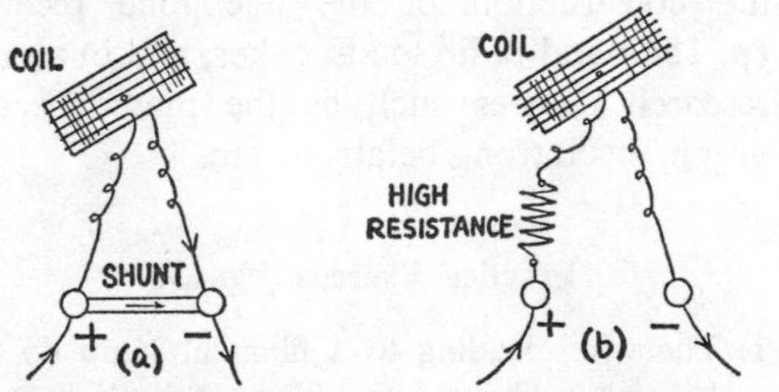

Fig. 139. Moving-coil meters

EXPERIMENT 52: Make a simple current-indicating instrument having a fixed coil and a moving needle. Wind about 25 turns of bell wire on a small glass or bottle, leaving about a foot of straight wire at each end. Slip the windings off, tape them together and mount the coil in an upright position on a piece of wood (Fig. 140). Place a pocket compass opposite the center of the coil and set the arrangement in a north-south direction, so that the face of the coil is parallel to the compass needle. When the coil is connected to a dry cell the flow of current will be indicated by the swinging aside of the needle. Reversing the battery connections makes the needle swing the other way. Check the coil rule for this case. Save the set-up for use in Experiment 53 (p. 153).

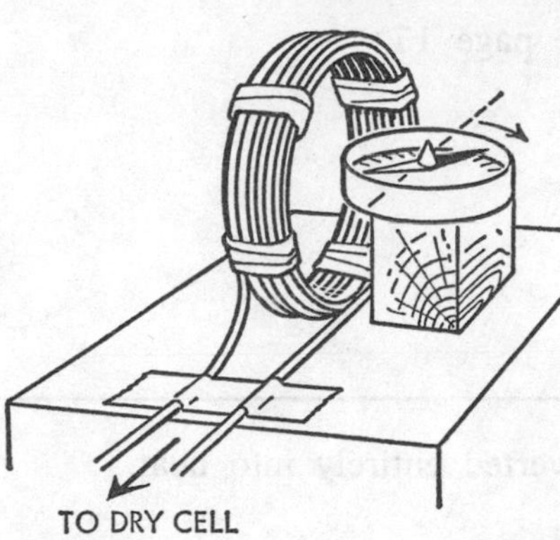

Fig. 140. Homemade current-indicating instrument

Motors

If a current-carrying coil is allowed to turn freely in a magnetic field as in the current meters described above, it will acquire kinetic energy. If this turning could be made to continue we would have a steady conversion of electrical into mechanical energy. Any device for doing this is called an electric **motor.** The operating principle of a motor that uses steady currents is shown in Fig. 141a. For simplicity, suppose the coil consists of only a single loop. If continuous turning is to take place, the current can no longer be led into and out of the coil by fixed wires; instead, this is done through a split ring, called a **commutator,** on which sliding contacts **(brushes)** bear. When the current is going through the loop in the direction shown in the figure, the loop will turn until its plane is vertical. At that moment, however, the current through the loop is automatically reversed by the switching around of connections as the commutator gaps pass the brushes. This reversal lets the coil make another half turn, when reversal occurs again, etc., with the result that the coil turns continuously in one direction.

A practical motor, such as the "starter" of an automobile engine or the motor of a battery-operated appliance, differs in design from the simple device just described. The single loop is replaced by a set of separate coils wound into recesses spaced around the curved surface of a soft-iron core, and the commutator has two opposite segments for each coil. The field magnet is usually an electromagnet, and all or part of the current supplied to the motor is passed through its windings (Fig. 141b).

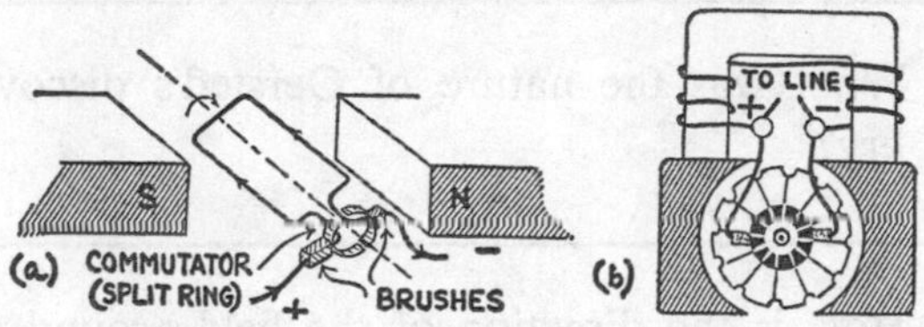

Fig. 141. Principle of the steady-current electric motor

Commercial motors convert about three-quarters of the electrical energy supplied to them into mechanical work. They vary in size from those of household devices (a small fraction of a horsepower) to the ones installed in electric locomotives and in electrically-propelled ships, which may be rated at many thousands of horsepower.

Practice Exercise No. 37

1. Apply the coil rule to Fig. 138 and check the indicated direction of motion of the coil.
2. Two current-carrying wires are side by side a short distance apart. What effect do they have on each other? (HINT: Either current can be considered to be in the magnetic field due to the other). Make a sketch showing the direction of the force on each wire (a) when the two currents are in the same direction and (b) when opposite.
3. If an ammeter whose coil has a resistance of 0.09 ohm is used with a shunt of resistance 0.01 ohm, what current actually will flow through the coil when 10 amp flows into the instrument?
4. If a voltmeter has a coil of resistance 0.1 ohm and a series resistor of 500 ohms, what will be the PD across the coil itself when the instrument is connected to the terminals of a 10-volt battery?
5. What is the effect, if any, on the direction of rotation of the motor diagrammed in Fig. 141, of reversing the connections to the line?

SUMMARY *Instructions:* (see page 17)

1. In a circuit containing only pure resistive elements (no motors, electrolytic cells, etc.), what becomes of all the energy originally supplied by the battery?	
2. What was the nature of Oersted's discovery?	It is converted entirely into heat.
3. How is the direction of the field around a straight wire found?	An electric current gives rise to a magnetic field in its neighborhood.
4. Define a) solenoid; b) electromagnet.	By using the right hand wire rule: Grasp the wire with the right hand, the thumb extended in the direction of the (conventional) current. Then the fingers encircle the wire in the sense of the magnetic lines of force.
5. What kind of mechanical effect appears when current is passed through a straight wire that extends perpendicular to the lines of force of a uniform magnetic field?	a) A spiral, or helical coil; b) A coil equipped with a soft-iron core for increasing the strength of the magnetic field within it.
6. In a moving-coil electrical instrument, what is the difference in the way the coil is connected to the circuit if it is to serve as a) an ammeter, or b) a voltmeter?	The wire is acted upon by a force whose line of action is perpendicular to both the wire and the direction of the field.
7. In general terms, what is an electric motor?	a) A low-resistance shunt is connected across the coil itself; b) A high-resistance unit is connected in series with the coil.
8. In a steady-current motor, how is continued rotation in one direction achieved?	A device for changing electrical energy into mechanical energy.
	By the use of a commutator and brushes, which automatically reverse the direction of the current through the coils every half turn.

Chapter XIX

INDUCED CURRENTS

Following Oersted's discovery that magnetism could be produced by electricity, many scientists looked for the reverse effect—the possible production of electric currents by means of magnetism. This was accomplished almost at the same time by Joseph Henry in the United States and by Michael Faraday in England. Their discovery is the basis of the electric generator, the transformer, and other devices which for the first time made the commercial development of electricity possible about a century ago. The fundamental discoveries and some of their applications will now be described.

FARADAY'S EXPERIMENTS

In one of Faraday's experiments he connected a coil directly to a meter, as in Fig. 142, and found that when one pole of a bar magnet was quickly moved toward the coil a momentary current was registered by the meter. When the magnet was jerked away, there was again a brief current, but in the opposite direction. As long as the magnet was held still in any position, no current was observed. The magnitude of the current was found to increase with the strength of the magnet, with its speed of motion and with the number of turns of wire on the coil.

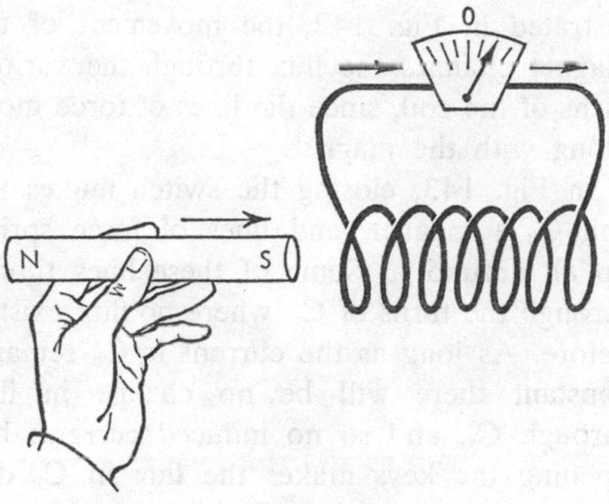

Fig. 142. Faraday's experiment

In another experiment, it was found that a meter connected directly to a coil showed current at the instant that a current was started or stopped in an entirely separate circuit nearby. Thus, in Fig. 143, when the key is closed in the **primary circuit** containing the coil C_p, a momentary "kick" of current is registered by the meter in the nearby **secondary circuit** containing the coil C_s. With a steady current flowing in the primary, nothing further happens, but now, if the key is opened, there is a momentary impulse of current in the secondary, *opposite* in direction to the original current.

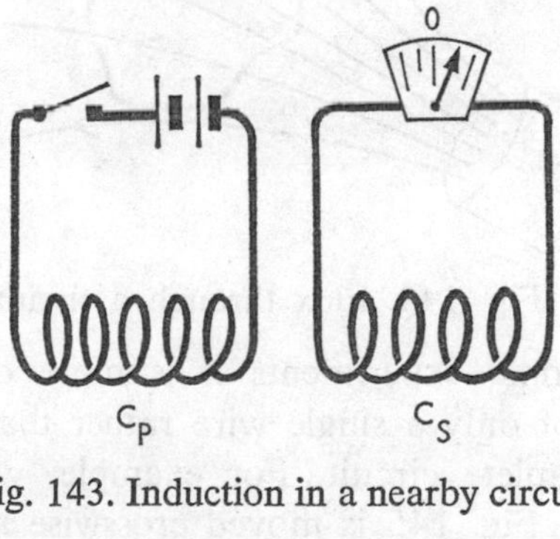

Fig. 143. Induction in a nearby circuit

ELECTROMAGNETIC INDUCTION

In all such experiments, where currents arise through the use of magnets and coils, they are said to be produced by **electromagnetic induction.** Faraday was able to find a simple way of describing the general conditions under which this happens. First, consider what is meant by **magnetic flux.** This is merely a convenient name for the **total number of lines of force** that pass through any closed loop located in a magnetic field (Fig. 144). In every one of the experiments in which a current is induced in a coil it is found that there is a **change of the flux** through it. For instance, in the experiment illustrated in Fig. 142, the movement of the magnet changes the flux through the various turns of the coil, since the lines of force move along with the magnet.

In Fig. 143, closing the switch makes the coil C_p a magnet, and lines of force spring up all around it. Some of these lines thread through the turns of C_s, where no flux existed before. As long as the current in C_p remains constant there will be no change in flux through C_s, and so no induced current; but opening the keys makes the flux in C_p disappear, meaning that the flux through C_s *changes,* and there is again an induced current.

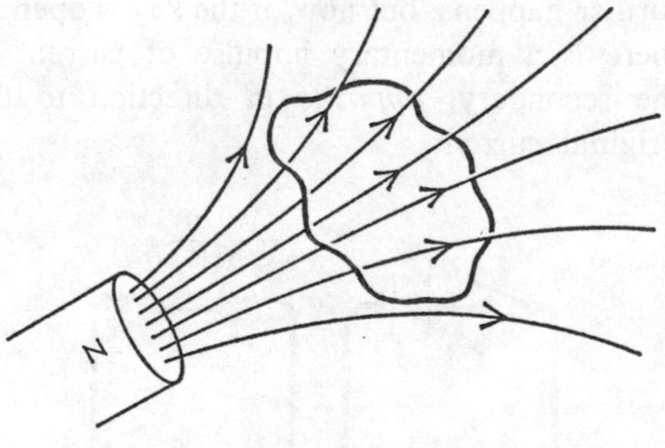

Fig. 144. Flux through a circuit

In some experiments it is more direct to think of only a single wire rather than a coil or complete circuit. For example, when the wire in Fig. 145 is moved crosswise near one pole of a stationary magnet, it can be shown that a PD exists between the ends of the wire. If the wire is connected into a complete circuit, the resulting current will be registered on a meter. It is convenient to think of the current in this instance as being due to the **cutting of lines of force** by the wire.

It is still true, of course, that the flux through this circuit is changed by the motion of the wire, and that this flux change is the cause of the induced current.

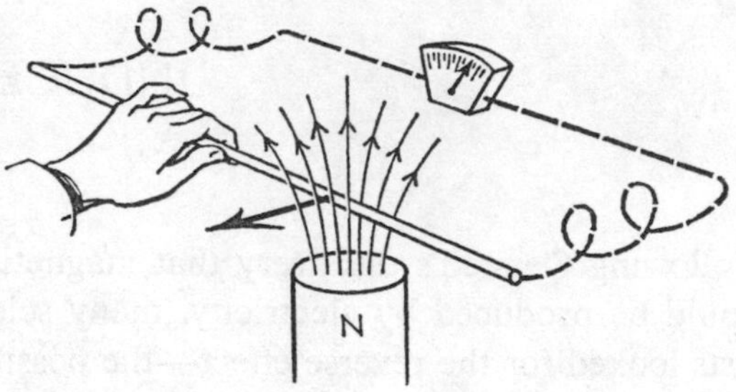

Fig. 145. Cutting lines of magnetic force by a conductor

LENZ'S LAW

In describing Faraday's experiments it was pointed out that there is a definite relation between the direction of the induced current and the direction of the action that causes it. Consider the experiment of Fig. 142. If the magnet is pushed toward the end of the coil, the flux through the turns increases and a current is induced in it. This current makes the coil magnetic. Suppose the direction of the induced current is such that the upper end of the coil becomes an *S* pole. Then the approach of the bar magnet will be helped along by the attraction between the *S* pole of the coil and the *N* pole of the bar. It would then be unnecessary to continue to push the bar magnet into the coil; the motion would reinforce itself, and unlimited amounts of mechanical as well as electrical energy would be produced without expending any further effort. By the Conservation of Energy (p. 77), we know that this does not happen and so the top end of the coil must, instead, become an *N* pole, whose repulsion would *oppose* the movement of the bar magnet. Similarly, when the magnet is pulled away from the coil, the induced current must be in the opposite direction, making the top end of the coil an *S* pole whose attraction opposes the removal of the bar. Experience bears these facts out. **The di-**

rection of an induced current is always such that its magnetic field opposes the operation that causes it. This generalization is called **Lenz's Law,** after its discoverer.

EXPERIMENT 53: Observe induced currents, using the meter you made for Experiment 52 (p. 148). Make a small coil of about 20 turns of bell wire and connect it to the coil of the meter by wires about a yard long. Thrust one pole of a bar magnet rapidly into the coil and verify the creation of a momentary current in the motor. Withdraw the magnet quickly and see if there is a current in the opposite direction. Trace the directions of the windings of the two coils and make use of the coil rule (p. 146) to see if you can check Lenz's Law for each of the above cases. Save the entire set-up for the next experiment.

Practice Exercise No. 38

1. A closed wire hoop is slid around in various directions while lying flat on a table located in a uniform vertical magnetic field. Is any current induced in the hoop? Explain.
2. Feeble induced voltages, due to motion in the earth's magnetic field, are to be expected in the axles of a moving railroad car. If a train is moving northward, in what direction will the induced voltage be?
3. In Experiment 53, would it make any difference if the magnet were held stationary and the coil moved toward and away from it?
4. If all other conditions were kept constant, how would the induced voltage at any stage of Experiment 53 be changed if the coil had 40 turns instead of 20?

GENERATORS

The induced currents that Henry and Faraday were able to produce in their experiments were feeble and temporary. The utilization of the principle of electromagnetic induction on a practical scale was realized only when it was found possible to construct continuously operating **generators.** As in the electric motor, the essential parts of a generator are a coil, a magnetic field in which the coil can be rotated, and some means for connecting the coil to the outside circuit. In fact, with slight adjustments, the same machine may be used either as a motor or a generator: If a current from some outside source is passed into the coil, it rotates and acts like a motor; if the coil is mechanically turned, as by a steam engine or water turbine, an induced current results and the machine becomes a generator.

Fig. 146 shows several positions of a coil that is made to turn in a magnetic field. Lenz's Law will show how the induced voltage changes as the coil is rotated. Starting with the plane of the coil perpendicular to the field (Fig. 146a), turning the coil onward in the direction shown must make its right-hand face an *N* pole and the other an *S* pole, in order that the forces between the poles of the coil and the poles of the field magnet should act to *hinder* the motions. The coil rule then shows that the direction of the induced voltage (or the current it gives rise to) will be as indicated by the arrows. By the time the coil has turned through a right angle (as in sketch b), the voltage has increased to its maximum value because the horizontal wires of the coils have been cutting more and more squarely across the lines of force. As the coil now approaches position (c), the voltage falls again to low values, and when it passes this place the voltage actually *reverses.* During the next quarter turn the voltage gets larger and larger in this reverse direction, and in the final quarter turn it lapses back to zero. Then the whole cycle of events repeats.

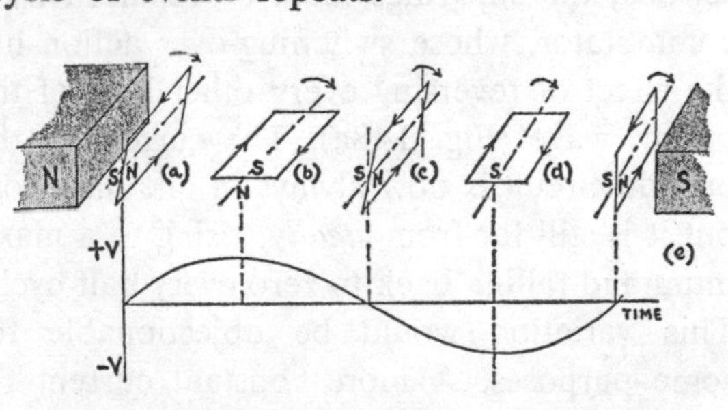

Fig. 146. Voltage induced in a rotating coil

The voltage graph at the bottom of the diagram shows that the voltage is **alternating**—that is, it goes first in one direction, then in the opposite. If now, the coil is connected to an outside circuit by means of **slip rings** and brushes (Fig. 147), the current furnished to this circuit will be an **alternating current** (AC). The number of complete cycles per second will be the same as the number of rotations per second of the coil. Thus an alternating current is the kind that naturally results from the continued turning of a coil in a fixed magnetic field.

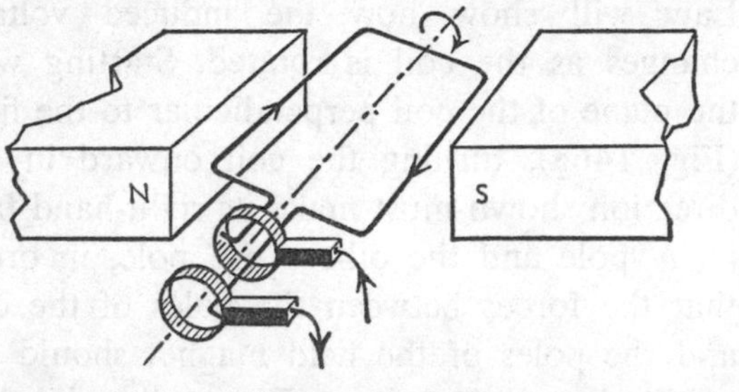

Fig. 147. An AC generator (schematic)

In all generators except very small ones the field magnets are electromagnets rather than permanent ones.

Generating DC

Alternating currents are perfectly satisfactory for some purposes, such as heating and lighting, but unsuitable for others, such as electroplating or charging storage batteries. For these uses, **direct current** (DC), which flows always in one direction, is required. To get DC from a generator of the kind described, the slip rings must be replaced by a commutator, whose switching-over action has the effect of reversing every other loop of the output wave (Fig. 148a). The current in the outside circuit is now always in one direction, but it is still far from *steady*, rising to a maximum and falling back to zero every half cycle. This variation would be objectionable for some purposes. A more constant current results if, instead of having only a single coil, the rotating part of the generator is wound with several coils set at various angles with each other. Then the output of each coil reaches its maximum when the others are at intermediate positions, and the combined output current shows relatively little variation. In Fig. 148b the effect of adding the outputs of three equally-spaced coils is shown. With a larger number of coils, hardly any "ripple" would remain.

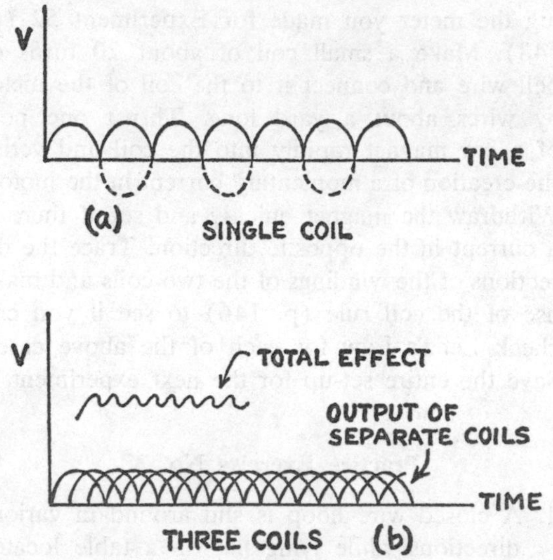

Fig. 148. Multiple coils make the output current steadier

Back Voltage

When an electric motor is in operation its rotating windings cut the lines of force of the field magnet, and so the motor will at the same time act as a generator. The direction of the induced voltage will be opposite to the PD that supplies current to the motor, and so is called **back voltage.** The back voltage increases with the speed of rotation, and the difference between the applied PD and the back voltage at any time determines how much current actually enters the motor. When a motor is just starting up, its back voltage will be very small because the rotation is slow. Without this back voltage, a large current would surge through the windings and perhaps burn them out. For this reason a **starting box,** consisting of a chain of several resistors (Fig. 149), is placed in series with the motor. As the motor picks up speed and its back voltage comes up to the operating value these protective resistors are cut out of the circuit one after another until, finally, the full line voltage is applied to the motor.

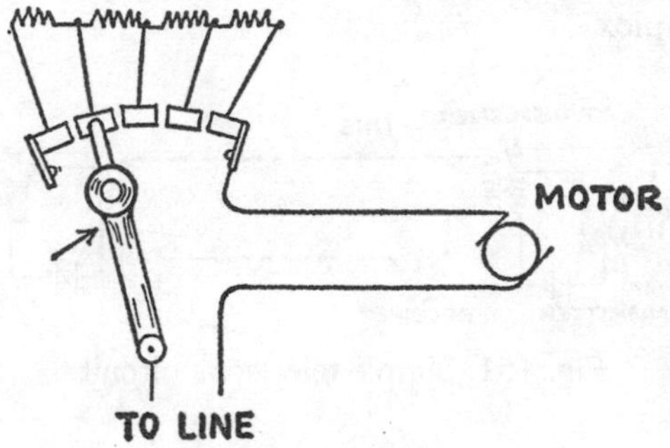

Fig. 149. A starting box

THE TRANSFORMER

One of the reasons for the widespread use of alternating current is the fact that voltage and current values may be readily and efficiently changed by the use of a device called the **transformer.** In principle, the pair of coils in Fig. 143, p. 151, is a transformer. Any change in the current in the primary coil induces a voltage in the secondary. If an alternating current is supplied to the primary there will be a corresponding variation of magnetic flux through the secondary. As a result, an alternating current of the same frequency will be induced in the secondary. In this country, the frequency used on domestic power lines is 60 **cycles**—that is, the current makes 60 complete vibrations per second.

Simple "air-cored" transformers are used in radio and TV circuits, but for power transmission the two coils are wound on a closed ring of special steel which increases and concentrates the magnetic flux (Fig. 150). With this design the flux at any time is the same for all turns, and the result is that the voltages in the two coils are proportional to the number of turns, or

$$\frac{V_s}{V_p} = \frac{n_s}{n_p}$$

If there are more turns in the secondary than in the primary, the voltage of the secondary will be greater than the primary voltage and the device is called a "step-up" transformer; if the other way around, a "step-down" transformer.

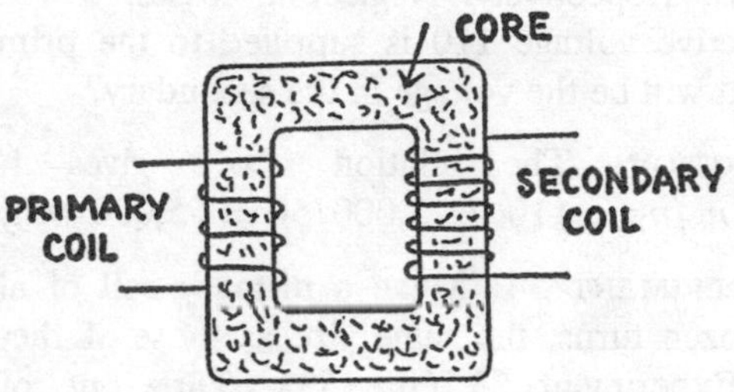

Fig. 150. The transformer (schematic)

When electric power is to be used at great distance from the generator it is transmitted in the form of high voltage AC, for the following reason: According to p. 144, the heat loss in a line is proportional to I^2R, so if the losses are to be reduced the current should be as small as possible. With a given power, this means making the voltage high, since $P = IV$. These current and voltage changes can be made economically only through the use of AC, which permits the use of transformers. In a power plant the generator voltage may be about 10,000. A transformer steps it up to perhaps 230,000 and puts it on the transmission line. At the edge of a city, a step-down transformer may reduce the PD to about 2,300 and small step-down transformers located on power-line poles throughout the city then reduce it to a safe value of about 110 volts for use in homes.

There are no moving parts in a transformer, and when properly designed the energy losses may be as low as 2 per cent. This means that, practically, the same amount of power is developed in each coil. As in the case of direct currents, the power developed in either one is given by current multiplied by voltage, so that $I_P V_P = I_S V_S$, or $I_S/I_P = V_P/V_S$. Combining with the relation above, we have

$$\frac{I_S}{I_P} = \frac{n_P}{n_S},$$

so that the currents in the two coils are inversely proportional to the number of turns in each.

EXAMPLE 1: The primary and secondary coils of a power-line transformer have 50 and 25,000 turns, respectively. Neglecting losses, if AC of effective voltage 110 is supplied to the primary, what will be the voltage in the secondary?

SOLUTION: The relation above gives $V_S = V_P\ n_S/n_P = 110 \times 25{,}000/50 = 55{,}000$ volts.

EXPERIMENT 54: Make a primary coil of about a dozen turns, the same size as those of the coil in Experiment 53 (p. 153). Tape one of its lead wires to the bottom terminal of a flashlight cell. Lay this coil on top of the one used in the last experiment, which now becomes the secondary coil of your experimental transformer. Connect the secondary to your current meter, as in the last experiment. Touch the other lead wire of the primary to the top terminal of the cell and observe the momentary kick of the meter. Take the wire away and notice that there is a kick in the opposite direction. Insert an iron core, consisting of a dozen large nails taped together, into the pair of coils and compare the size of the meter indications with the previous ones.

THE TELEPHONE

Basically, the telephone consists of a **transmitter** for changing sound vibrations into similar variations of an electric current and a **receiver** for changing these currents back into audible sounds at the far end of the line. The operation of the usual carbon-button transmitter is based on the fact that loosely packed carbon granules have less electrical resistance when pressure is applied to them. Sound waves hitting a thin metal diaphragm (Fig. 151) change the pressure on the capsule of carbon granules and cause corresponding changes in the current sent through it by a battery. These variations pass through a transformer, go over the line to a transformer at the other station and are duplicated in the windings of the receiver. This makes the soft-iron diaphragm vibrate to give a fair reproduction of the original sound. On long lines, repeating devices boost the energy of the impulses as they are transferred from one section of line to the next. The equipment required for modern telephony is extremely complex.

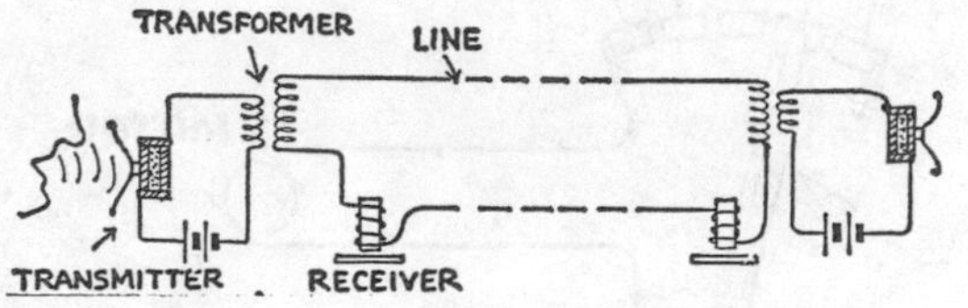

Fig. 151. Simple telephone circuit

Other Sound Reproducers

In all forms of electrical sound-reproducing and recording apparatus, as in the telephone, the first step in the process is the conversion of sound vibrations into variations of an electric current. In a **tape-recorder,** a plastic tape coated with magnetic oxide passes beneath the core of a coil that carries the varying "voice current" and so becomes permanently magnetized in the pattern of the original sound waves. To reproduce the sound, the tape is run past another coil and the magnetic pattern is changed by induction into a variable current once more. This current is amplified and led into a loudspeaker to convert it back into sound. The magnetic pattern impressed on a tape may be "erased" by passing it between the poles of a magnet, after which the tape may be re-used.

The Hammond **electric organ** uses electromagnetic induction to produce tones closely resembling those of a pipe organ. A set of tone wheels, one for each note, is mounted on a rotating shaft. Each wheel, made of magnetic material, has a certain number of evenly-spaced bumps or projections on its edge. Near the rim of each wheel is mounted a small magnet with a coil wound on it. The regularly-passing bumps disturb the magnetic field and so induce currents of the same frequency in the coil. These currents are amplified and fed into a speaker in the usual way.

EDDY CURRENTS

These are induced currents arising in the metal parts of electrical machinery. They flow in small closed paths, and their energy comes at the expense of the electrical energy in the main circuits. These losses are minimized in transformers, for instance, by making the core out of many separate strips of iron rather than in one piece. This makes it difficult for eddy currents to flow. On the other hand, eddy currents are useful in heating metal parts that are difficult to reach—for example, those inside a vacuum tube. The tube is placed inside a coil carrying a strong alternating current. Only the metal parts, which are conducting, will be heated, the glass remaining unaffected. Induction heating has many industrial applications.

If a sheet of conducting material is moved rapidly past the pole of a magnet, the eddy currents produced will, by Lenz's Law, be in such a direction that their magnetic effect tends to hold back the moving body. This **eddy current drag** is used as a sort of flexible coupling for turning the needle on the speedometer of a car, and as a speed regulator in the watt-hour meters used for measuring the electrical energy used in the home.

Most electric motors intended for use on AC are **induction motors.** They are not constructed like the machines described in the previous chapter. Instead, there is a set of stationary field coils, producing what amounts to a **rotating magnetic field.** The mechanically rotating part has no current lending to it, but consists merely of a cage of heavy copper bars. Eddy currents induced in these bars by the rotating field act to drag the cage around, thus producing rotation of the cage.

Practice Exercise No. 39

1. What is the effect on the voltage delivered if the speed of rotation of a generator is increased?
2. Find the ratio of the number of turns in the primary to the number in the secondary of a toy transformer that steps down the 110-volt house current to 22 volts for operating a model electric railroad.
3. In a **spot welder,** where very large currents are needed for producing the required heat, a transformer having a 100-turn primary and a 2-turn secondary is used. If a current of 1 amp is admitted to the primary, what current can be obtained from the secondary?
4. A generator turns very easily when no current is being drawn from it, but becomes very hard to turn as soon as the switch connecting it to the outside circuit is closed. Explain.
5. The rotating coils of a motor that is used on a 50-volt line have a total resistance of 2 ohms. What current flows in them when the back voltage of the motor amounts to 45 volts? If connected directly to the line while standing still, how large a current would flow in the windings? What might then happen?

SUMMARY *Instructions:* (see page 17)

1. Oersted's discovery and that of Henry and Faraday are said to be reciprocal or complementary in nature. Explain what this means.

2. What is meant by electromagnetic induction?

The first involves the production of magnetism by means of electricity; the other, the production of electric currents by means of magnetism.

3. State Lenz's Law.

The production of a current in a circuit when the magnetic flux through the circuit changes.

4. What kind of current will be induced in a simple, rectangular coil rotating in a uniform magnetic field?

The direction of an induced current is always such that its magnetic field opposes the operation that causes it.

5. What is meant by the back voltage of an electric motor?

An alternating current (AC).

6. Describe, basically, the nature of an electrical transformer.

The induced voltage resulting from the fact that the rotating coils act as a generator. This voltage is in a direction opposing the applied voltage.

7. In a closed-core transformer, in which the flux in both coils may be assumed the same, what is the relation between the voltages in the two coils at any time?

A pair of coils so positioned that magnetic flux produced by the current in one threads through the other.

8. What are eddy currents?

Voltages are directly proportional to the respective numbers of turns of wire:
$$V_s/V_p = n_s/n_p.$$

Induced currents, flowing in small closed paths, in any conducting material placed in a varying magnetic field.

SECTION SEVEN

ELECTRONICS AND NUCLEAR PHYSICS

Chapter XX

ELECTRONICS

Although the electron was discovered hardly more than half a century ago, the consequences have been tremendous in their effect on the development of pure and applied science and especially on the technique of communication. The following sections outline the circumstances of this discovery and trace the development of some of its main applications.

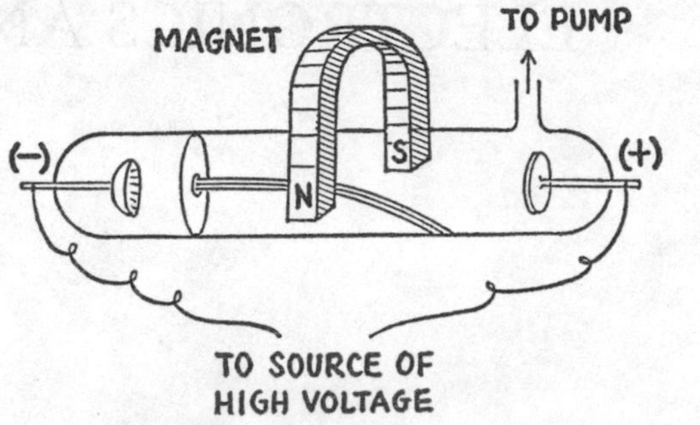

Fig. 152. Cathode rays bend aside in a magnetic field

CATHODE RAYS

The early experiments that led to the identification of the electron were done nearly a century ago by passing high-voltage direct current through a tube containing air at very low pressure. When the pressure of the gas is reduced to about 1/100,000 of normal atmospheric, the glow that existed previously in the gas (p. 100) disappears, and instead the glass of the tube begins to glow with a greenish light. This is found to be caused by something that appears to come out of the negative terminal in straight lines. The early experimenters called these emanations **cathode rays.** Besides causing fluorescence in the glass, these rays were found to deliver energy by impact, and it was concluded that they consist of streams of particles. Also, they could be bent aside by applying a magnetic field (Fig. 152). This could happen only if the rays were equivalent to an electric current, and by applying the right hand wire rule, it was seen that they must consist of negatively charged particles. This is also what would be expected from the fact that they originate at the negative terminal of the tube.

The English experimenter J. J. Thomson constructed a tube in which the rays could be bent by electric as well as magnetic fields and found that each particle could be assumed to carry an amount of charge equal to that on a hydrogen ion in solution (p. 137). The mass of each cathode ray particle turned out to be much smaller than that of any known atom —about 1/1840 of the mass of a hydrogen atom. No matter what gas was used in the tube or what metal the terminals were made of, these values always turned out the same. Thomson concluded that these small, subatomic particles were part of every atom. They were named **electrons.** Later, other workers were able to experiment with electrons and obtained better measurements of their charge and mass. Thus it is established that **cathode rays consist of electrons,** each one of which carries a charge of negative electricity. These electrons play a fundamental part in the structure of the atom. No particle that is lighter than an electron or that carries less charge has ever been shown to exist.

PRODUCTION OF X RAYS

Under the influence of the electric field in a tube of the kind described, electrons attain very high speeds since they travel almost without hindrance through the high vacuum. The German experimenter Röntgen found that X rays were produced when a cathode ray beam struck the end of the tube. X rays, which are electromagnetic waves, have already been described to some extent on p. 120. In a modern X-ray tube, the vacuum is higher than in a cathode ray tube and the electron stream is allowed to hit a metal "target" rather than the glass (Fig. 153). Theory shows that the X rays are produced by the sudden stopping of the electrons as they hit the target. The frequency of the rays—and so their penetrating power—increases with the PD applied to the tube.

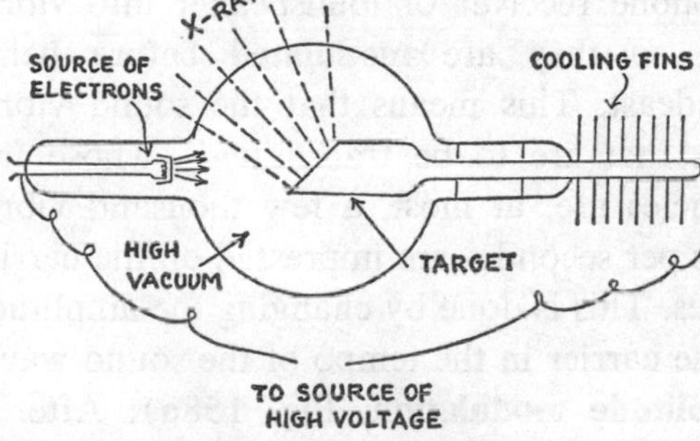

Fig. 153. X-ray tube

Special medical X-ray tubes using voltages up to 2 million are in use, but it is not feasible to go much higher. A new type of machine for speeding up electrons for the generation of X rays was devised a few years ago by the American physicist D. W. Kerst. In place of using high voltages, this device, called a **betatron** (pronounced BAY-ta-tron), gives energy to the electrons by means of a changing magnetic field. The electrons are whirled in a circular path in a large doughnut-shaped vacuum tube. After several hundred thousand revolutions the electrons, now moving almost with the speed of light, are allowed to strike a target, producing X rays. Betatrons are used in physics research as well as in medicine.

ELECTRON TUBES

When a piece of metal is placed in a vacuum and heated, some of the free electrons get speeds high enough to enable them to break away and form a cloud near the surface. This "boiling-out" of electrons from a metal is called **thermionic emission.*** Edison noticed this effect when he was experimenting with filament lamps. Later, Fleming, in England, showed that electrons were sent out from the hot filament and could be attracted to a positively-charged plate nearby. A vacuum tube containing a heated emitter and a plate is called a **diode;** it can be used to **rectify** an alternating current—that is, change it to DC.

In Fig. 154, the filament is heated in the usual way by passing a current through it. If a source of alternating voltage is connected between filament and plate, electrons will move from filament to plate whenever the plate is positive with respect to the filament, but not when the PD is the other way around. In this way an alternating voltage that is put on the tube results in an interrupted DC in the outside circuit. By using two diodes, both loops of the AC cycle can be used, and by passing the output through suitable circuits consisting of coils and capacitors, the pulsations can be

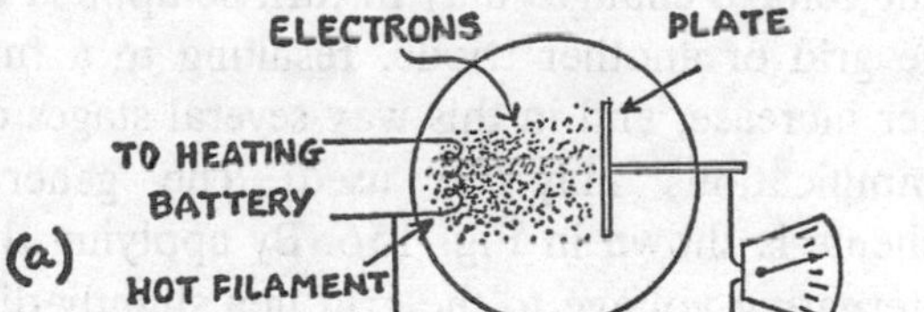

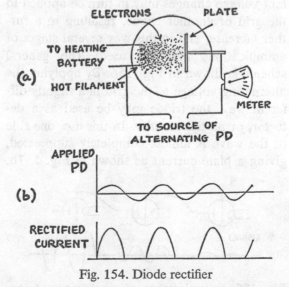

Fig. 154. Diode rectifier

* Other suitable emitters, such as certain metallic oxides, are used in practice.

smoothed out almost completely. Vacuum tube rectifiers are used to charge batteries from an AC line and to furnish direct voltages for operating X-ray tubes, radio sets, etc.

Shortly after the beginning of this century the American experimenter Lee De Forest made an important addition to the diode by inserting a wire mesh, or **grid,** between emitter and plate. The tube, consisting of emitter, grid and plate is called a **triode** (Fig. 155). With this arrangement it is necessary to apply only small PD's to the grid in order to get large changes in the electron current, so that the grid provides a sensitive control of this electron stream.

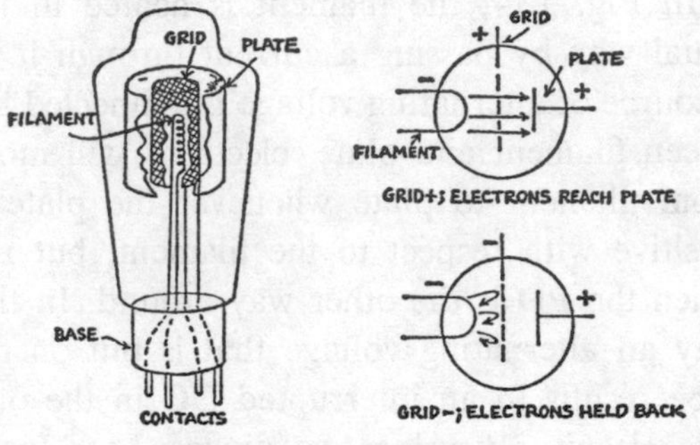

Fig. 155. The triode

A feeble alternating voltage can be greatly amplified in the way just described; the resultant voltage changes may in turn be applied to the grid of another triode, resulting in a further increase, and in this way several stages of amplifications may be used. The general scheme is shown in Fig. 156. By applying the alternating voltage to the grid in a slightly different way, the triode may be used as a **detector,** or partial rectifier. In this use, one side of the wave is almost completely suppressed, giving a plate current as shown in Fig. 157b.

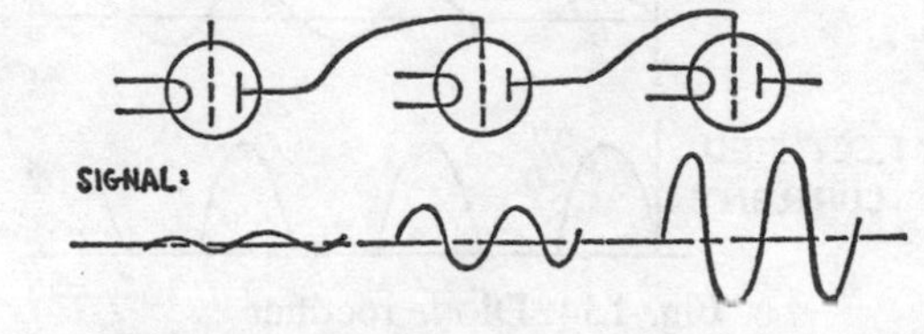

Fig. 156. Several stages of amplification (schematic)

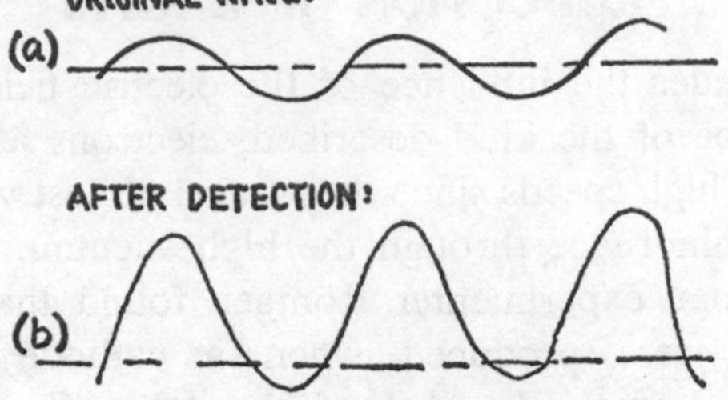

Fig. 157. Detector action

RADIO

The alternating voltage in question may be that induced in the collecting wire, or antenna, of a radio receiving set by electrical waves coming from a broadcasting station. Oscillations having frequencies of around a million per second are used. These **carrier waves** are too rapid to set the diaphragm of a telephone receiver or loudspeaker into vibration, so they are **modulated** before being broadcast. This means that the sound vibrations that are to be transmitted—whose frequencies are, at most, a few thousand vibrations per second—are impressed on the carrier waves. This is done by changing the amplitude of the carrier in the tempo of the sound waves **(amplitude modulation,** Fig. 158a). After it has been partially rectified as described above, the modulated wave is able to operate a loudspeaker to reproduce the original sound vibrations.

In the **frequency modulation** system, the carrier wave has a constant amplitude, but its *frequency* is changed according to the pattern of the sound waves (Fig. 158b). Advantages

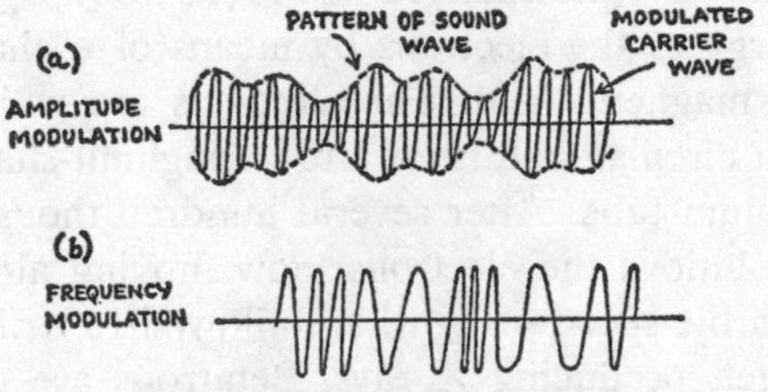

Fig. 158. Amplitude- and frequency modulation

of this scheme are the almost complete elimination of "static" and fading.

The triode serves a third purpose, that of an **oscillator,** in the sending circuit, where it acts as a valve that regulates the feeding of energy from a battery to the circuit. The frequency of the oscillations is fixed by the electrical constants of the circuit. A microphone changes the pattern of the sounds to be broadcast into a corresponding voltage pattern, as in the telephone. This signal is amplified and then combined with the carrier wave to give the modulated wave form described above. Some of the energy of the circuit is thrown out from the antenna into the surrounding space in the form of electromagnetic waves.

A diagram of a very simple receiving circuit is shown in Fig. 159. By tuning the circuit it can be made to respond by resonance (p. 92), to waves of a selected frequency coming from a given broadcasting station. The tuning is usually done by turning the knob of a variable capacitor (p. 133). The variations in potential of the grid cause the triode, acting as a detector, to send a signal current through the telephone receiver or loudspeaker, which reproduces the sound.

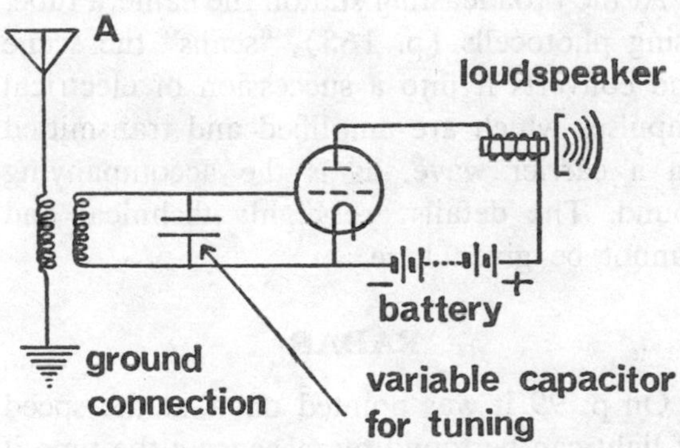

Fig. 159. Simple receiving circuit

EXPERIMENT 55: Get a discarded glass radio tube (a metal one will not be suitable). Wrap a cloth around the tube and carefully break the glass. Remove the cloth and break away enough of the remaining glass so that you can examine the metal parts to see how they are assembled. The source of electrons may be a small cylinder coated with special chemicals, heated by the filament inside it. Also, some tubes have one or two extra grids serving special purposes. Descriptions of the great variety of tubes made at the present time will be found in technical books or in the tube manuals issued by the manufacturers.

THE TRANSISTOR

The **transistor** is a comparatively recently-invented electronic device that will probably replace vacuum tubes for many purposes. Its operation depends on the motion of electrons in a small piece of silicon or germanium. These materials are typical **semiconductors,** intermediate in conductivity between good conductors and insulators.

A transistor requires no hot cathode or vacuum enclosure. In addition to its small size, it has the advantages over vacuum tubes of using much less power, developing practically no heat, and having no warm-up time. Transistors are increasingly taking the place of vacuum tubes in telephone circuits, electric phonographs, radio sets, hearing aids, etc.

Practice Exercise No. 40

1. The fact that cathode rays can be swerved aside by both electric and magnetic fields shows that they

— (A) are small magnets.
— (B) carry an electric charge.
— (C) are electromagnetic waves.
— (D) contain atoms.

2. A metal plate located near a hot filament will acquire a negative charge because

— (A) the plate gives positive atoms.
— (B) the filament gives off protons.
— (C) the plate loses electrons by thermionic emission.
— (D) the filament releases electrons.

3. The betatron is a device for

— (A) giving electrons high speeds.
— (B) rectifying A.C.
— (C) detecting weak radio signals.
— (D) charging storage batteries.

4. X rays are produced when electrons are

— (A) suddenly stopped.
— (B) sent through a wire.
— (C) neutralized.
— (D) made to leave a hot wire.

5. A vacuum tube that contains a filament, a grid and a plate is called a

— (A) diode.
— (B) X-ray tube.
— (C) cathode ray tube.
— (D) triode.

TELEVISION

The tube used to reproduce the picture in a TV receiver is a refinement of the apparatus used by Thomson in his experiments on cathode rays. Electrons from a hot filament (Fig. 160) are accelerated electrically and the narrow beam is made to pass between two pairs of plates. Voltages applied to one pair can deflect the beam vertically; to the other pair, horizontally. Because the electrons have small inertia and high speed they can respond immediately, and the path of the beam is marked by the luminous curve it traces on the fluorescent coating on the end of the tube. One pair of plates makes the beam move rapidly *across* the screen at regular intervals while the other jerks it *down* a short distance after each sweep, so that the path of the spot of light on the screen is like that followed by

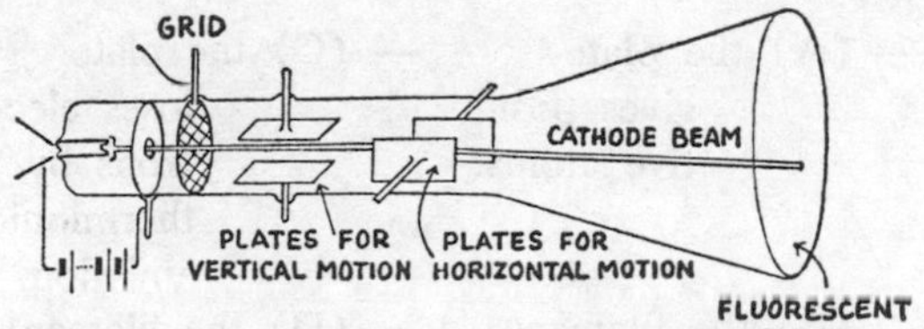

Fig. 160. Diagram of TV picture tube

the eyes in reading a book (Fig. 161). In this way a rectangle of light is "painted" on the end of the tube, all of this taking place in about 1/30 sec. But while it traces over the lines, the brightness of the spot is made to vary by the application of the incoming signal to the grid, and this reproduces the details of the picture. As in viewing motion pictures, the impression of each complete picture remains on the retina until the next picture is formed, giving the illusion of continuous motion.

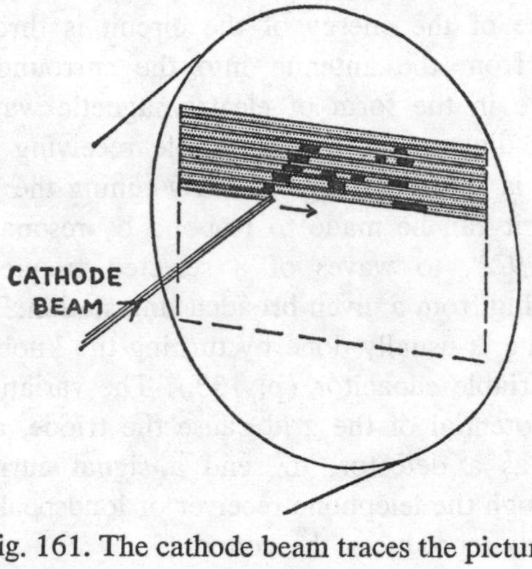

Fig. 161. The cathode beam traces the picture

At the broadcasting station the camera tube, using photocells (p. 165), "scans" the scene and converts it into a succession of electrical impulses which are amplified and transmitted on a carrier wave, as is the accompanying sound. The details are highly technical and cannot be given here.

RADAR

On p. 99 it was pointed out that the speed of light can be found by measuring the time it takes to travel a known distance. In principle, **radar** turns this method around and finds the distance of an object by determining the time it takes a radio signal (which, like light, travels with the speed *c* in empty space) to go there and back. The sending circuit sends out regular, short pulses, using electromagnetic waves only a few inches long. During the interval between pulses the device "listens" for reflections of these pulses from objects in the surroundings. The direct and reflected pulses are shown visually on the face of a picture tube, and observation of their distance apart gives the distance of the object directly. In another system, a rough actual picture of the territory surrounding the station is shown on the face of the tube. This gives the direction as well as the distance of each reflecting object.

Because the electric waves can penetrate fog, smoke and rain, radar has a number of important uses. It can locate and guide ships and planes in bad weather, and detect icebergs and ships at sea. Recently, astronomers found that they can use this method to track meteors high in the atmosphere. The movement of storm centers can be followed by radar, thus contributing to the prediction of weather conditions.

THE ELECTRON MICROSCOPE

Cathode rays coming from a point can be brought to a focus at another point by either electrostatic or magnetic means. A device for doing this is called an **clectron lens** because it does for cathode rays exactly what a glass lens does for light rays. A combination can be arranged to form an **electron microscope** (Fig. 162). The form and structure of objects placed in the path of the rays can be seen in the image formed on a fluorescent screen. Magnifications ten to a hundred times those of the best light microscopes can be attained, revealing the structure of viruses, crystals and even large molecules.

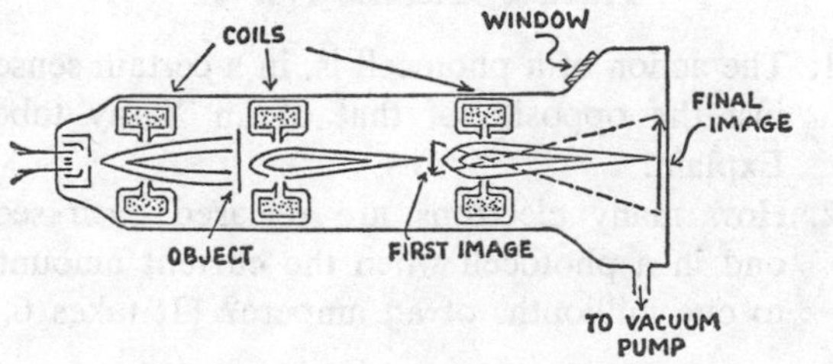

Fig. 162. Electron microscope

THE PHOTOELECTRIC EFFECT

In the previous sections you have seen how the release of electrons from a solid substance by heat is put to practical use. There is another way of freeing electrons in quantity, and that is by shining light on suitable materials. This process is called the **photoelectric effect.** The construction of a typical **photocell** is shown in Fig. 163. The inner coating may be a metal such as potassium. When light of suitable wavelength is allowed to fall on the coating, electrons immediately begin to stream out of the metal and can be attracted to the positive terminal, giving rise to a current in the outside circuit. The strength of this current is found to be proportional to the intensity of the incoming light, and this makes it possible to use a photocell as an illuminometer (p. 101) in photography, astronomy, etc.

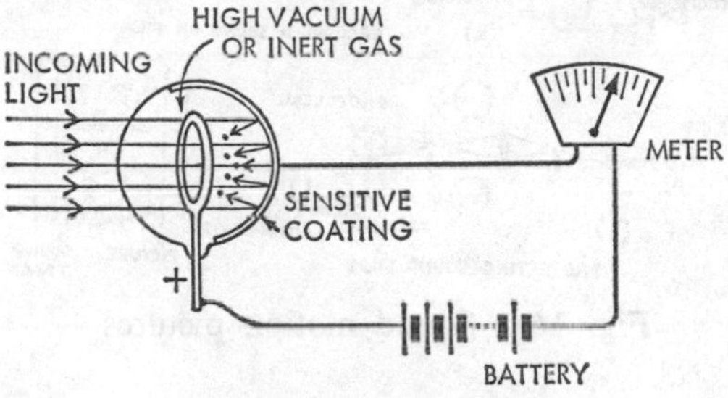

Fig. 163. Photocell

Other applications of the photoelectric effect, where it is used merely as a light-controlled relay, are numerous and familiar. By leading the amplified current into a suitable device, a cell may be made to operate a burglar alarm, door opener, smoke detector, sorting or counting mechanism, etc. The kind of cell used in most photographic light meters produces its own voltage and needs no battery. Such a **photronic cell** is made by depositing a layer of copper oxide on a copper plate, or a film of selenium metal on an iron plate. The two elements are connected directly to a sensitive meter whose scale is marked in illumination values.

In making **sound motion pictures,** a **sound track** is recorded photographically along the edge of the film to accompany the pictures. To do this, the sound is picked up by a microphone (Fig. 164a), the resulting current variations are amplified and applied to some type of light valve. This device, usually a metal slit whose width can be varied magnetically, controls the amount of light that falls on the moving film to form the sound track. Development converts this track into a succession of light and dark places corresponding to the sounds recorded. When the film is projected in a theater, the sound track controls the amount of light falling on a photocell (Fig. 164b), and the resultant current variations are amplified and fed into a speaker to reproduce the original sound.

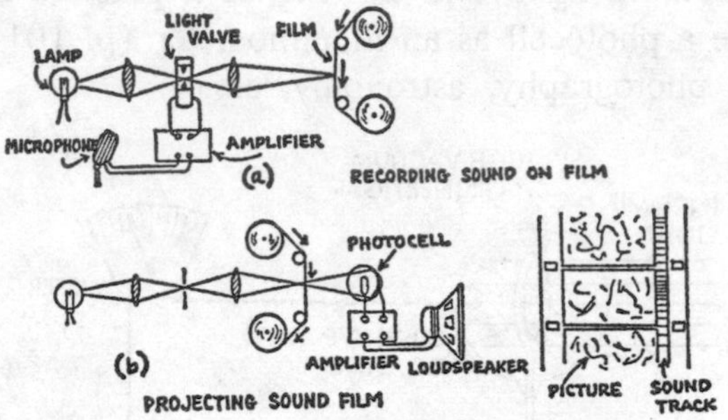

Fig. 164. Sound motion pictures

THE QUANTUM THEORY

Besides having useful practical applications, such as those described above, the photoelectric effect played an important part in the development of one of the outstanding ideas of modern physics—the **Quantum Theory.**

In all cases of energy transfer considered up to this point, it was quite naturally assumed that such processes are continuous—that is, it is always possible to measure out and transport any desired amount of energy, within available limits, just as one might measure out a quantity of liquid. But at the beginning of this century, the German physicist Max Planck found that a theoretical explanation of the radiation from a hot solid body could be worked out only by making the unusual assumption that the energy is given off in separate "chunks" which he called **quanta.** These quanta are not all of the same size; instead, **the amount of energy carried by each is proportional to the frequency of the radiation** in question. A single quantum of red light, for example, carries about 1/400 of a billionth of an erg of energy; a quantum of violet light, having about twice the frequency of red light, would carry twice as much.

The experimental facts about the photoelectric effect also remained unexplained until, a few years later, Einstein saw that this was another case where the quantum idea was called for.*

In the course of time other sub-atomic processes were found to require a quantum explanation, and the Quantum Theory has become an accepted part of modern science. But how can this idea be made to fit with the well-established Wave Theory of light, which says that radiation is a *continuous* process? The answer seems to be that *both* theories are needed to explain all that is known about radiation: Single quanta are so small that, as long as we deal with any ordinary amount of radiation, everything seems to be perfectly continuous, and the wave idea explains perfectly the passage of light through space. But when we consider what happens when radiant energy is given off or taken in by matter, we realize that this energy comes in very small but distinct bundles rather than as a steady flow. Einstein gave the name **photon** to a single quantum of radiant energy.

Practice Exercise No. 41

1. The action of a photocell is, in a certain sense, just the opposite of that of an X-ray tube. Explain.
2. How many electrons are released each second in a photocell when the current amounts to one millionths of an ampere? (It takes 6.3

* Most people, having heard only of Einstein's work on Relativity, are not aware that he was given the Nobel Prize, in 1921, largely for his work on photoelectricity.

billion billion electrons to carry one coulomb of charge.)

3. Make a diagram showing how to connect a lamp, a photocell, a relay, a battery and an alarm bell to act as a smoke detector.
4. An electron microscope forms the image of a virus at a magnification of 80,000. If the image measures 0.24 in. across, how big is the virus?
5. Which is the larger amount of energy, an X-ray quantum or a quantum of infra-red light? From the information given in Fig. 105, p. 120, what would be the approximate ratio of their energies?

SUMMARY *Instructions:* (see page 17)

1. In modern terminology, what are cathode rays?	
2. How does the mass of an electron compare with the masses of atoms?	Streams of fast electrons traveling through a vacuum.
3. Define thermionic emission.	It is only 1/1840 of the mass of the lightest atom—hydrogen.
4. What is a diode?	Ejection of electrons from a hot metal or other suitable emitter in a vacuum.
5. What are the principal parts of a triode?	A vacuum tube containing a heated emitter and a plate.
6. Describe the function of the grid.	It contains an emitter, a grid and a plate.
7. What is meant by modulation of a carrier wave used in radio transmission?	It controls the number of electrons that reach the plate.
8. What is meant by the photoelectric effect?	Changing either the amplitude or the frequency of the carrier wave in the pattern of the sound wave that is to be transmitted. This is called amplitude modulation (AM) or frequency modulation (FM), respectively.
9. State the basic idea of the Quantum Theory.	Emission of electrons from a material by incident radiation.
10. Are all quanta of energy the same size?	Whenever energy is given off or absorbed by matter, the energy comes in tiny bits called quanta.
	No. The energy of a quantum is directly proportional to the frequency of the radiation of which it is a part.

Chapter XXI

NUCLEAR PHYSICS

In the last chapter you saw how the discovery of the electron led to great advances in science and to astonishing technical developments. Electrons form the outer parts of atoms; however, until relatively recently very little was known about the **nucleus,** or innermost portion, of an atom. The rapid developments of the last half century, reaching a dramatic climax in the discovery of how to release "atomic" energy on a large scale, will be the subject of this final chapter.

POSITIVE RAYS; MASS SPECTRA

The nineteenth-century experimenters discovered cathode rays by observing what happened when a high voltage was applied to a tube containing a gas at very low pressure, as described on p. 160. Similar experiments proved to be the starting point in the search for knowledge about the atomic nucleus. At moderately low pressures, the left-hand part of the tube shown in Fig. 165 is filled with a soft glow; but, in addition, faintly luminous straight beams can be seen beyond the small holes in the negative terminal plate. They proved to be streams of positive ions—gas atoms which had lost one or more electrons after being hit by electrons or by other ions in the main discharge between the plates. These streams were called **positive rays.**

Thomson was able to identify the ions more exactly by bending the rays in electric and magnetic fields. He found that the positive charge on each ion was always a whole number of times the electron charge, never a fraction.

Among the ions he detected were singly-ionized hydrogen atoms (H^+), doubly-ionized

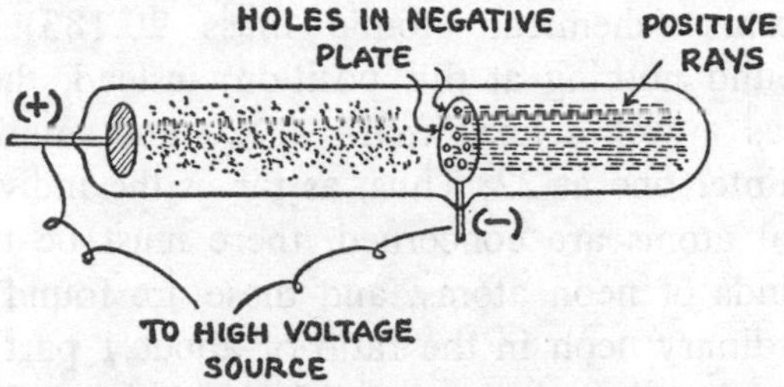

Fig. 165. Positive rays

oxygen atoms (O^{++}), singly-ionized carbon monoxide molecules (CO^+), etc. Here, in effect, was a method of identifying individual atoms and molecules. An instrument that does this is called a **mass spectrograph,** because it sorts out ions according to their different masses in a way that suggests the sorting-out of wavelengths of light by an optical spectrograph.

In principle, a mass spectrograph uses a strong magnetic field to bend the ion beam (Fig. 166). If the ions are all moving with a given speed, the amount that a given kind swerves aside will depend only on its charge and its mass. The charge carried will always be exactly 1, 2, 3 . . . times the electron charge, and so is easy to recognize. This means that each mass will fall at a definite point on

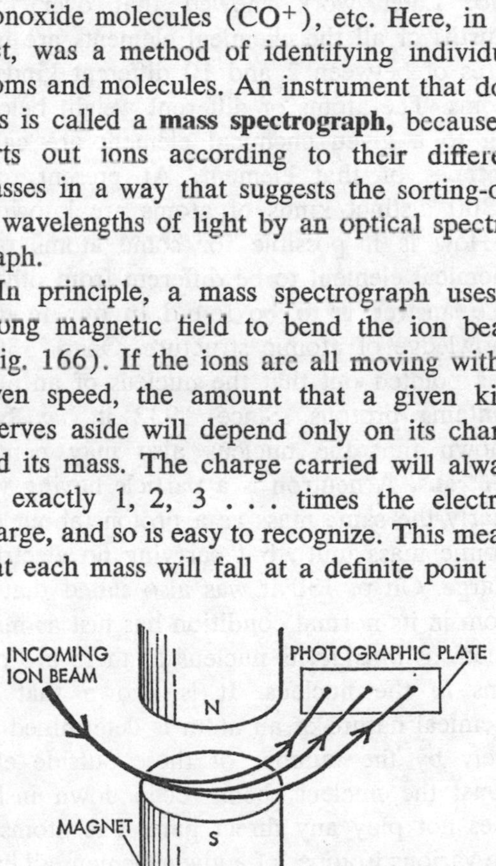

Fig. 166. Principle of the mass spectrograph

the photographic plate, and measurement of the position of any spot on the plate will give the mass value very accurately. The results are stated in **atomic mass units** rather than, say, in grams. The standard is set by calling the mass of the carbon atom exactly 12 units.

ISOTOPES

When Thomson measured the mass of neon atoms (chemical atomic mass 20.183) he found nothing at this position; instead, there was a well-defined mark at 20 and another fainter one at 22. Thus, as far as the individual atoms are concerned, there must be two kinds of neon atoms, and these are found in ordinary neon in the ratio of about 1 part of the heavier to 9 parts of the lighter. The chemically determined mass of 20.183 is simply the average for the natural mixture of the two. Later work showed that over three fourths of all the chemical elements are mixtures of between 2 and 10 different kinds of atoms. The atoms of different weight belonging to a given chemical element are called **isotopes** of that element. At present, over 1,300 distinct kinds of atoms are known.

How is it possible for some atoms of a chemical element to be different from others? The answer is to be found in our modern knowledge of atomic structure. On p. 130 it was pointed out that the nucleus of an atom contains protons. Since 1932 it has been known that the nucleus also may contain **neutrons.** A neutron is a particle having very nearly the same mass as a proton (about one atomic mass unit), but carrying no electrical charge. On p. 130 it was also stated that an atom in its normal condition has just as many electrons *outside* its nucleus as there are protons *in* the nucleus. It is known that the chemical nature of an atom is determined entirely by the number of these outside electrons; the nucleus, being deep down inside, does not play any direct part. The atoms of the various isotopes of a given element all have the same number of outer electrons, but their nuclei differ in containing different numbers of neutrons, and so having different masses.

An example will make this more definite: Chlorine has two isotopes, mass numbers 35 and 37, occurring in a ratio of about 3:1. The fact that characterizes both of these as chlorine atoms is that each has 17 outer electrons. To hold these 17 electrons, each nucleus must have 17 protons. To make up the total masses of 35 and 37 units one of the nuclei must contain, in addition to the protons, 18 neutrons, the other 20 neutrons. The scheme of the arrangement is shown in Fig. 167a. Even hydrogen, the lightest element, has 3 known isotopes (Fig. 167b). The double-weight one is also called **deuterium.** "Heavy water" is the name usually given to H_2O in which the H's are deuterium atoms.

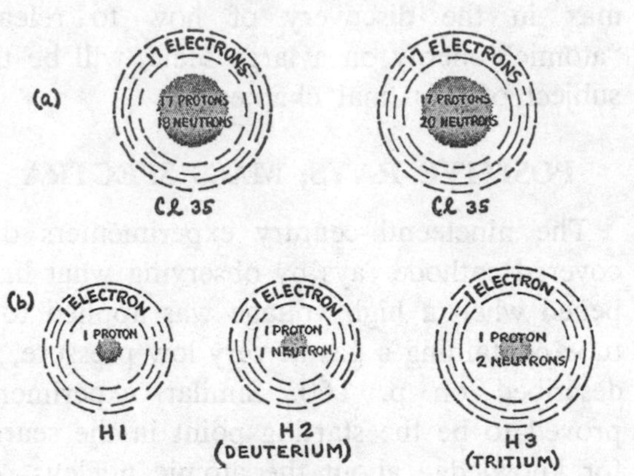

Fig. 167. Scheme of the structure of certain atoms

Two numbers completely identify any atom:

1) The **atomic number** *P* is the normal number of outer electrons, which is also the number of nuclear protons. It is the same as the number of the element in the chemical table—1 for hydrogen, 2 for helium, 3 for lithium, etc.

2) The **mass number** *A* gives the mass of any particular atom to the nearest whole number, in atomic mass units (Carbon = 12).

In the usual chemical shorthand, an atom is designated by writing its chemical symbol and attaching the mass number at the upper right and the atomic number at the lower left.

For example, Uranium 235, used in one form of atomic bomb (see below) has the symbol $_{92}U^{235}$.

NATURAL RADIOACTIVITY

In 1896 the French physicist A. H. Becquerel found that a sample of natural uranium-bearing rock gave off a highly penetrating radiation capable of affecting a photographic plate. Pierre and Marie Curie found that the activity was not due to uranium itself but to some much more powerful radiating material which must be present in small amounts in such ores. After a long, laborious process they succeeded in extracting a small quantity of a new active element, which they named polonium, and later a tiny amount of a still more energetic element, radium. Further experiments by the Curies and by others soon revealed many other radioactive substances. We now know that the last dozen or so elements, beginning with atomic number $P=84$, are radioactive.

The British scientist Ernest Rutherford made a thorough study of the radiations from these materials and found that there are, altogether, three kinds of radiation given off. Fig. 168 shows what happens when samples of radioactive minerals are put in a magnetic field: One type of ray is bent slightly in one direction, another much more strongly in the opposite direction, and a third kind not at all. These rays are designated by Greek letters as α (alpha), β (beta) and γ (gamma) rays, respectively.

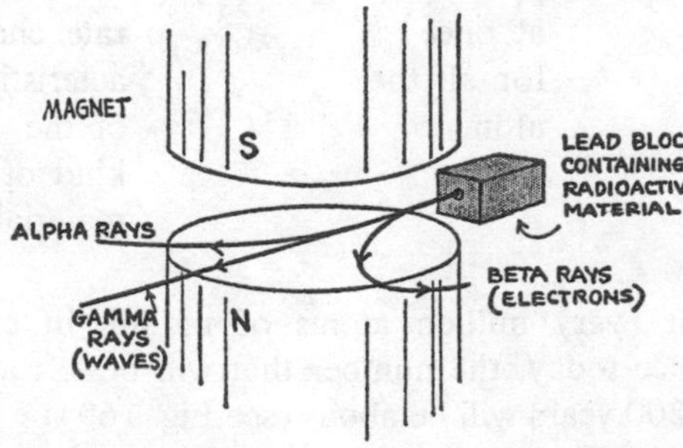

Fig. 168. Radioactive rays can be separated in a strong magnetic field

Alpha rays are found to be streams of + charged particles, each having a mass number of 4 and carrying a charge of +2 electron charges. In fact, an alpha particle is identical with the nucleus of a helium atom. The **beta rays** are streams of very fast electrons, with speeds up to within a few tenths of a per cent of the speed of light. **Gamma rays,** already described on p. 120, are very penetrating electromagnetic waves.

All radioactive atoms give off either alpha or beta rays, and either kind may have gamma rays along with it. Some materials emit all three kinds. The gammas are the most penetrating and destructive of all, and can go through as much as a foot of metal. Beta particles can penetrate about a sixteenth of an inch of metal, while the fastest alphas are stopped by a sheet of paper.

Because of their enormous energies, all three types of rays are known to come from the nucleus. An alpha, consisting of 2 protons and 2 neutrons, is always thrown off as a unit; individual protons or neutrons are never shot out. A beta particle (electron) is believed to be formed when a neutron in the nucleus splits up into a proton and an electron. The proton stays behind. Gamma radiation arises from the shake-up produced when a nucleus throws out a particle.

When a radioactive element breaks down, the product may itself be radioactive, and the process can be traced through a series of elements. Each time a nucleus gives off a particle it becomes a different nucleus, and the end product of all such breakdowns is usually some isotope of lead ($P=82$).

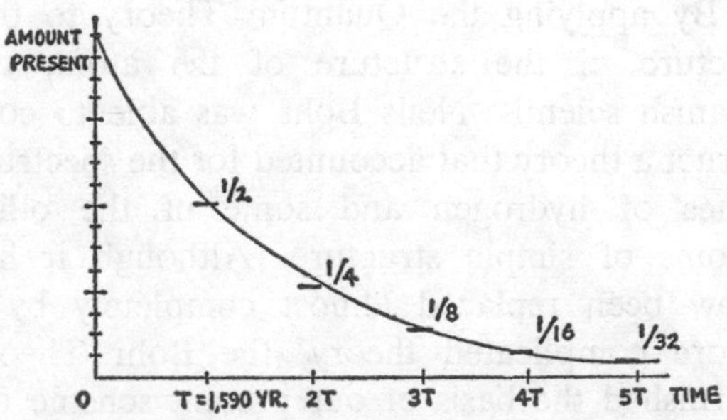

Fig. 169. Breakdown of radium

The rate of breakdown of a given element is not affected by outside conditions, but depends only on the nature of the element in question. The rate follows a geometric law: For each kind of active nucleus, there is a characteristic time T, the **half-life,** such that after the passage of this time, just half as much of the element remains as before (see Fig. 169).

EXPERIMENT 56: You can observe, indirectly, the breakdown of a radium nucleus by looking at a luminous watch dial with a high-powered magnifier. The luminous paint is a fluorescent material containing a very small amount of a radium compound. After resting your eyes in a completely dark room for several minutes, look at the luminous figures with the lens. In place of the soft, uniform glow seen with the eye alone you will now see shimmering pin-point flashes of light, each one produced by an alpha particle from a radium nucleus.

SIZE OF THE NUCLEUS; BOHR'S THEORY

Rutherford and his associates used alpha particles from natural radioactive materials as probes to find out the size of the nucleus. They let a narrow beam of alphas hit a thin metal foil and found that particles were thrown off at all sorts of angles, some even in the backward direction. The scheme used to count the number coming off was the one used in your last experiment with the watch dial. From a study of the results, Rutherford proved that the nucleus is extremely small—less than a ten-thousandth the diameter of the whole atom.

By applying the Quantum Theory to this picture of the structure of the atom, the Danish scientist Neils Bohr was able to construct a theory that accounted for the spectrum lines of hydrogen and some of the other atoms of simple structure. Although it has now been replaced almost completely by a more complicated theory, the Bohr Theory furnished the basis of our present scheme for explaining spectra.

Practice Exercise No. 42

1. Two atoms may have different atomic mass numbers and yet

— (A) belong to the same element.
— (B) contain the same total number of protons and neutrons.
— (C) have electrons in their nuclei.
— (D) have no protrons in their nuclei.

2. The atomic number of oxygen is 8. Then the nucleus of the oxygen isotope of mass 15 must contain

— (A) 15 protons.
— (B) 8 electrons.
— (C) 7 protons.
— (D) 7 neutrons.

3. Beta rays are

— (A) fast protons.
— (B) electromagnetic waves.
— (C) high speed electrons.
— (D) able to penetrate heavy armor plate.

4. The breakdown of a sample of radioactive material

— (A) can be speeded up by applying heat.
— (B) happens all at once for all the atoms.
— (C) is always accompanied by gamma rays.
— (D) goes at a rate characteristic of the kind of material.

5. For every million atoms of radium in existence today, the number that will be left after 3,200 years will be about (see Fig. 169):

— (A) 999,999.
— (B) 250,000.
— (C) 500,000.
— (D) 125,000.

ARTIFICIAL NUCLEAR CHANGES

Whenever the nucleus of a natural radioactive atom breaks down it does so of its own accord, shooting out an alpha or beta particle in the process. In 1919, Rutherford succeeded in producing nuclear changes *artificially* for the first time by letting alpha particles hit nitrogen nuclei. An alpha particle first combines with the nitrogen nucleus, and the unstable composite nucleus thus formed immediately breaks down into an isotope of oxygen and a fast proton. This can be written in the form of a nuclear chemical reaction equation

$$_{2}He^{4} + {}_{7}N^{14} \rightarrow {}_{8}O^{17} + {}_{1}H^{1}.$$

The alpha particle is represented by $_{2}He^{4}$, since it is the same as a helium nucleus, and the proton by $_{1}H^{1}$, since it is a hydrogen nucleus. The equation expresses the fact that the total mass is the same before and after the action,* since $4 + 14 = 17 + 1$. It also says that the total electrical charge remains unchanged: $2 + 7 = 8 + 1$.

Rutherford and his co-workers followed this up later by producing nuclear changes with electrically-accelerated protons. Since that time, many other nuclear changes have been produced using protons, alphas, deuterons (deuterium nuclei), neutrons, photons and other particles. The devices that give high speeds to charged particles so that they can be used for such purposes are popularly known as "atom smashers." In the **linear accelerator,** the particles travel down a long tube, getting a series of electrical boosts in speed as they proceed. In the **cyclotron,** the moving particles are bent around in a large circle by a strong magnetic field, meanwhile getting two boosts in speed during each revolution. In a very short time, this brings their speed up close to that of light, giving them enough kinetic energy to produce nuclear changes when they are then allowed to hit the target material.

* This statement will have to be qualified.

MASS-ENERGY EQUIVALENCE

In describing Rutherford's alpha particle-nitrogen reaction above, it was pointed out that the total mass is the same before and after the change. However, if the exact mass values gotten from mass spectrograph measurements are put in, this is found to be no longer quite true. The total mass of the H and the O that are formed turns out to be 0.0013 mass unit *more* than the total mass of the original alpha particle and nitrogen atom. This difference is small, but still very much bigger than the expected error of measurement. Also, it is found that the total kinetic energy of the particles formed is very slightly, but unmistakably, *less* (by about 0.000002 erg) than the energy of the particles to begin with.

Einstein's Theory of Relativity provides an explanation. According to this theory, mass and energy are no longer to be considered independent things; instead, one can be converted into the other. Matter can, under certain circumstances, be converted into energy, and—the other way around—energy can be "frozen" into the form of matter. The relation between the two is given by the famous **mass-energy equation**

$$E = mc^2,$$

where E is a quantity of energy, in ergs, m is the equivalent amount of mass, in grams, and c is the speed of light, in centimeters per second.

One result of this relation is that whenever energy is given to a body (by heating it, by setting it into motion, etc.) its mass must increase. But for any ordinary physical process, this increase would be far too small to detect. This is because the factor c^2 by which the energy must be divided to get the equivalent mass, has the enormous value of 900 billion billion. But, going the other way around, the destruction of even a tiny amount of matter produces tremendous amounts of energy. If the atoms of a piece of coal could be completely destroyed, the energy produced would be about 3 billion times that obtained by merely burning the coal. However, complete destruction of matter has not yet been attained; even the atomic bomb cannot do this, as you will see below.

Getting back to the nitrogen reaction, the Einstein mass-energy relation is found to explain the observed energy loss. This has also been found to be true in dozens of other nuclear changes examined. In this way the mass-energy relation has become firmly established as a physical law: mass and energy must now be considered to be merely interchangeable forms of the same thing.

RADIO-ISOTOPES

The French physicist F. Joliot and his wife (the daughter of Madame Curie) found that when alpha particles were allowed to strike a piece of aluminum, **positrons** were given off. A positron is a particle identical with an electron, except that its charge is positive instead of negative. It is not permanent, but soon unites with an ordinary negative electron, both disappearing in a flash of radiant energy in accordance with the mass-energy relation. The positron activity did not stop at once when the alphas were cut off, but kept on for some time. It was found that some of the aluminum atoms had been changed into radioactive isotopes of other elements.

Other experimenters have found ways of making many hundreds of kinds of artificially radioactive atoms, or **radio-isotopes,** by bombarding matter in the cyclotron or by exposing it to radiation in a nuclear reactor (p. 175). Some of these radio-isotopes find application as tracers for checking the distribution of foods or fluids in plants and animals. Common salt in which some of the atoms have been made radioactive can be fed to a patient and followed through his system by an electronic detector (such as a **Geiger counter)** held near the surface of the body. Some radio elements can be used in place of radium or X rays for treating tumors and other growths. They can be injected and allowed to go to the affected part; and since they usually have an active life of only several hours, they become harmless after serving their purpose.

Radio-isotopes have found a large number of applications in industry and technology as well.

COSMIC RAYS

In every cubic centimeter of air there are ordinarily several hundred ions present. At the beginning of this century, physicists carried detecting instruments up in balloons and discovered that the intensity of this ionization increased greatly with distance above the earth. They concluded that the cause was some kind of penetrating radiation coming from all directions of outer space. This radiation, which has much greater penetrating power than the shortest known gamma rays, was called **cosmic radiation.** The incoming rays are now known to consist of particles—mainly protons, but also electrons, positrons, alpha particles and a few nuclei of heavier atoms. Some of these primary particles have millions of times as much energy as the fastest particles that can be produced in the big cyclotrons. The origin of these high-energy particles is still unknown. One idea is that they are charged particles that have been speeded up over long periods of time by magnetic fields out in space.

When these **primary** particles plunge into the earth's atmosphere they produce tremendous numbers of **secondary** particles and waves: electrons, positrons, protons, neutrons, alphas, gamma rays, etc.

ELEMENTARY PARTICLES

Electrons, positrons, protons, neutrons and photons form part of a group collectively called **elementary** or **fundamental** particles. Other sets of fundamental particles were first discovered in cosmic rays, and still others were first created in high-energy experiments using powerful particle accelerators ("atom smashers").

One set of such particles are **mesons,** with

masses between that of the electron and the proton. They may carry +1, −1 or zero electron charges. Mesons are not permanent, but break down into some of the lighter particles or simply become swallowed up in atomic nuclei. One kind of meson appears to have something to do with holding the parts of the nucleus together.

A group of heavier particles, called **baryons,** begins with the proton and neutron and includes particles of mass several times as great. Baryons, too, may have charges of either sign or may be electrically neutral, depending on their kind. They are extremely short-lived, and decay into lighter particles of various kinds.

The scheme of fundamental particles of matter, originally thought to be made up of only the electron and the proton, has now had to be enlarged to comprise perhaps more than 80 distinct varieties. The explanation of the existence and properties of these particles is one of the outstanding problems before scientists today.

NUCLEAR FISSION

All the nuclear changes so far mentioned, with the exception of some of those produced by cosmic rays, involve the chipping-off of fairly small pieces of the nucleus of an atom. In 1939, Hahn and Strassmann in Germany found that uranium nuclei can apparently be split into two parts of roughly the same mass, releasing huge amounts of energy in the process. The change was produced by bombarding uranium with neutrons, which are ideal nuclear bullets because—unlike the other heavy particles—they have no charge, and so are not repelled by the target nucleus. The breaking down of a nucleus into two parts of comparable size was called **fission.**

It was found that the uranium isotope of mass 235, rather than the more abundant 238, is the one that undergoes fission. In natural uranium there are only about 7 U^{235} atoms to 1,000 of U^{238}. Fig. 170 shows one possible way that U^{235} can undergo fission. The entering neutron shakes up the structure, making it pinch in two. An important feature of the action is that perhaps two or three neutrons are thrown off at the same time. It was recognized that this makes possible a **chain reaction:** If more than one of the neutrons produced were able to cause fission of another nucleus, the process would go ahead faster and faster until, after a very short time, all the nuclei would be transformed, with the release of an enormous amount of energy.

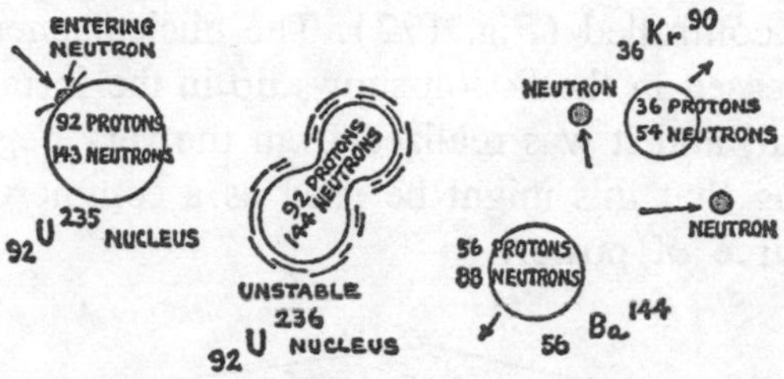

Fig. 170. Stages in the fission of U-235

EXPERIMENT 57: In order to get an idea of how a chain reaction goes, set up a model of one using matches, as shown in the sketch. Lay out the pattern on a pavement or on gravel, and apply a lighted match to the base of the "tree." Notice that one match sets off two, two set off four, etc., so that the activity builds up rapidly.

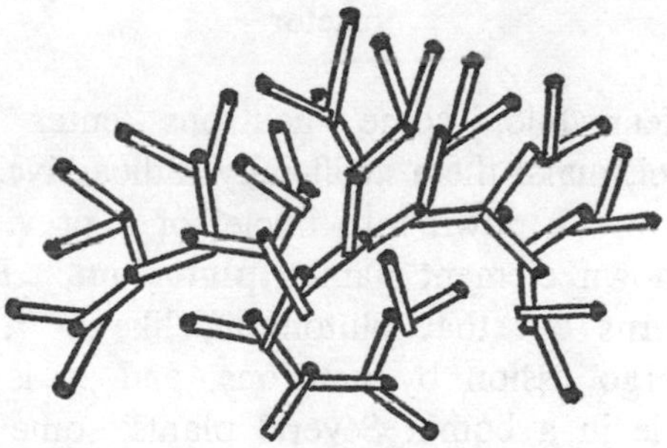

Fig. 171.

NUCLEAR REACTORS; FISSION BOMBS

A chain reaction does not happen in natural uranium. The reason is that a detached neutron has a good chance of entering a U^{235}

nucleus only if it is moving relatively slowly. The fission-produced neutrons, however, are fast, and in a piece of natural uranium most of them would be swallowed up by the more abundant U^{238} before they could find atoms of U^{235}. It was suggested that lumps of uranium metal could be inserted between blocks of graphite, which would act as a **moderator** to slow up the neutrons. Such an arrangement, called a **nuclear reactor,** was first operated successfully in 1942. By inserting or removing rods of cadmium metal, which strongly absorbs neutrons, the activity of the reactor can be controlled (Fig. 172). The nuclear energy released in the fission shows up in the form of heat, and it was realized from the very beginning that this might be used as a commercial source of power.

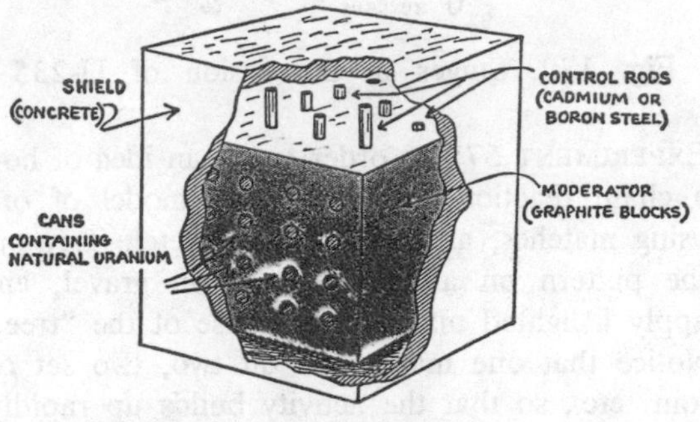

Fig. 172. Cutaway view of one type of nuclear reactor

Meanwhile, some neutrons enter U^{238} nuclei, make them artificially radioactive, and they break down into nuclei of a previously unknown element named **plutonium,** ${}_{94}Pu^{239}$. It turns out that plutonium, like U^{235}, can undergo fission by neutrons, and so is also usable in a bomb. Several plants, some containing reactors that can develop hundreds of thousands of kilowatts of power, are now in operation in this country and elsewhere.

In a small piece of U^{235} or Pu^{239}, many neutrons will escape, and the chain reaction will not develop.* In a larger lump, the chance of a neutron escaping without meeting fission nuclei is much less. So there must be a **critical size**—any smaller piece will not be able to maintain a chain reaction, a larger one will. In an atomic bomb there are two (or more) samples each smaller than the critical size, perhaps a few pounds in mass. In each of these a few fissions are going on, since there are always some neutrons around to start things off. The firing mechanism of the bomb forcibly rams the sub-critical masses together into a single lump, and in something like a hundred millionth of a second the chain reaction is under way, releasing energy equivalent to the explosion of millions of tons of TNT.

* Perhaps in your experiment, some of the matches failed to burn completely and so did not succeed in setting off the next pair.

Uses of Reactors

The controlled release of nuclear energy is now being put to peaceful use as a source of industrial power to take the place of our rapidly decreasing supply of chemical fuels such as coal and oil. The main technical obstacle here, apart from economic considerations, is the fact that human beings must be protected from the deadly radioactivity—mainly gamma rays—produced in nuclear reactors. This protection can be obtained only by surrounding the reactor with a shield of concrete, water or steel several feet thick, which weighs many tons. This makes it unlikely that nuclear power plants will soon come into general use for ordinary vehicles such as cars, trains and airplanes; however, nuclear-powered submarines and ships are already in operation.

In existing nuclear power plants the heat generated in the reactor is conveyed to some ordinary type of heat engine, such as a steam engine or steam turbine. Fig. 173 shows a possible arrangement. The liquid for transferring heat from the reactor may be a molten metal that is kept separate from the steam or hot water that circulates to the engine in order to avoid radioactive contamination. All controls for the device are operated from a place outside the shield.

Possibly more important than its use for generating power is the use of the nuclear re-

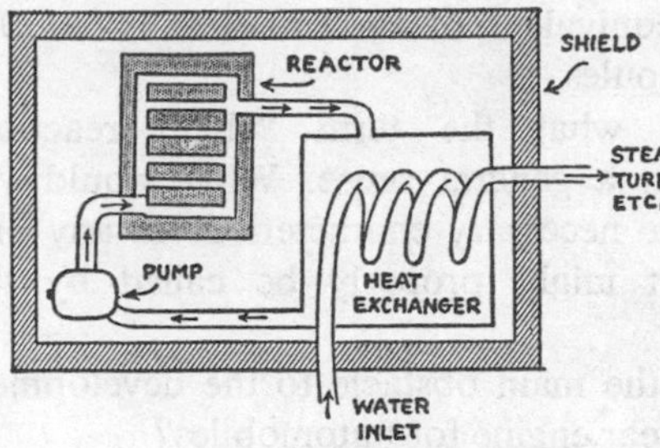

Fig. 173. Arrangement for a nuclear power plant

actor as an activator. Samples of various materials inserted into the reactor receive intense neutron bombardment, converting them into radioactive sources far more powerful than natural ones or than any that can be made by particle accelerators like the cyclotron. The use of radioactive tracers in medicine has already been referred to on p. 174. Many other applications—to biology, chemistry, metallurgy, physics, and engineering—are extremely valuable and important.

NUCLEAR FUSION

You have seen from the preceding sections that the fission of heavy atomic nuclei can yield enormous quantities of energy. There is another process, even more powerful, called **nuclear fusion.** It involves the combination of light-weight nuclei into heavier ones; in this sense it is just the opposite of fission. From the point of view of energy delivered, the most profitable fusion reaction would be the putting together of four hydrogen atoms to form one helium atom according to the scheme

$$4\ {}_1H^1 \rightarrow {}_2He^4 + 2 \text{ positrons.}$$

When accurate mass spectrograph values are used, it turns out that the total mass beforehand is 0.03 mass units greater than that afterward. If the difference were converted into energy according to Einstein's mass-energy relation, it would amount to about 0.00004 erg per helium atom formed. This is seemingly not a great amount of energy, but for any sizable quantity of hydrogen it is enormous, something like a hundred million kilowatt hours per pound!

In 1939, Weizsäcker in Germany and Bethe in the United States independently concluded that the hydrogen fusion action could account for the heat of the sun and the stars. No other source ever suggested is at all large enough to furnish the huge quantities of energy that the sun has been pouring out into space for several billion years. The Einstein formula tells us that as a result of this energy output the sun is losing mass at the rate of over 4½ million tons each second. Yet the sun is so large that even after 150 billion years it will have lost only 1 per cent of its present mass.

The **thermonuclear** bomb (H-bomb) produces energy by a fusion reaction. For the same mass of reacting material, a fusion bomb produces about 30 times as much energy as a fission bomb. In addition, there is no upper limit to the size of such a weapon.

The possibility of a controlled fusion reaction is the subject of much current research, and limited success has been attained. Because of the existence of temperatures of millions of degrees, no known material is suitable for containing such a reaction. This has led to attempts to carry out the process in an electrical **plasma,** confined by magnetic fields (Fig. 174). A plasma is a mass of ionized atoms or molecules mixed with free electrons so that the whole region is essentially electrically neutral. Fusion actually has been made to occur in such an apparatus for brief instants of time.

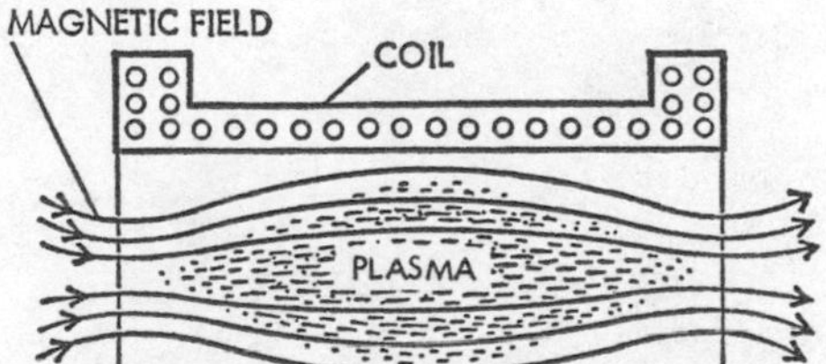

Fig. 174. Plasma confined by a magnetic field

Practice Exercise No. 43

1. Satisfy yourself that the total number of protons and the total number of neutrons are the same before and after the fission reaction diagrammed in Fig. 170.
2. The smallest mass difference that can ordinarily be detected with a sensitive chemical balance is about 0.00001 gm. Show that the energy equivalent of this mass is about 900 million joules.
3. Describe what the term "chain reaction" means in a general sense. What would you say is the necessary characteristic of any process that might properly be called by this name?
4. What is the main obstacle to the development of a nuclear engine for automobiles?

SUMMARY *Instructions:* (see page 17)

1. Describe the essential function of a mass spectrograph.	
2. What number, assigned to a given kind of atom, specifies the number of protons in the nucleus?	A magnetic field is used to separate the components of a beam of ions and to measure their masses.
3. Define the mass number of an atom.	The atomic number *P*.
4. Of what do the alpha, beta and gamma radiations from radioactive atoms consist?	The mass number, *A*, states the mass of the atom to the nearest whole number, based on a value of 12 for carbon.
5. In any nuclear change, what two quantities remain the same?	Streams of a) helium nuclei (alpha particles) b) electrons, and c) very penetrating electromagnetic waves, respectively.
6. What is Einstein's principle of mass-energy equivalence?	a) the sum of the mass numbers on both sides; b) the total electrical charge on both sides.
7. Distinguish between mesons and baryons.	Mass and energy are interconvertible according to the relation $E = mc^2$.
8. What is meant by nuclear fission?	Mesons are fundamental particles of matter with masses between that of the electron and the proton. Baryons are fundamental particles with masses equal to or greater than the proton mass.
9. What is meant by nuclear fusion?	The splitting of a heavy atomic nucleus into two parts of comparable mass, plus some free neutrons.
10. Describe the most promising way of realizing a controlled fusion reaction.	The combination of light nuclei, such as hydrogen, to form heavier nuclei, such as helium.
	By using a plasma confined by means of magnetic fields.

ANSWERS AND SOLUTIONS TO THE EXERCISES

Exercise No. 1

1. C.
2. B.
3. A.
4. D.
5. B.

Exercise No. 2

1. Since there are 36 in. to a yard, 38.7 yd will contain $38.7 \times 36 = 1{,}390$ in. (rounded off to three significant digits).
2. There are 39.4 in. to one meter, so 1.34 m will amount to $1.34 \times 39.4 = 52.8$ in.
4. Since 2.54 cm = 1 in. this will be 25.4 threads per inch.
5. 3000 m $= 3000 \times 39.4/12$ ft. The cost per foot is 0.14 cent, so the above length will come to $3000 \times 39.4 \times 0.14/12 = 1379$ cents or $13.79.

Exercise No. 3

1. The volume of the tank, in liters, is $16 \times 231 \times (2.54)^3/1000 = 60.6$.
2. According to Table 3, the weight would be 1,200 lb.
3. The volume of the room is $20 \times 15 \times 8 = 2400$ ft³. Each cubic foot weighs 0.08 lb (Table 3), so this volume weighs $2400 \times 0.08 = 192$ lb.
4. The volume of a cylinder is given by π (radius of base)$^2 \times$ (height). Here, this is $3.14 \times 1 \times 10 = 31.4$ cm³. The density is then $250/31.4 = 7.96$ gm/cm³.
5. $V = M/D$. Using the Table, $V = 200/0.0055 = 36{,}400$ ft³, about.

Exercise No. 4

1. Since pressure increases with depth, the pressure would be greater under the hump and as a result the water would flow outward from it in all directions, until everything is at the same level.
2. This, too, is due to the fact that pressure increases with depth, so the tank walls must be made progressively stronger toward the bottom.
3. See answer to preceding question.
4. No. The pressure is the same in each case, since the depth is the same. The *extent* of the body of water makes no difference.

Exercise No. 5

1. Use the relation $p = hD$: $p = 30 \times 1 = 30$ gm/cm².
2. The pressure is given by $p = 100 \times 64 = 6{,}400$ lb/ft². The total force is found by multiplying by the area: $F = 6400 \times 1500 = 9{,}600{,}000$ lb, 4,800 tons force.

Exercise No. 6

1. C, since $100/80 = 1.25$.
2. C, since water is denser than gasoline.
3. C.
4. C.

Exercise No. 7

1. According to Table 3, aluminum and lead will, while gold will not.
2. Cork is much less dense than water—about ¼ as much.
3. Salt water being denser than fresh, will the hull have to displace as great a volume of salt water?
4. The boat will have to displace an additional 20 tons of water, whose volume, given by $V = M/D$ is $20 \times 2000/62.4 = 641$ ft³. With a 5,000 ft² area, the thickness of this layer of water would have to be $641/5000 = 0.13$ ft, or about an inch and a half.
5. From the Table, the ratio of the density of ice

to that of sea water is $57/64 = 0.89$; therefore, about 89% of the bulk of an iceberg is under water.

Exercise No. 8

1. The computation goes: $p = 30 \times 850/1728 = 14.7$ lb/in².
2. The difference in pressure is $14.7 - 5.0 = 9.7$ lb/in² and the area of the lid is $\pi(2.5)^2 = 19.6$ in². The whole force is then $19.6 \times 9.7 = 190$ lb.
3. By Boyle's law,

$$\frac{100}{7.35} = \frac{p_2}{14.7}, \text{so } p_2 = 200 \text{ lb/in}^2.$$

4. Archimedes' principle says that the buoyant force is equal to the weight of the displaced air, which is $4000 \times 0.08 = 320$ lb. Also, the hydrogen weighs $4000 \times 0.0055 = 22$ lb. This, together with the bag, makes a total weight of 72 lb. The difference, $320 - 22 = 298$ lb, is the "pay load."

Exercise No. 9

1. Strictly speaking, you do not *suck* the air in, you merely enlarge your lungs and normal outside air pressure *pushes* more air into them.
2. What does the pressure of the outside air do when the middle of the cup is pulled away slightly from the surface to which it has been applied?
3. Refer back to the remarks on p. 24.
4. Decide what effect the pumping will have on the resultant pressure on the balloon.
5. The parachute in effect greatly increases the cross-section area of the falling body. How does this affect the resistance to motion through the air?
6. Between the boats there is what amounts to a swift current of water toward the stern. Recall Bernoulli's principle.

Exercise No. 10

1. C; force is a vector.
2. A.
3. C.
4. D, for then the amount of the resultant force is the sum of the two.
5. B.

Exercise No. 11

1. Compare the height of the center of gravity in the two cases.
2. If the load is 4 ft. from the left-hand end, then taking torques around this end gives us $150 \times 4 = R \times 9$, or $R = 66.7$ lb, where R is the force with which the right-hand end is supported. Then the force at the other end must be simply $150 - 66.7 = 83.3$ lb.
3. 2.7 lb.
4. Since the force is inversely proportional to the square of the distance, it would be reduced to $1/3^2 = 1/9$ of its present amount.
5. Substituting in the gravitational formula,

$$F = \frac{(0.000000000033) \times (15000 \times 2000)^2}{(150)^2} = 1.3 \text{ lb.}$$

Exercise No. 12

1. The first part of the trip takes 1/12 hr. The average speed is the total distance divided by the total time, or

$$\frac{3\tfrac{1}{2}}{\frac{1}{12} + \frac{1}{4} + \frac{1}{10}} = \frac{105}{13} = 8.1 \text{ mi/hr.}$$

2. The aceleration on the moon will amount to $32/6 = 5\tfrac{1}{3}$ ft/sec². At the end of 2 sec, the stone will have gained a speed of 2 times this figure, or 10.7 ft/sec.
3. During the first second, the average speed is $\tfrac{1}{2}(0 + 32) = 16$ ft/sec, so the body goes 16 ft during this time. The speed at the beginning of the 2nd second will be 32 ft/sec, and at the end of the 2nd second it will be 64 ft/sec. Hence the average speed in this interval will be $\tfrac{1}{2}(32 + 64) = 48$ ft/sec. Therefore, the body will go 48 ft during the 2nd second, or 3 times as far as in the first second.
4. Average speed would be increased, time required decreased.
5. Since the bullet "drops off" as it goes along, the aim must be high.

Exercise No. 13

1. If the accelerations involved are high, what about the forces?
2. What happens is that the hammer is brought to

rest in a very short time interval. What about the magnitude of its acceleration during this time?

3. The gun is much more massive than the bullet, hence what must be true of its recoil speed?
6. No. The air blast would hit the sail and deliver its forward momentum to the boat in this way, but in setting this air into motion, the fan experiences an equal backward momentum. Being attached to the boat, the fan gives the latter an equal rearward momentum, and nothing happens.
7. Is there a centrifugal force acting on the body? What direction does this have with respect to the weight of the body? What is your conclusion?

Exercise No. 14

1. B.
2. A.
3. D.
4. B.
5. C. According to the result of the example, the car had a KE of 363,000 ft lb. This will equal the work done in stopping it, so $363{,}000 = F \times 11$, or $F = 33{,}000$ lb force.

Exercise No. 15

1. 40 lb.
2. 80 lb.
3. The area ratio of the two pistons is 100, so the load force will be 1,000 lb.
4. At each stage, work done *on* machine equals work done *by* machine. Thus the two rates of working are equal.

Exercise No. 16

1. C.
2. C.
3. B.
4. A.
5. B.

Exercise No. 17

1. When the gas is highly compressed, for them the molecules are much closer together.
2. $4/0.01 = 400$.
3. One mile of this wire would have a volume of $5280 \times 12/(12)^3$ ft³. This would weigh $5280 \times 490/(12)^2 = 18{,}000$ lb, much less than 200 tons (400,000 lb), the tensile strength of steel.

Exercise No. 18

1. The ratio is 5/9, since there are $212 - 32 = 180$ Fahrenheit degrees between the ice and steam points, while there are 100 Celsuis degrees in the same interval.
2. From the relation on p. 67 we find $C = 37.0°$. The absolute value is $37 + 273 = 310°$.
6. Larger. The metal expands outward from the center at every point. Another way to look at it: What must happen to any imaginary band of metal surrounding the cavity as the metal is heated? Therefore, what happens to the size of the cavity?
7. The temperature of the piston rises by 160 Celsius degrees. By Table 6, the fractional increase in length for aluminum, per degree, is 0.000024, so the actual increase in length will be $0.000024 \times 160 \times 2\frac{3}{4} = 0.011$ in., about.

Exercise No. 19

1. B.
2. C.
3. B.
4. D.
5. A.

Exercise No. 20

1. Since they have very small mass, the quantity of heat they carry is small in spite of their high temperature.
2. Using $Q = smt$ we get $Q = 0.11 \times 5 \times 265 = 146$ Btu.
3. Heat needed to melt the ice: 144 Btu.
   Heat to raise the resulting water by 180° F to its boiling point: 180
   Heat to change the water to steam: 970
   Total: 1,294 Btu.
4. a) Any heat supplied after the water has begun to boil is carried off in the steam produced instead of going toward a further increase of temperature. b) Heat is needed to melt ice; thus heat must be given up when water freezes.
6. No. If the air is at the same temperature as the object, the only way cooling could be produced would be by evaporation.
7. Condensed from vapor in the air.
8. The ice formed eventually evaporates. Melting is not involved.

Exercise No. 21

1. Do the brakes become warmed?
2. Since 778 ft lb is equivalent to 1 Btu, the quantity of heat amounts to $160 \times 3900/778 = 802$ Btu.
3. Calling the distance in feet *d*, the work needed will be 3000*d* ft lb. One fourth of 30,000 Btu is equivalent to $30{,}000 \times 778/4$ ft lb. Setting the two equal and solving, $d = 1{,}945$ ft.
4. Higher.
5. How is the heat taken from the inside of the box disposed of? Also, what is the effect of the driving motor or the gas flame?

Exercise No. 22

2. Is a tune played by a band recognizable by a listener even if he is some distance away? What can you conclude from this?
4. $d = \frac{1}{2}(3.5)(4700) = 8{,}200$ ft.
5. Compare Experiment 39, p. 107.

Exercise No. 23

1. Dividing the distance in feet by 1100 and by 86,400 (the number of seconds in a day) gives about 13 days as the result.
2. B.
3. The speed in ft/sec is $5280/4.8 = 1100$. According to Table 10, the speed in air at 20° C is 1126 ft/sec. The speed of sound decreases about 2 ft/sec for each degree drop in temperature, so the temperature must have been 13° lower than 20, or 7° C.
4. $1100/256 = 4.3$ ft.
5. The frequency stays the same, even if the waves pass into another material. Since $V = nl$, going into water where V is about 4 times as great will make l about 4 times as great.

Exercise No. 24

1. A.
2. B.
3. C.
4. B.
5. C.

Exercise No. 25

2. One half and twice this value, respectively.
3. To increase their weight.
4. What happens to the length of the air column in the jar?
5. These are doubtful cases, but the tendency is to call the piano a stringed instrument and to refrain from putting the voice in any of these classes.

Exercise No. 26

1. C. It is the only self-luminous source.
2. A.
3. The number of minutes is given by $93{,}000{,}000/(186{,}000 \times 60) = 8\frac{1}{3}$.
4. The image will become $12/8 = 1.5$ times as large when he comes to the position 8 ft from the camera.
5. Illumination being inversely as the square of the distance, it will amount to $1/(\frac{1}{3})^2 = 9$ times as much.
6. The lamp must be $5^2 = 25$ times the strength of the candle.

Exercise No. 27

1. Do you know of any ways of detecting light energy besides the human eye?
4. Suppose the corpuscles were given off equally in all directions. The illumination would be expected to depend on the number striking each square inch of a surface held perpendicular to the "rays." Does this lead to the illumination law?

Exercise No. 28

1. C.
2. C.
3. A. Make a diagram showing a side view of the situation. A ray coming from the man's toe to the mirror and then to his eye must hit the mirror in such a way that the angles of incidence and reflection are equal. The same for a ray from the top of his head and to his eye. The mirror will have to extend from one of these places on the wall to the other. How big is this distance in terms of the man's height? Does his distance from the wall make any difference in the result?
4. A.
5. D.

Exercise No. 29

1. It has no dimensions, since it is the ratio of two speeds. It is merely a pure number.
2. Consider the type, size and positions of the images that can be formed.
4. $1/p + 1/10.5 = 1/10$, or $1/p = 1/210$, $p = 210$ in., which is 17½ ft.
5. $2500/14 = 179$ in., or nearly 15 ft.

Exercise No. 30

1. B. Consider the directions in which the various rays come to the eye.
2. A. (See Fig. 102).
3. C. Only white light will give the true colors.
4. D. The first observation shows that it reflects red light, the second shows that it does not reflect blue at all. Hence it cannot be either blue or white.
5. A.

Exercise No. 31

1. From p. 99, $c = 30{,}000{,}000{,}000$ cm/sec, about. Then $n = c/l = 500{,}000{,}000{,}000{,}000$ (500 trillion) vib/sec.
2. (a) Moonlight is merely reflected sunlight. (b) Line spectrum. (c) Continuous spectrum.
4. The wires running each way act as a coarse diffraction grating.
5. Are these colors due to pigments or to something else?

Exercise No. 32

1. C.
2. B.
3. B.
4. C.
5. C. (see Fig. 114).

Exercise No. 33

1. What kind of charge will be induced on the near end of the object? The force at the near end will dominate because of the smaller distance.
2. After touching, the force is no longer due to induced charges only. What else happens?
3. Is there, in a sense, any rubbing involved?
5. a) Note that they have opposite kinds of charge. b) The act of touching leaves a balance of 1 billion electron charges, and these are shared equally by the two, leaving half a billion (500 million) on each. The force is one of repulsion.

Exercise No. 34

1. Dividing the charge by the time gives $1/0.0002 = 5000$ amp.
2. No; two *different* metals must be used.
3. Nine storage cells in series would have a total PD of about 18 volts. Therefore $18/1.5 = 12$ dry cells would be needed.
4. A fully-charged one.

Exercise No. 35

1. According to p. 139, the resistance is proportional to length divided by cross-section. The cross-section, in turn, is proportional to (diameter)^2. Then, if length and diameter are both doubled, the resistance will be multiplied by $2/2^2 = ½$; it will be half as much as before.
2. The PD across each lamp is $120/8 = 15$ volts. Then, using $R = V/I$, R turns out to be 75 ohms.
3. Call the value of the resistor r. Then Ohm's law for the resistor and appliance together is $2 = 120/(25 + r)$ and $r = 35$ ohms.
4. The current flowing in the smaller resistance will be 3 times that in the larger; that is, ¾ of the *total* current goes through the former.
5. The equivalent resistance of the two coils in parallel is given by $1/R = ⅓ + ⅙$, or $R = 2$ ohms. Then, using Ohm's law for the whole circuit, $I = 12/(2 + 2) = 3$ amp, and this is also the current in the 2-ohm coil.
6. The current in the 3-ohm coil will be twice as great as that in the 6-ohm coil, and since the total current is 3 amp, ⅔ of this, or 2 amp will pass through the 3-ohm coil.
7. If we substitute the value of I from Ohm's law ($I = V/R$) into the expression for power ($P = IV$), we get $P = V^2/R$. Putting in the numbers, $30 = 144/R$, or $R = 4.8$ ohms.

Exercise No. 36

1. C.
2. B. Since 1 watt is 1 joule/sec, the number of joules of energy expended in 5 min is $100 \times 5 \times 60 = 30{,}000$. The quantity of heat delivered when the temperature rises t C° is $Q = 1$

$\times 225 \times t$ cal, or $225 \times 4.18 \times t$ joules. Setting this equal to 30,000 and solving for *t*, we get 32 C°.

3. B.

4. A.

5. D.

Exercise No. 37

2. Attract each other when currents are in same direction; repel when in opposite directions.

3. Since the coil has 9 times as much resistance as the shunt, 1/10 of the total current, or 1 amp, will flow in the coil.

4. The coil constitutes 0.1/500.1, or about 1/5000, of the total resistance, and so the PD across the coil will be $10/5000 = 0.002$ volt.

5. None, since *both* the current in the field magnets and that in the coils will be reversed. Convince yourself by sketching the field lines.

Exercise No. 38

1. Remembering that the field is uniform, is there any *change* in the flux through the loop when moved as described?

2. North of the equator the lines of the earth's field have a downward direction. In order to oppose the motion of the wire (Lenz's Law) the lines of force of the induced current would also have to be downward on the front side of the wire, so the current would have to be toward the west (Right-hand wire rule). South of the magnetic equator, the result would be just the opposite.

3. No; it is only the relative movement of the two that matters.

4. It would be twice as great.

Exercise No. 39

1. It is increased in the same proportion.

2. 5 to 1.

3. According to the relation on p. 155 the secondary current will be 50 amp.

4. The electromagnetic forces act only when current actually flows in the windings, since these forces are really between two magnetic fields—that of the field coils and that of the rotating coils. The work done against this opposition accounts for the energy of the current produced.

5. With a back voltage of 45 volts, the actual voltage applied to the coils is $50 - 45 = 5$ volts. Then, by Ohm's law, the current will amount to 2.5 amp. If the motor is not turning, the back voltage will be absent and the current in the coils will be $50/2 = 25$ amp. This would likely burn out the windings, since the heating effect is proportional to I^2, and so would become 100 times as great as normal.

Exercise No. 40

1. B.

2. D.

3. A.

4. A.

5. D.

Exercise No. 41

1. Both involve the interaction between radiation and electrons. Can you state explicitly how each operates in these terms?

2. One millionth amp is 6,300,000,000,000,000,000/1,000,000 = 6,300,000,000,000 (6.3 trillion) electrons per second.

4. 0.24/80,000 = 3 millionths of an inch.

5. Since the energy of a quantum is proportional to the frequency of the radiation, the X-ray quantum would have far greater energy. The energy ratio is proportional to the frequencies, which in turn are inversely proportional to the wavelengths. This ratio turns out to be 0.001/0.00000001, or about 100,000.

Exercise No. 42

1. A.

2. D.

3. C.

4. D.

5. B. The time given is about that required to drop to ¼ the original amount.

Exercise No. 43

2. Using $E = mc^2$ and dividing by ten million to change ergs to joules, the computation would be $(0.00001) \times (30{,}000{,}000{,}000)^2/10{,}000{,}000$, or 900 million joules.

4. The excessive size and weight of the shielding required for safety of the occupants.

IMPORTANT FORMULAS AND RELATIONS

Chapter 2

Density of a substance: $D = \frac{M}{V}$, where D is the density, M is the mass of a sample of the material and V is the volume of that sample.

Chapter 3

Pressure: $p = \frac{F}{A}$, where p is the pressure acting on a surface, F is the total force and A is the area to which it is applied.

Pressure beneath the surface of a liquid: $p = hD$, where p is the pressure at any point, h is the depth of that point below the surface and D is the density of the liquid.

Archimedes' law: Buoyant force on a body immersed in a liquid = Weight of liquid displaced by the body.

Chapter 4

Boyle's law: If the temperature of a gas remains constant, $\frac{V_1}{V_2} = \frac{p_2}{p_1}$, where p_1 and V_1 are the pressure and volume, respectively, in one case and p_2 and V_2 are the values in another.

Chapter 5

Torque, or turning effect, of a force about a given pivot point: $T = Fh$, where T is the torque, F is the amount of the force and h is the perpendicular distance from the pivot to the line of the force.

Equilibrium of torques (condition for no rotation): Sum of torques tending to turn body in one direction = Sum of torques tending to turn it in the opposite direction.

Law of Gravitation: $F = \frac{Gm_1m_2}{d^2}$, where F is the force of attraction, m_1 and m_2 are the two masses and d is their distance apart.

Chapter 6

Average speed of motion: $v = \frac{d}{t}$, where v is the average speed, d is the distance covered and t is the elapsed time.

Acceleration: $a = \frac{v}{t}$, where v is the change in speed and t is the time required to produce that change.

Newton's Second Law: $\frac{F}{W} = \frac{a}{g}$. Here F is the force acting on a body of weight W, g is the acceleration due to gravity, and a is the acceleration of the body's motion. F and W must be measured in the same units.

Momentum: $M = mv$, where M is the momentum, m is the mass of the body and v is its velocity.

Chapter 7

Work done by a force: $W = Fd$. W is the amount of work done, F is the magnitude of the force and d is the distance moved in the direction of the force.

Kinetic Energy of a moving body:

$$KE_{ft\ lb} = \frac{m_{lb} v^2_{ft/sec}}{64}$$

$$or\ KE_{gm\ cm} = \frac{m_{gm} v^2_{cm/sec}}{1960}$$

where KE is the kinetic energy, m is the mass and v is the speed of the body.

Power: $P = \frac{W}{t}$, where P is the average power expended, W is the amount of work done and t is the time required to do it. In horsepower,

$$P_{HP} = \frac{W_{ft\ lb}}{550 \times t_{sec}}.$$

CHAPTER 9

Celsius and Fahrenheit temperatures: Readings on the two scales are related by $F = \frac{9}{5}C + 32$, where C is any temperature on the Celsius scale and F is the corresponding one on the Fahrenheit scale.

CHAPTER 10

Quantity of heat: $Q = smt$. Here Q is the quantity of heat taken on or given off, s is the specific heat of the material, m is the mass of the body and t is its temperature change.

Heat-work equivalent: 1 cal is equivalent to 4.18 joules, or 1 Btu is equivalent to 778 ft lb.

CHAPTER 11

Wave equation: $V = nl$, where V is the speed of the waves, n is their frequency and l is their wave length.

CHAPTER 13

Illumination produced by a small light source on a surface held perpendicular to the rays:

$E = \frac{C}{d^2}$. E is the illumination, C is the intensity of the source and d is its distance from the illuminated surface.

CHAPTER 14

Index of refraction: $n = \frac{c}{V}$, where n is the index of refraction of a material in which the speed of light is V, and c is the speed of light in a vacuum.

Location of image formed by a converging lens:

$\frac{1}{p} + \frac{1}{q} = \frac{1}{f}$, where p is the distance of the object from the lens, q is the distance of the image from the lens, and f is the focal length of the lens.

Size of the image: $\frac{h_i}{h_o} = \frac{q}{p}$, where h_i is the height of the image, h_o the height of the object, q is the image distance and p is the object distance.

CHAPTER 17

Strength of an electric current: $I = \frac{Q}{t}$, where I is the current strength, Q is the total quantity of charge passing any point in the conductor and t is the time during which it passes.

Ohm's law: $I = \frac{V}{R}$, where I is the strength of the current flowing in a conductor, V is the PD applied to its ends and R is its resistance.

Resistors in series: $R = R_1 + R_2 + R_3$ etc.,

Resistors in parallel: $\frac{1}{R} = \frac{1}{R_1} + \frac{1}{R_2} + \frac{1}{R_3}$ etc.

Here R is the combined resistance, and R_1, R_2, etc. are the separate values.

Power expended in an electric appliance:

$$P_{\text{watts}} = I_{\text{amp}} \times V_{\text{volts}}.$$

CHAPTER 18

Heat produced in a conductor by a current:

$$Q = 0.24\ I^2Rt.$$

Here Q is the quantity of heat, in calories, I the current in amperes, R the resistance of the conductor, in ohms, and t the time the current flows, in seconds.

CHAPTER 19

Transformer: $\dfrac{V_S}{V_P} = \dfrac{n_S}{n_P}$, where V_P is the voltage in the primary coil, V_S that in the secondary, and n_P and n_S are respectively, the numbers of turns in each.

CHAPTER 21

Mass-energy equivalence: $E = mc^2$, where E is the energy, in ergs, equivalent to a mass m, in grams, and c is the speed of light in cm/sec.

INDEX

Absolute scale, 69
Absolute zero, 69
Absorption
  of heat radiation, 71
  of paints, 118
AC (alternating current), 153–57
Acceleration, 46–47
  constant, 46, 48–49
  due to gravity, 47
  formula for, 186
Acoustics, 88–95
  See also Sound
Action and reaction, 50
Air, 30–36
  moisture in, 77
  molecular magnitudes for, 60
  pressure of, 30–33
  refraction of light in, 110
  resistance of, 33–34
  See also Gases
Air conditioning, 77
Airplane, 33–35
  wing principle, 34
Alpha rays, 171–74
Alternating current, 153–57
Altimeter, 31
AM (amplitude modulation), 162
Ammeters, 139, 148
Ampere, 136
Ampère, A. M., 136, 146
Amplitude, 89
Amplitude modulation, 162
Appliances, power in, 188
Archimedes' law, 27, 33, 186
Area, measurement of, 19–20
Aristotle, 46, 102
Astigmatism, 113
Atmosphere, 31–32
Atomic bomb, 176
Atomic mass units, 170
Atomic number, 170
Atomizer, 35
Atoms, 14, 170–71
  electricity and, 130
  molecules and, 58
  particles of, 174–75
  radioactive, 171–72, 174

Back voltage, 154–55
Barber chair, 26
Barometer, 30–31
Baryons, 175
Baseball, curving of, 35
Batteries, 136–38
  car, 28
  See also Electric circuits
Becquerel, A. H., 171
Bernoulli's Law, 34–35
Beta rays, 171
Betatron, 161
Bethe, Hans, 177
Bimetal, 67–68
Binocular, prism, 110, 114
Bohr, Niels, 172
Boiling, 76
  at reduced pressure, 76
Boiling point, 66
Bombs
  atomic, 176
  thermonuclear, 177
Boyle, Robert, 32
Boyle's Law, 32–33, 59, 186
Brownian motion, 58
Brushes (motors), 149
Btu, 75, 187
Buoyancy
  in gases, 33
  in liquids, 26–27

Calorie, 75
Cameras, 112, 120
  pinhole, 98–99
Capacitance, 132–34
Capacitor, 133–34
Capillarity, 62
Carbon arc, 99–100
Carburetor, 35
Car lift, 26
Cathode rays, 160, 164
Cells, 136–37
  dry, 137
  lead storage, 138
  photronic, 165
  voltaic, 137
Celsius system, 66–67, 187
Center of gravity, 40–41
Centigrade system. *See* Celsius system
Centrifuge, 48
Centripetal force, 48
Chain reaction, 175–76
Charges. *See* Electric charges
Chemical changes, 14
Circuits. *See* Electric circuits
Clarinet, 92, 94
Cloud chamber, 77
Clouds, 77
Coal, 71
Coal mines, 70
Coefficients
  heat-conduction, 70
  of linear expansion, 67
Cohesion in solids, 61
Coils, 146–57
  in generators, 153–54
  resistance of, 140
Cold, 71
  See also Heat; Temperature
Colloidal suspension, 14
Color, 116–24
  mixing of, 117, 118
  in photography, 118
  primary, 117
  printing processes for, 118
  spectrum of, 116–17, 119
  white light and, 116–17
Commutator, 149
Compass needle, 128, 145
Compounds, chemical, 14
Conduction of heat, 69–70
Conductors of electricity
  heat developed in, 144–45, 188
  insulators and, 130–31
Conservation of energy, 53, 55, 77–78
Convection, 70–71
Corpuscular theory, 102
Cosmic rays, 174
Coulomb, 132
Critical size, 176
Crystalline structure, 59
Curie, Marie, 171
Curie, Pierre, 171
Currents. *See* Electric currents
Cyclotron, 173

Davy, Sir Humphry, 70
Day, measurement of, 20
DC (direct current), 154
Decibel, 89
De Forest, Lee, 162
Democritus, 58
Density, 27, 28
  formula for, 21, 186
  measuring, 20–21
Depth and liquid pressure, 24–25
Derived units, 20
Detector (electronics), 162
Deuterium, 170
Diamonds, 61
Diffraction, 120–21
Diffraction gratings, 121
Diode, 161
Direct current, 154
Dispersion of color, 116–17
Displacement, 27
Dissociation, chemical, 137
Domains, magnetic, 127
Doppler effect, 88
Drag, 157
Dry cell, 137
Ductility, 61

Echo, 83
Eclipse, 98
Eddy currents, 157
Edison, Thomas A., 161
Einstein, Albert, 166, 173
  theory of relativity of, 173
Elasticity, 61
Electric appliances, power in, 188
Electric charges, 129–31
Electric circuits, 138–39
  fuses and, 145
  measurement of, 139
  Ohm's law, 139–41, 187
  resistors in, 140–41
  "short" in, 141
Electric currents, 130, 136–58
  batteries and, 136–38
  heating effects of, 144–45
  induction of, 151–57
  magnetic effects of, 145–49
  stepping up and down, 155–56
  strength of, 136, 187
  See also Electric circuits
Electric fields, 132
Electric generators, 153–55
Electric motors, 149, 154–55
  induction, 157
Electric organ, 156
Electric power and energy, 142, 187

Electricity, 129–58
atoms and, 130
photo-, 165
static, 129–30
Electrolysis, 138
Electromagnetic waves, 102, 119–20
Electromagnets, 146, 147
Electronics, 160–68
Electron microscope, 113, 165
Electrons, 130, 160
Electron tubes, 161–62
Electrophorus, 132
Electroplating, 138
Electrostatic force, 131–33
Electrotypes, 138
Elementary particles, 130, 174–75
Elements, 14
See also Atoms
Emulsion, 14
Energy, 16, 53–54
chemical, 16, 71
conservation of, 53, 55, 77–78
electrical, 16, 142
of heat, 74–80
kinetic, 53–54, 187
mass-energy equivalence, 173–74, 177, 188
mechanical, 16, 52, 53
potential, 53, 71, 133
in Quantum Theory, 166
radiation and, 71
Engines
heat, 78
jet-propulsion, 49–50, 78
Equilibrium
of forces, 39–40
of torques, 186
Erg, 52
"Ether," 102
Evaporation, 59, 76
Exponents, 19
Exposure meters, 101
Eye, human, 112–13

Fahrenheit, 66–67, 187
Falling motion, 46–47
Faraday, Michael, 128, 151
Far-sighted eye, 113
Fathometer, 84
Fields
due to current, 145–49
electric, 132
magnetic, 127–28
rotating magnetic, 157
Filament lamp, 99, 100, 139, 144–45
Fission, nuclear, 175–77
Fleming, Sir John, 161
Flotation, 26–28
Fluorescent lamps, 100
Flute, 92, 94
Flux, magnetic, 152
FM (frequency modulation), 162–63
Foam, 14
Focal length, 107, 111
Focus
principal, 107, 111
virtual, 112
Fog, 77
Foot-candle, 100–1
Foot pounds, 41
Force (forces), 38–44
centripetal, 48
compared, 133
drag, 36
electric fields and, 132
equilibrium of, 39–40
lines of, 152
liquid pressure and, 23
magnetic lines of, 128
molecular, 61
motion and, 47–50
representation of, 38
resultant of, 38–39
torque and rotation, 41–42
work and, 52, 186
See also Gravity
Formulas, 186–88
Franklin, Benjamin, 130
Freezing, 75–76
Freezing point, 66
Frequency
pitch and, 88
ultrasonic, 88
wavelength and, 85–86
Frequency modulation, 162–63
Frost, 77
Fundamental tone, 91
Fundamental particles, 130, 174–75
Fundamental units, 20
Fuses, 145
Fusion
heat of, 75
nuclear, 177
of a solid, 75–76

Galileo, 30, 46, 48
Galvani, Luigi, 136
Gamma rays, 120, 171, 176
Gases, 14
buoyancy in, 33
expansion of, 68–69
pressure of, 59–60
See also Air
Gas refrigerator, 78
Gas thermometer, 68
Geiger counter, 174
Generators, 153–55
electrostatic, 132
Glass
non-reflective coatings for, 121
radiation and, 71–72
See also Light; Mirrors
Glass tubes, 62
Gold, 61
Golf ball, "sliced," 35
Gravity, 40–43, 133
acceleration due to, 47
atmosphere and, 31
center of, 40–41
Law of Gravitation, 43, 186
specific, 27
Greenhouse, 72
Grounding (electricity), 130–31
Guitar, 91
Guns and bullets, 49
Gyroscope, 50

Hail, 77
Hahn, Otto, 175
Half-life, 172
Hardness, 61
Harmonics, 91, 93
H-bomb, 177
Heat, 66–80, 144–50
conduction of, 69–70
conductor - developed, 144–45, 188
convection and, 71–72
engines, 78
of filament lamps, 144
of fusion, 75
nature of, 66–73
quantity of, 74–75, 187
specific, 74
units of, 75
of vaporization, 76
See also Temperature
Heat energy, 74–80
Heat-work equivalent, 77, 187
Helicopter, 35
Henry, Joseph, 151
Hooke, Robert, 102
Horsepower, 54
Hot-air heating system, 70
Human eye, 112–13
Huygens, Christian, 102
Hydraulic press, 25–26
Hydrometer, 28

Ice point, 66–75
Illumination. *See* Lamps; Light
Illuminometers, 101
Image, 106
Image formation, 111–12, 187
Incidence, angle of, 105
Induction
electromagnetic, 151–57
electrostatic, 131–32
Induction motors, 157
Inertia, 15
Law of, 47–48
rotational, 50
Infra-red rays, 119
Insulators
electrical, 130–31
heat, 70
Intensity
of light, 100–1
of sound, 89
Interference of light, 121–22
Interferometers, 122
Ions, 136–38, 169, 174
Isotopes, 170–71
radio-, 174

Jet engines, 49–50, 78
Joliot, F., 174
Joule, 52, 54

Kelvin scale, 69
Kepler, Johannes, 42
Kerst, D. W., 161
Kilogram, 20
Kilometer, 19
Kilowatt, 54
Kilowatt-hour, 142
Kinetic energy, 53–54, 187
Kinetic Theory, 58–60, 68

Lamps
filament, 99, 100, 139, 144–45
fluorescent, 100
intensity of, 100–1
miners', 70
in series, 140
tube-type, 100
Lead storage cell, 138
Length
focal, 107, 111
measurement of, 18–19
metric units of, 19
Lenses, 110–12
converging, 110–12, 187
cylindrical, 113
diverging, 110, 112
electron, 165
Lenz's Law, 152–53
Lever, 55
Light, 98–124
behavior of, 98–99
diffraction of, 120–21
formulas for, 187
interference of, 121–22
measurement of, 100–1
needed for various purposes, 101
polarization of, 122
reflection of, 105–8, 110
refraction of, 108–10
speed of, 99
theories of, 102–3, 109, 166
white, 116–17
See also Lamps; Lenses; Mirrors

Light-gathering power, 114
Lightning rod, 131
Linear accelerator, 173
Linear expansion, 67
Liquids, 14, 23–29
  buoyancy and flotation in, 26–29
  evaporation of, 59, 76–77
  expansion of, 67–68
  pressure of, 23–26, 186
  See also Water
Liter, 20
Loops (acoustics), 91
Loudness, 89–90
Luminous intensity, 100
Luminous watch dial, 172

Machine parts, flaws in, 128
Machines, 55
Magnaflux method, 128
Magnetic fields, 127–28
  current-produced, 145–49
  rotating, 157
Magnetic flux, 152
"Magnetic storms," 128
Magnetism, 126–28, 133
  comparative force of, 133
  earth's, 128
  electric currents and, 145–50
  induced, 127
Magnifier, simple, 11
Malleability, 61
Mass, 15–16, 21
  atomic, 170
  measurement of, 20
  velocity and, 49
Mass-energy equivalence, 173–74, 177, 188
Mass number, 170–71
Mass spectrograph, 169–70, 177
Matter, 14–36
  forms of, 14
  general characteristics of, 15
  Kinetic Theory of, 58–60, 68
Mayer, J. R., 77
Measurement, 18–22
  of length, 18–19
  of temperature, 66–67
Mechanical energy, 16, 52
  conservation of, 53, 55
Mechanics, 47–50
Melting, 59
Mesons, 174–75
Meters, moving-coil, 148–49
Metric system, 18–20, 52, 75, 100–1
Microscopes, 113–14
  compound, 113
  electron, 113, 165
Mirages, 110
Mirrors, 105–8
  curved, 107–8
  plane, 105–7
Modulation, 162–63
Moisture, forms of, 77
Molecules, 14, 58–64
  atoms and, 58
  Kinetic Theory and, 58–60, 68
Momentum, 49, 186
Mothball, 59
Motion, 45–51
  accelerated, 46–49
  average speed of, 45, 186
  falling, 46–47
  formulas for, 186
  laws of, 47–50, 186
  of molecules, 58–59
Motion pictures, sound, 165–66
Motors, electric, 149, 154–55
  induction, 157
Musical instruments, 91–94

Near-sighted eye, 113
Neon lighting, 100
Neutrons, 170, 175
Newton, Sir Isaac, 102, 116
  Law of Gravitation, 42–43
  Laws of Motion, 47–50, 186
Nodes (acoustics), 91
Noise, 88
Non-reflecting coatings, 121
Nuclear fission, 175–77
Nuclear fusion, 177
Nuclear physics, 169–79
Nuclear reactor, 176–77
Nucleus, 130, 169, 170
  artificial changes in, 173
  radioactive rays from, 171
  size of, 172

Objective (optics), 113
Octave, 91
Ocular (optics), 113
Oersted, H. C., 145
Ohm, G. S., 139
Ohm's law, 139–41, 187
Optics, 105–22
  wave, 116–22
Organ, electric, 156
Organ pipe, 92–93
Oscillation, 84
Oscillator (electronics), 163
Particles, fundamental, 130, 174–75
PD. *See* Potential difference
Pendulum, 53
Percussion instruments, 93
Perpetual-motion machines, 55
Photocell, 164, 165
Photoelectric effect, 165–66
Photography, 112
  color, 118
Photometers, 101
Photon, 166
Photronic cell, 165
Physical changes, 14
Piano, 91, 93, 94
Pigment mixing, 118–19
Pinhole camera, 98–99
Pitch and frequency, 88
Pivot, 41
Planck, Max, 166
Plasma, electrical, 177
Plasticity, 61
Platinum, 61
Plutonium, 176
Polarization of light, 122
Poles
  magnet, 126–27
  North and South Magnetic, 128
Positrons, 174
Potential difference (PD), 132–33
  in a circuit, 138–40
Potential energy, 53, 71
  capacitance and, 133
  gravitational, 53
Power
  electric, 142
  in electric appliances, 188
  light-gathering (telescopes), 114
  nuclear, 176–77
  work and, 54
Power lines, 155
Precipitator, smoke and dust, 131
Pressure, 23–26
  air, 30–33
  formulas for, 186
  gas, 59–61
  liquid, 23–26
  reduced, 76
Pressure cooker, 76
Principal focus, 107, 111
Printing processes
  color, 118
  electrotypes in, 138
  type metal in, 76
Prism, 116–117
Prism binocular, 110, 114
Projectiles, 46–47, 49–50
Protons, 130, 175
Quantum theory, 166, 172

Radar, 164–65
  Doppler effect and, 88
Radiation, heat, 71–72
Radio, 162–63
Radioactivity, 171–77
  cosmic rays, 174
  natural, 171–72
Radio capacitor, 133
Radio-isotopes, 174
Radio tubes, 163
Radium, 171, 172
Rain, 77
Rainbow, 117
Rays
  alpha, 171–74
  beta, 171
  cathode, 160, 164
  cosmic, 174
  gamma, 120, 171, 176
  positive, 169–70
  X, 119–20, 161
  See also Light
Reaction
  action and, 50
  chain, 175–76
Reactors, nuclear, 175–77
Recoil, 50
Reflection
  of light, 105–8, 110
  of waves, 83–84
Refraction of light, 108–9
  index of, 109, 187
  wave theory of, 109
  See also Lenses
Refrigerators, 70, 78
Relativity, Theory of, 173
Relay, 147
Resistance, air, 33–34
Resistance thermometer, 140
Resistors, 140–42
  in parallel, 141–42, 187
  in series, 140, 187
  starting box, 154–55
Resonance, 92–93
Retina, 113
Reverberation time, 89
Right Hand Rules, 146
Rockets, 49–50, 78
Röentgen, W. C., 161
Römer, Olaus, 99
Rotation, 41–42, 186
Rotational inertia, 50
Rutherford, Ernest, 171–73

Satellites, 48
Searchlight, 107
Second (unit of time), 20
Semiconductors, 163

Ships
displacement of, 27
sinking, 28
Short-circuit, 141–42
Shunt, 141–42
Significant digits, 19
Slip rings, 153
Smoke and dust precipitator, 131
Snow, 77
Soap film, 121
Solenoid, 146
Solids, 14, 61
crystalline structure of, 59
evaporation of, 59
expansion of, 67–68
fusion of, 75–76
molecular forces in, 61
molecular properties of, 61
Sound, 82–95
indoor, 89
intensity of, 89
in musical instruments, 91–94
pitch and frequency, 88
quality of, 93–94
reflection of, 83–84
reproducers of, 156
speed of, 82
temperature and, 83
vibrations and, 86
See also Waves
Sound track, 165–66
Specific gravity, 27
Spectrochemical analysis, 119
Spectrograph, 119
mass, 169, 177
Spectroscope, 119
Spectrum, 116–19
electromagnetic, 120
continuous, 119
Speed, 45–46, 186
air resistance and, 33
conversion factors for units of, 45
of colors, 117
of light, 99
of sound, 82
velocity and, 45–46
Spray gun, 35
Spring scale, 16
Standard candles, 100
Standard meter, 19
Standard Yard, 18
Standpipe, 25
Stars, twinkling of, 110
Starting box, 154–55
Stationary waves, 90–92
Steam point, 66
Steel, 61
Stereoscope, 113
Stratosphere, 32
Streamlining, 33–34
Submarines, 27–28
Sunken ships, 28
Surface tension, 62

Tape-recorder, 156
Telephone, 156
Telescopes, 113–14
reflecting, 108, 114
refracting, 113–14, 116
Television, 164
Temperature, 66
absolute, 68–69
Celsius, 66–67, 187
Fahrenheit, 66–67, 187
measurement of, 66–67
sound and, 83
of various objects, 69
See also Heat
Tensile strength (tenacity), 61
Tension, surface, 62
Thermal Unit, British, 75, 187
Thermionic emission, 161
Thermometers
gas, 68
mercury, 66–67
resistance, 140
Thermonuclear bomb, 177
"Thermos" bottle, 70
Thermostat, 68
Thomson, J. J., 160, 164, 169, 170
Thunder, 83
Tides, 43
Time, 20
Tone, 88
fundamental, 91
quality of, 93–94
Torque, 41–42, 186
equilibrium of, 186
Torricelli, Evangelista, 30–31
Transformer, 155–56, 157, 188
Transistor, 163
Triode, 162, 163
Turning effect, 41
Type metal, 76

Ultrasonic frequencies, 88
Uranium, 175–76

Vacuum, 30, 70
Vacuum bottle, 70
Vacuum tube, 161–62, 163
Vaporization of a liquid, 59, 76–77
Vectors, 38–39
Velocity, 45–46
mass multiplied by, 49
resultant, 45–46
See also Acceleration
Vibrations, 84
forced, 92–93
of strings, 91
Violin, 91, 93, 94
Volt, 137
Volta, Alessandro, 136–37
Voltage
alternating, 153
back, 154–55
Voltaic cell, 137
Voltmeters, 139, 148
Volume, 21
measurement of, 19–20

Water, 14
density of, 21
freezing of, 75–76
in standpipe, 25
surface tension of, 62
See also Liquids; Waves
Watt, 54, 100
Watt, James, 54
Wave equation, 86, 187
Wavelength, 85–86
color as, 117
Wave optics and color, 116–24
Waves
amplitude of, 89
compressional, 82, 85
continuous, 84–86
diffraction of, 120
electric, 120
electromagnetic, 102, 119–20
infra-red, 119
longitudinal, 85
patterns of, 91
reflection of, 83–84
stationary, 90–92
transverse, 85
ultraviolet, 119
See also Light
Weather forcasting, 31, 165
Weight, 15–16, 21
of air, 30
measurement of, 20
of ships, 27
Whispering galleries, 84
White light, 116–17
Wind, 70–71
Wind instruments, 93
Work, 52–57
defined, 52
formulas for, 52, 54, 186–87
heat and, 77, 187
mechanical energy and, 53
rate of doing, 54

X rays, 119–20
production of, 161

Yard, Standard, 18